1 e4 c5 2 ♘f3 e6 3 d4 cxd4 4 ♘xd4 ♘c6

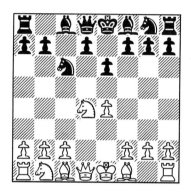

*To Arnie, KGB, Seven-Horned, Helen Fiona Pitt-Kethley and particularly Alexander Michael with the assurance that I shall never play him so much as one game of chess.*

# The Sicilian Taimanov

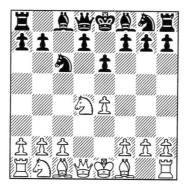

# CHESS PRESS OPENING GUIDES

## Other titles in this series include:

For further details for Chess Press titles, please write to The Chess Press c/o Cadogan Books plc, 27-29 Berwick Street, London W1V 3RF.

Chess Press Opening Guides

# The Sicilian Taimanov

## James Plaskett

The Chess Press, Brighton

First published 1997 by The Chess Press, an imprint of First Rank Publishing, 23 Ditchling Rise, Brighton, East Sussex, BN1 4QL, in association with Cadogan Books plc

Copyright © 1997 James Plaskett

Distributed by Cadogan Books plc, 27-29 Berwick Street, London WIV 3RF

A CIP catalogue record for this book is available from the British Library

ISBN 1 901259 01 3

Cover design by Ray Shell Design
Printed and bound in Great Britain by BPC Wheatons, Exeter

# CONTENTS

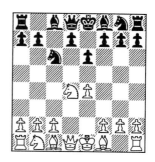

**1 e4 c5 2 ♘f3 e6
3 d4 cxd4 4 ♘xd4 ♘c6**

# BIBLIOGRAPHY

## Books

*Encyclopaedia of Chess Openings vol. B (ECO)*, Sahovski Informator 1984
*Batsford Chess Openings 2 (BCO)*, Kasparov & Keene (Batsford 1989)
*Sicilian Defence: Taimanov System*, Taimanov (Batsford 1989)
*Sicilian Taimanov*, Jacobs (Chess Player 1991)
*Winning with the Sicilian*, Taimanov (Batsford 1991)
*Beating the Sicilian 2*, Nunn (Batsford 1990)
*Sicilian Love*, Polugayevsky, Piket & Guéneau (New in Chess 1995)
*Taimanov's Selected Games*, Taimanov (Cadogan 1995)
*Timman's Selected Games*, Timman (Cadogan 1995)

## Periodicals

*Informator*
*ChessBase Magazine*
*New In Chess Yearbook*
*British Chess Magazine*
*Chess Monthly*

# INTRODUCTION

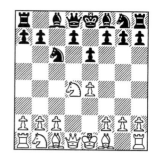

The move-order 1 e4 c5 2 ♘f3 e6 3 d4 cxd4 4 ♘xd4 ♘c6 (or 1 e4 c5 2 ♘f3 ♘c6 3 d4 cxd4 4 ♘xd4 e6) has always associated with the Russian concert pianist and former World Championship Candidate, Mark Taimanov. Many of the seminal games of this variation, which is often distinguished by very fast queenside development for Black, are by Taimanov himself from the 1950s and 1960s. And he was pretty successful too. In one USSR Championship he made a score of 7½ out of 9 with his pet system!

Current Taimanov players include Kasparov, Karpov, Anand, Salov, Adams, Timman and many others from the world's best, and in the last game of the famous Fischer-Spassky World Championship match in 1972, Fischer won, and thus took the title, by using the Taimanov Sicilian.

This work concerns itself purely with the system 1 e4 c5 2 ♘f3 e6 3 d4 cxd4 4 ♘xd4 ♘c6 and does not cover the related Paulsen variation (1 e4 c5 2 ♘f3 e6 3 d4 cxd4 4 ♘xd4 a6) and as far as possible steers clear from Scheveningen formations with ...e7-e6 and ...d7-d6, even though there are frequent, and often quite good, opportunities for transposition into such set-ups.

## Typical Themes in the Taimanov Sicilian

The Sicilian Defence remains the most popular reply to the king's pawn at all levels of the game. Strategically the semi-open c-file and his extra central pawn are clear pluses for Black. His problem is that *tactically* the Sicilian is slightly suspect, as many a practitioner has discovered when some sacrifice blew him away in the middlegame.

In general, Sicilian endgames tend to favour Black because of the aforementioned strategical features. They are especially pleasant if White has extended, or hopefully over-extended, himself with pawn advances on the kingside in the middlegame.

From the starting position of the Taimanov, let us take a look at each of Black's typical development moves in turn:

**...a7-a6 and ...b7-b5**

These moves are hardly ever omitted from a Taimanov formation, the only common exception being when White captures ♘xc6.

**...b7-b6**

A much less frequent fianchetto.

**...♘a5-c4**

This ambitious manoeuvre is often effected when the white queen's bishop is on e3. It can prove so effective that Black may take time out for it whilst his development is still incomplete.

**...♘e5**

Again this move is most often used against a ♗e3 formation, perhaps most frequently when the king's bishop sits alongside it on d3 (see Chapter 2). There Black of course has the option of capturing the bishop or just taking an alternative route to c4.

**...♘xd4**

The general rule is that in a cramped position one should seek exchanges, and very often Black makes the exchange of knights on d4 when he has played his king's knight to e7. This affords him the chance to instantly drop the other knight to c6, often with tempo, e.g. after White has recaptured with the queen.

**...♕c7**

On the very rare occasions when Black does not develop the queen here, it will probably go to a5. After ...♕c7 an exchange of knights on c6 will usually met by recapturing with the queen.

**...♗b7**

Also an almost mandatory stationing.

**...♖c8**

GM Andrew Soltis observed that the Taimanov Sicilian 'runs on active piece play'. True enough, and Black often plays this natural move early on, completing a queen and rook battery on the c-file before mobilising his kingside. Occupation of the c-file often occurs far earlier in the Taimanov than in other types of Sicilian.

### ...d7-d6

As stated above, we are concerned here with Taimanov formations, and although there is frequently nothing amiss with ...d7-d6, this move usually takes play into a Scheveningen. Accordingly when ...d7-d6 is played in the Taimanov, it probably comes at a stage which might be described as the early middlegame rather than the opening.

### ...d7-d5

This move is perhaps seen less often than it ought to be!? It is often said that if Black can achieve ...d7-d5 in the Sicilian, then he has solved most of his problems. Would life were that simple! In Chapters 6 and 10 we shall see some liberating ...d7-d5s from customary Sicilian formations, and in Chapter 7 from the very different structure that arises from White taking on c6 and Black recapturing with the b-pawn.

### ...e6-e5

We shall see this restructuring particularly in Chapters 1, 8, 9 and 10. It is probably fair to say that Black does not usually undertake this change to the central pawns unless it is forced upon him.

### ...♘f6

Always a natural square for this piece in any Sicilian.

### ...♘ge7

The 'hip' way to play the Taimanov, and one favoured by the maestro himself. After this move Black sometimes swaps knights on d4 and then installs the other one at c6 from e7. On other occasions the king's knight goes to g6 or is deposited on c8. A still more exotic plan arises when White retreats his knight from d4 to b3: Black can 'chase' it with ...♘(c6)-a5, and then ...♘(e7)-c6. My comments upon the metatheory of ...♘ge7 are somewhat vague, since although the idea has been known for decades, there is still surprisingly little theory upon it! But it can be said that this is the move most apt to stamp a definitive Taimanov character upon the game, for after ...♘ge7 there remain no possibilities for subsequent angling back into a Scheveningen, and this is the way that most true Taimanov devotees want to handle their baby.

### ...♘h6

A rarity, usually only cropping up after White has advanced e4-e5, when the knight aims at the tempting f5-square. Frequently such an occupation is buttressed with ...h7-h5 to dissuade White from playing g2-g4.

### ...♗e7

The normal square for this piece.

### ...♗b4

Occasionally you do see the bishop used to pin the white queen's knight, perhaps even doubling the white pawns with ...♗xc3, although the downside of this is the weakening of the dark squares in the black camp. Another plausible effect of the pin is to exert pressure on the e4-pawn, in conjunction with the fianchetto of the queen's bishop.

### ...♗c5

This move particularly comes into its own in Chapter 8, where it will usually temporarily stop White from castling kingside. It also crops up after an exchange of knights on d4 in Chapter 1 and in conjunction with ...♘e5 in Chapter 2. Generally speaking, this move constitutes an ambitious development which has the drawback of removing a potentially important defender from the black king, but if Black can get away with it, the a7-g1 diagonal can be very significant.

### ...♗d6

Most often seen where White has played a system with ♗d3. Sticking a bishop in front of an unmoved d-pawn looks irregular, yet White frequently removes that problem in such lines by capturing on c6, allowing Black to take back with ...d7xc6. The bishop move often involves a tempo gain through the threat of ...♗xh2+, after which Black may continue ...♗f4 or ...♗e5. The d6-square is very unlikely to represent a permanent post.

### ...h7-h5

This pawn advance can serve as a method for either holding up further developments on the kingside from White and/or of securing the outpost on f5 for the black king's knight. When in the mood an audacious player of the black pieces may even venture this move very early on, hoping to use it as part of an attack on a castled white king, e.g. by using g4 for his king's knight in conjunction perhaps with the queen on c7, the fianchettoed queen's bishop, and the king's rook still on its initial square.

### ...f7-f6

This move is hardly ever seen, except when Black plays ...♘ge7 and later ...♘g6. That curious defensive formation can prove extraordinarily resilient and appropriate against either White advance e4-e5 or f4-f5; in the latter case the knight can instantly hop into the newly created hole at e5.

### ...f7-f5

An even rarer method, usually used to stop a white kingside demonstration from growing any larger. As one might imagine, this advance involves the acceptance of weaknesses, but it can sometimes be made to work.

# CHAPTER ONE

## 5 ♘c3 a6 6 g3

**1 e4 c5 2 ♘f3 e6 3 d4 cxd4 4 ♘xd4 ♘c6 5 ♘c3 a6 6 g3**

Fianchetto developments are often associated with slow, positional build-ups. Don't let that fool you! White can still launch the pawns in front of his fianchettoed king's bishop to start a mighty attack in this line, and it is included within the repertoires of such aggressive players as Anand, Short, Topalov and Timman.

The first four games of this chapter involve an early ...♕c7. Games 1 and 2 show a line which became rehabilitated in the early 1970s through the device of ...♚e7(!) in a position where castling, although clearly not satisfactory, had been thought to be essential. It is obviously hazardous to stick the king in the centre, but Anand managed to outplay Short with this idea, so it is certainly worthy of scrutiny. In Games 3 and 4 Black plays ...♕c7 and ...d7-d6, reaching a Scheveningen type of position. White pursues an edge through exchanging knights on c6 and then tries to work with a superior pawn structure, but Black can generate sufficient activity to compensate fully. Note that in the second of these games (and in Game 10) Tim-

man plays ♕g4, which is met by ...h7-h5!, forcing an immediate retreat. Although this approach has been popular for White, I really fail to see why. In each of these games something of an impasse develops.

The next four games involve ...♘ge7 rather than ...♕c7. In Game 5 Black swaps on d4 and moves the other knight to c6 with tempo because of the attack on the white queen. However, I believe that White has more hope of gaining an edge by retreating with ♘b3 against ...♘ge7 in this line, as evinced in Games 6 and 7. If Black wishes to avoid 7 ♘b3, he can play 6...♘xd4, as in Game 8.

The final two games are examples of a Scheveningen 6...d6 (without ...♕c7). In Ivanov-De Firmian White starts off one of those kingside pawn storms and Nick de Firmian's unique method of holding it up, by the fianchetto of the king knight, is extraordinary and efficient.

*Game 1*
**Short-Anand**
*Tilburg 1991*

**1 e4 c5 2 ♘f3 ♘c6 3 d4 cxd4 4**

♘xd4 ♕c7 5 ♘c3 e6 6 g3 a6 7 ♗g2 ♘f6

For 7...d6, see Game 4.

**8 0-0 ♘xd4**

8...♗e7 used to be the regular choice here, and after 9 ♖e1 only then 9...♘xd4 (since 9...0-0 is met by 10 ♘xc6 dxc6 11 e5, claiming space in the centre). But then Paul Motwani produced the amazing 10 e5!? and the line fell out of fashion, even though Tal, for one, told me that after 10...♘b5! he was not sure that White really had anything. The solid 8...d6 is considered in Game 3.

**9 ♕xd4 ♗c5 10 ♗f4**

Here 10 ♕d3 is well met by 10...♘g4 followed by ...♘e5.

**10...d6 11 ♕d2**

11 ♕d3 can be met by 11...♘d7, again intending ...♘e5 and ready to meet 12 ♘a4 with 12...e5 13 ♗d2 b5.

**11...h6**

Black must be very careful here: 11...0-0? 12 ♖ad1 e5 13 ♗g5 ♗g4 14 ♗xf6 gxf6 15 ♘d5 ♕d8 16 ♕h6 graphically illustrates the danger of allowing White to gain control of the d5-square.

**12 ♖ad1 e5 13 ♗e3 ♔e7!?**

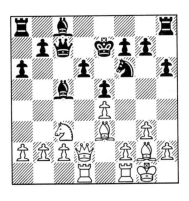

This move has rehabilitated the line with an exchange on d4. Now if White were to capture on c5, Black could take back with the queen, whereas after 13...0-0 14 ♗xc5, 14...dxc5 is forced, when White can invade the black position with 15 ♕d6.

**14 f4**

14 h3 is seen in the next game.

**14...♗e6 15 fxe5 dxe5 16 ♘d5+**

This action in the centre certainly seems logical, when Black's king is stuck there.

**16...♗xd5 17 exd5 ♖hd8!**

Black has to be careful. On 17...♖ad8 18 ♔h1 ♖he8 White can prove an edge after 19 ♕c3! ♗d6 (19...♔d6 20 ♗xh6) with either a queen exchange and 21 c4, getting his pawn roller moving, or by playing for attack with 20 ♕b3.

**18 ♔h1 ♖ac8!**

This was a new move (*yes, theory does go a heck of a long way these days!*). Prior to this game 18...♗xe3 had been tried, but Anand's move looks better.

**19 c4 ♕d6! 20 ♗xc5 ♖xc5 21 ♕e2 ♖dc8 22 ♗h3 ♖8c7**

**23 b3?!**

After this move White's queenside majority is in danger of being frozen, and may become a liability. It would have been better for Short to turn his attention towards the black king with 23 ♖fe1!, when after 23 ...♔d8 24 b3 b5 White could take play into an equal ending with 25 cxb5 axb5 26 ♕xe5 ♕xe5 27 ♖xe5 ♖c1.

**23...b5**

Starting to chisel.

**24 ♖f5?**

Here to 24 ♖fe1! bxc4 25 bxc4 ♔d8 26 ♕b2!? (fishing for complications) 26...♖xc4 27 ♕b8+ ♔e7 would have left White with some chances, due to the uncertain placement of the black king.

**24...bxc4 25 ♖xe5+ ♔f8 26 ♖e1 g6 27 bxc4 ♖xc4**

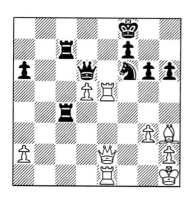

Now White will have a hard time to draw. His minor piece is inferior, his d-pawn is vulnerable and his king position is insecure.

**28 ♕b2 ♖c2 29 ♕d4 ♔g7 30 ♗g2 ♖7c4 31 ♕a1 ♕a3 32 ♖5e3 ♕xa2**

A very tasty morsel to grab for the coming ending.

**33 ♕xa2 ♖xa2 34 ♗f3 ♖cc2 35 h4**

**♖d2 36 ♖e7 ♘xd5 37 ♗xd5 ♖xd5 38 ♖f1 ♖f5 39 ♖xf5 gxf5**

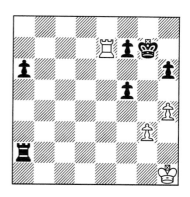

This is a technical win, the most significant feature being the presence of the f-pawns. Vishy demonstrates why.

**40 ♖c7 a5 41 ♖c6 a4 42 ♖a6 a3 43 ♔g1 h5 44 ♔f1 ♖a1+ 45 ♔g2 a2!**

There are only two more technical stages left now. First bring the king over...

**46 ♔h2 ♔f8 47 ♖a7 ♔e8 48 ♔g2 ♔d8 49 ♔h2 ♔c8 50 ♔g2 ♔b8 51 ♖a4 ♔b7 52 ♖a3 ♔b6 53 ♖a8 f4!**

...and then saddle White with an f-pawn.

**54 gxf4 f5 55 ♖a3 ♔c5 56 ♖a8 ♔c4 57 ♖a3 ♔d4 58 ♖a8 ♔e4 59 ♖a4+ ♔e3 0-1**

Zugzwang. White resigned, because first the pawn falls after, say, 60 ♔h2 ♔f3, and then, having taken it, Black may brazenly advance his own f-pawn until it reaches f3, even with check. If that is taken by the rook, Black plays ...♖b1 and his a-pawn promotes (providing ♖xf3 was not check!), while if it is taken by the king then ...♖f1+ and ...a2-a1♕, or if ♔h2, ...f3-f2 and again a pawn queens, or, finally, if ♔f2 then ...♖h1! and after ♖xa2 the skewer ...♖h2+ wins the white rook. These ideas reveal the significance of the f-pawn. If Black had had a g-pawn, after ...a3-a2 there would not have been a win.

Anand played this whole game in under an hour.

> **Game 2**
> **Suetin-Wyss**
> *Biel 1995*

**1 e4 c5 2 ♘f3 e6 3 d4 cxd4 4 ♘xd4 ♘c6 5 ♘c3 ♕c7 6 g3 a6 7 ♗g2 ♘f6 8 0-0 ♘xd4 9 ♕xd4 ♗c5 10 ♗f4 d6 11 ♕d2 h6 12 ♖ad1 e5 13 ♗e3 ♔e7!? 14 h3**

A slower treatment.

**14...♗e6 15 ♗xc5 ♕xc5 16 ♔h2**

16 ♘a4 is met by 16...♕c6 17 b3 b5 18 ♘b2 ♖hd8 with equal chances.

**16...♖ac8 17 f4 ♖hd8 18 ♖f2 ♔f8**

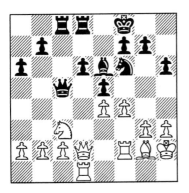

The outcome of the opening is fine for Black.

**19 ♕e1 ♕b4 20 ♖b1 b5 21 a3 ♕c5 22 ♖d1 ♕b6 23 ♖fd2 ♔e7!? 24 ♘d5+**

Transforming the pawn structure, but since White does not manage to gain any chances against the 'misplaced' black king, as he may have hoped, this was perhaps an unwise choice, because now Black will have the superior minor piece.

**24...♗xd5 25 exd5 ♘d7 26 ♕e4 ♔f8 27 ♕h7 ♘f6 28 ♕f5**

Acknowledging that he has no attack.

**28...exf4 29 ♕xf4 ♖e8 30 ♖f1 ♖e5**

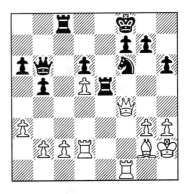

Starting to take over the position.

**31 ♖df2 ♖c4 32 ♕c1 ♕e3!? 33 ♕xe3 ♖xe3 34 c3 a5 35 ♖d1 b4 36 axb4 axb4**

The minority attack does serve to weaken the enemy pawns, but it also creates a passed pawn, a factor of some relevance later on. I suspect that Black's advantage was never quite enough for a win.

**37 ♗f1 ♖ce4 38 ♗g2 ♖e2 39 ♔g1 ♖e1+ 40 ♖f1 ♖xf1+ 41 ♔xf1 ♖c4 42 ♖d3 bxc3 43 ♖xc3 ♖d4 44 ♖c8+ ♔e7 45 ♖c7+ ♔e8 46 ♖b7 ♘h5 47 ♖b3 ♔e7 48 ♖e3+ ♔d7 49 ♔e2 ♘f6 50 ♖b3 ♘xd5 51 ♗xd5 ♖xd5**

*see following diagram*

White is struggling in this ending, but he just scrapes a draw.

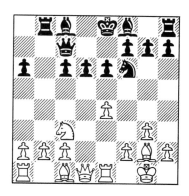

**52 ♖b7+ ♚e6 53 b4 ♖g5 54 ♚f3 ♖f5+ 55 ♚e3 ♖e5+ 56 ♚f3 ♖e1 57 b5 ♖b1 58 b6 ♖b3+ 59 ♚f2 d5 60 ♖b8 g6 61 b7 ♚e7 62 g4 g5 63 ♚e2 ♚d7 64 ♖f8 ♖xb7 65 ♖xf7+ ♚c6 66 ♖f6+ ♚c5 67 ♖xh6 ♚d4 68 h4!**

White generates the required counterplay just in time.

**68...♖b2+ 69 ♚f3 ♖b3+ 70 ♚e2 gxh4 71 ♖xh4 ♚e4 72 g5+ ♚f5 73 ♖d4 ♖b5 74 ♚e3 ♚xg5 75 ♖a4 ♖b1 ½-½**

<hr>

*Game 3*
**Leko-Lautier**
*Horgen 1994*

<hr>

**1 e4 c5 2 ♘f3 e6 3 d4 cxd4 4 ♘xd4 ♘c6 5 ♘c3 ♕c7 6 g3 a6 7 ♗g2 ♘f6 8 0-0 d6 9 ♖e1 ♖b8 10 ♘xc6 bxc6**

*see following diagram*

**11 e5! dxe5 12 ♖xe5**

A trick to remember.

**12...♗d6!**

Of course 12...♕xe5 is advantageously countered by 13 ♗f4 and 14 ♗xb8.

**13 ♖e1 0-0 14 b3 c5! 15 ♕e2**

White has the better structure, but Black sets about creating enough activity to compensate for this.

**15...♗b7 16 ♗xb7 ♕xb7 17 ♘e4 ♘xe4 18 ♕xe4 ♖fc8 19 ♗b2**

On 19 c4, 19...a5, aiming to play ...a5-a4, is fine for Black.

**19...c4 20 ♖ad1 ♗b4 ½-½**

<hr>

*Game 4*
**Timman-Milov**
*Biel 1995*

<hr>

**1 e4 c5 2 ♘f3 e6 3 d4 cxd4 4 ♘xd4 a6 5 ♘c3 ♕c7 6 g3 ♘c6**

We have transposed to the Taimanov via a Paulsen move-order, a common occurrence in practice.

**7 ♗g2 d6 8 0-0 ♗e7 9 ♖e1 ♗d7 10 ♘xc6 ♗xc6 11 ♕g4**

The only testing move. After 11 a4 ♘f6 12 ♗e3 0-0 Black has a satisfactory Scheveningen-type position.

**11...h5!**

A recurrent motif.

**12 ♕e2**

Taking the g-pawn was not a good idea (12...♗f6).

**12...h4**

The consistent follow-up to Black's

previous move, although 12...b5 is also playable.

**13 a4 hxg3 14 hxg3 ♔f8**

The opening of the h-file has complicated matters. Black foregoes castling, but because White has chosen a quieter positional deployment he is not well placed to commence immediate action. Gradually something of an impasse comes about, with neither side able to do much.

**15 a5 ♘f6 16 ♗e3 ♖e8 17 ♗d4 ♕c8 18 ♖ed1 ♖h7 19 ♗e3 ♘d7 20 f4 ♘f6 21 ♗f3 g6 22 ♔g2 ♔g7 23 ♖h1 ♖eh8**

**24 ♖xh7+ ♖xh7 25 ♖h1 ♖xh1 26 ♔xh1**

The purging of all the rooks brings the draw nearer.

**26...e5 27 ♔g2 ♗d7 28 ♘d5 ♘xd5 29 exd5 ♗b5 30 ♕d1 ♗f6 31 b3 ♗d7 32 c4 ♗h3+ 33 ♔f2 exf4 34 gxf4 ♕h8 35 ♕h1 ♕c8 36 ♕d1 ♕h8**
½-½

---

## Game 5
### Istratescu-Klarenbeek
*Cappelle la Grande Open 1993*

---

**1 e4 c5 2 ♘f3 e6 3 d4 cxd4 4 ♘xd4 ♘c6 5 ♘c3 a6 6 g3 ♘ge7**

True to Taimanov's original principles, Black intends ...♘xd4 followed by ...♘c6. The immediate 6...♘xd4 is discussed in Game 8.

**7 ♗g2**

This allows Black to carry out his planned exchange.

**7...♘xd4 8 ♕xd4 ♘c6**

The game Tiviakov-Frolov, Moscow Olympiad 1994, continued instead (by transposition) 8...d6 9 ♗e3 ♘c6 10 ♕b6 ♕xb6 11 ♗xb6 ♗d7 12 0-0-0 ♖c8 with a draw in 25 moves.

**9 ♕d1**

The queen is more active on e3 or d2, but there it would block the dark-squared bishop, while on d3 the queen is vulnerable to an attack from the black knight on e5 or even b4.

**9...♗e7**

A modest and logical development, but Black could have tried for more out of the opening with 9...♗c5!? (Compare this with Sion Castro-Ljubojevic, Leon 1994: 1 e4 c5 2 ♘f3 e6 3 d4 cxd4 4 ♘xd4 ♘c6 5 g3!? ♘xd4!? 6 ♕xd4 ♘e7 7 ♗g2 ♘c6 8 ♕d1 ♗c5!? 9 0-0 h5!? [some players love to get this in whenever they can!] 10 ♘c3 h4 11 ♘a4 ♗e7 12 c4 hxg3 13 hxg3 b6 14 ♗f4 ♗a6 15 ♖c1 ♖c8 16 b3 b5 17 cxb5 ♗xb5 with equal chances.)

**10 0-0 0-0 11 ♗e3 b5**

---

*see following diagram*

To avoid White's next Black preferred 11...♖b8 in Bielczyk-Tunik, Czech Republic 1995, with equal chances after 12 ♕e2 b5 13 ♖fd1 ♘e5 14 ♗a7 ♖b7 15 ♗d4 ♕c7 16 f4 ♘c4.

---

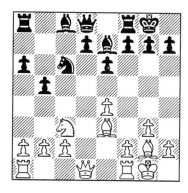

**12 ♘d5!?**

Black has equalised, and this flashy idea does nothing to alter that assessment. After the standard 12 f4 ♗b7 13 ♕e2 ♖c8, as in Mnatsakanian-Taimanov, Erevan 1986, Black is ready to start operations on the queenside with ...♘a5.

**12...exd5 13 cxd5 ♗b7! 14 dxc6 ♗xc6 15 c3**

15 ♗d4 ♖c8 16 c3 ♖e8 17 ♖e1 ♗f8 has been considered equal ever since the famous game Faibisovich-Taimanov, Leningrad 1973(!).

**15...♖e8 16 ♕d2 ♕b8! 17 ♖ad1 ♕b7**

An excellent manoeuvre which more or less insists that White correct his opponent's slight pawn weakness. Chances are now equal.

**18 ♗xc6 dxc6 19 ♕d7 ♕xd7 20 ♖xd7 ♔f8 21 ♖fd1 ♖ed8 22 ♗b6 ♖xd7 23 ♖xd7 ♔e8 24 ♖b7 c5 25 b3 ♖c8 26 a4**

White tries his best to wrest some advantage from his rook on the seventh rank, but Black has adequate counter-measures.

**26...c4 27 axb5 axb5 28 bxc4 ♖xc4 29 ♗a5 ♗f6 ½-½**

**1 e4 c5 2 ♘f3 e6 3 d4 cxd4 4 ♘xd4 ♘c6 5 ♘c3 a6 6 g3 ♘ge7 7 ♘b3**

It seems to make more sense for White to cut across his opponent's plan with this move, as the exchange of knights seems to be in Black's favour. Note that 7 ♘de2 can be met by 7...♘g6 9 0-0 ♗c5! 10 ♘f4 ♗b7 11 ♘d3 ♗d6, when Black was fine in Kapengut-Taimanov, USSR Championship 1971.

**7...d6**

The most solid move, though some players prefer to 'chase' the knight with 7...♘a5, when 8 ♕h5!? is the sharpest response. 7...b5 8 ♗g2 d6 simply transposes to the next note.

**8 ♗g2 ♗d7**

After 8...b5, 9 ♗e3 followed by f2-f4 is considered to be a little better for White.

**9 0-0**

Taking the d-pawn would not be a good idea (9...♘d5!).

**9...♘c8**

The customary repository for this guy in the ...♘ge7 line of the fianchetto system.

**10 a4**

Black is a little cluttered on the queenside, so this clamping move makes good sense.

**10...♗e7 11 ♕e2 0-0 12 a5**

A sharper line of kingside expansion with ♗e3, followed by f2-f4 and g3-g4, is considered in the next game, while in Kudrin-Zapata, Zamora 1990, a draw was agreed after 12 ♖d1 ♕c7 13 f4 ♗f6 14 ♗e3 ♘b4!? 15 ♗d4 e5 16 fxe5 ♗xe5 17 ♕f2 ♗e6 18 ♗xe5 dxe5 19 ♘c5 ♗g4 20 ♖d2 ♘d6.

**12...♕c7 13 f4 ♗f6**

This artificial fianchetto is a key idea, but frankly I mistrust this formation and would advocate either playing the knight to g6 or chasing the knight on b3 with ...♘a5.

**14 ♗d2**

Permitting a welcome simplification for Black

**14...♘d4! 15 ♘xd4 ♗xd4+ 16 ♔h1 ♘e7 17 ♖fc1 ♖ac8 18 ♘d1**

These are the not the sort of moves to set the world on fire.

**18...♗b5 19 ♕e1 ♗c6 20 c3 ♗a7**

**21 c4 f5! 22 ♘c3 fxe4 23 ♘xe4 ♘f5 24 b4 ♕d7**

The queen steps out of the way of b5, and Black's splendidly active forces give him by far the more comfortable game.

**25 g4?!**

Kristiansen starts to over-extend himself.

**25...♘d4 26 ♖a3 d5! 27 cxd5 exd5 28 ♘c5 ♗xc5 29 ♖xc5 ♕xg4! 30 ♗h3 ♕h5 31 ♗xc8 ♖xc8**

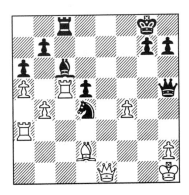

For his slight material investment Black keeps splendid attacking chances.

**32 h3 ♘e2 33 ♖e3 ♘xf4**

The black activity is too much too handle.

**34 ♔h2 ♖f8 35 ♖g3 ♘e2 36 ♖e3 ♘d4 37 ♔g2 ♘f3**

This chap has certainly put in the legwork in this game!

**38 ♕e2 ♕g6+ 0-1**

> *Game 7*
> **Topalov-Illescas**
> *Alcobendas (match) 1994*

**1 e4 c5 2 ♘f3 ♘c6 3 d4 cxd4 4 ♘xd4 e6 5 ♘c3 a6 6 g3 ♘ge7 7**

♘b3 d6 8 a4 ♗d7 9 ♗g2 ♘c8 10 0-0 ♗e7 11 ♕e2 0-0 12 ♗e3 ♕c7

In De Firmian-Zapata, Tunis Interzonal 1985, White had a slight edge after 12...♘a5 13 ♘xa5 ♕xa5 14 ♗d4.

**13 f4 ♖b8?!**

The setting is deceptively calm, but in fact by simply advancing on the kingside White can place his opponent in a critical position. Here 13...b6, keeping some control on the queenside, or even 13...♗f6!?, contemplating ...♗xc3, would have been a wiser course of action.

**14 g4! ♖e8 15 g5 ♘b4**

By now Illescas had probably realised the trouble that he was in. On 15...♗f8, 16 a5! keeps absolute control.

**16 ♕f2 b5 17 axb5 axb5 18 f5**

And now after 18...♗f8, 19 g6! is dangerous.

**18...♘xc2 19 ♕xc2 b4 20 g6! e5**

Or 20...hxg6 21 fxg6 fxg6 22 e5! bxc3 23 ♕xg6 and the queen enters into the thick of things with decisive effect. With all his pieces huddled on the back ranks, Black can hardly hope to create enough activity to justify his sortie at move 18.

**21 ♘c5! bxc3**

Or 21...dxc5 22 ♘d5 ♕d8 23 gxf7+ ♔xf7 24 ♘xe7 ♕xe7 25 ♕c4+ ♔f8 26 ♗xc5 and wins.

**22 ♘a6! ♖xb2 23 ♘xc7 ♖xc2 24 ♘xe8 ♗xe8 25 f6! ♖xg2+**

25...♗xf6 is met by 26 ♗h3 ♘e7 27 ♖a8, winning.

**26 ♔xg2 ♗xf6 27 ♖a8 ♗d7 28 ♖c1 1-0**

An unusual and powerfully played game.

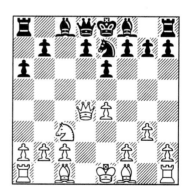

## Game 8
## Kindermann-Wilder
### Dortmund 1988

**1 e4 c5 2 ♘f3 ♘c6 3 d4 cxd4 4 ♘xd4 e6 5 ♘c3 a6 6 g3 ♘xd4!?**

In this example Black accelerates the exchange on d4 in order to avoid 6...♘ge7 7 ♘b3.

**7 ♕xd4 ♘e7**

**8 ♗f4**

The disadvantage of this move-order is that White has time to play this move, followed by ♕d2, instead of having to retreat the queen to d1 or d3.

**8...♘c6 9 ♕d2 b5 10 ♗g2 ♗b7 11**

**0-0**

In De Firmian-Morovic, Linares 1994, White chose 11 ♖d1, and after 11...♘a5 12 b3 ♖c8 13 ♘e2 ♗b7 14 0-0 d6 15 c3 ♕b6 16 ♗e3 ♕c7 17 f4 ♘c6 the game was drawn in 40 moves.

**11...♘a5!?**

As so often in this opening, we see Black concentrating on rapid queen-side development. The threat of the knight dropping into c4 with tempo induces White's next. Previous games had seen 11...♗e7 and 11...♖c8.

**12 b3 ♖c8 13 ♘e2 ♘c6 14 ♖fd1 f6!?**

Hoping to use the e5-square as a base and at the same time preventing White from advancing his pawn there.

**15 c3 ♗c5!? 16 ♗e3 ♗xe3 17 ♕xe3 ♕c7 18 ♖d2 0-0 19 ♖ad1 ♘b8**

Not the preferred mode of covering the d-pawn, but Black can still make it work.

**20 ♖d3 f5!?**

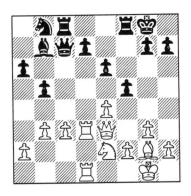

**21 e5 ♗xg2 22 ♔xg2 ♕b7+ 23 ♔g1 ♖c7 24 ♖d6 ♘c6 25 ♘f4 ♖fc8?!**

Up to this point Black has organised himself efficiently, but here-

abouts he starts to dither. 25...♖f7 would have been better.

**26 ♖1d3 ♘d8?**

Compounding his previous error in an attempt to trade his d-pawn for the white e-pawn. Black had to play 26...♖f8 and then ...♖f7.

**27 ♕d2 ♘f7 28 ♖xd7 ♖xd7**

Not 28...♘xe5 29 ♖xc7 ♖xc7 30 ♖e3 ♖d7 (30...♘f3+ 31 ♖xf3 ♕xf3 32 ♕d8+) 31 ♔e2 and wins.

**29 ♖xd7 ♕c6**

Now White cannot prevent ...♘xe5, whereupon the knight will coordinate with the queen to create some counter-chances.

**30 ♘h5 ♘xe5 31 ♖xg7+ ♔h8**

On 31...♔f8 32 ♕f4! ♘f3+ 33 ♔g2, Black is lost. Now both kings are a bit exposed, but White is to move and he can do the damage first.

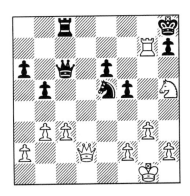

**32 ♕h6?**

Getting it wrong. With 32 ♕f4! White could have set his opponent insuperable problems, e.g. 32...♖d8 33 ♖g8+! ♔xg8 34 ♕g5+ ♘g6 (or 34...♔f7 35 ♕g7+ ♔e8 36 ♘f6 mate) 35 ♕xd8+ and White will pick up at least another pawn, which will do, or 32...♘f3+ (instead of 32...♖d8) 33 ♔g2

♘e1+ 34 ♔f1, when Black's draughty king and scattered men mean that he must lose:

a) 34...♘d3 35 ♕d4 ♕h1+ 36 ♔e2 ♘c1+ 37 ♔d2 and it is all over.

b) 34...♕xc3 35 ♖d7! (the most precise) 35...♘f3 36 ♕h6 ♘xh2+ (if 36...♕e1+ then the white king can escape the checks thus: 37 ♔g2 ♕g1+ 38 ♔xf3 ♕h1+ 39 ♔e2 ♖c2+ 40 ♖d2 ♕e4+ 41 ♔d1) 37 ♔g1 ♕e1+ 38 ♔xh2 ♕xf2+ 39 ♔h3 ♕f1+ 40 ♔h4 ♕h1+ 41 ♔g5 and the king hunt fails after 41...♕c1+ 42 ♘f4 ♖g8+ 43 ♔f6 ♕c3+ 44 ♔xe6 or 41...♖g8+ 42 ♔f6! ♖g6+ 43 ♔f7!, when the prey becomes hunter, e.g. 43...♕a8 44 ♕xg6! hxg6 45 ♘f6, intending 46 ♔xg6 and 47 ♖h7.

**32...♘f3+**

But now Black has just about has enough to draw.

**33 ♔f1**

Or 33 ♔g2 ♘g5+.

**33...♘xh2+ 34 ♔g1 ♘f3+ 35 ♔f1 ♘h2+ 36 ♔g1 ♘f3+ ½-½**

---

### Game 9
### A.Ivanov-De Firmian
### *New York Open 1989*

---

**1 e4 c5 2 ♘f3 d6 3 d4 cxd4 4 ♘xd4 ♘f6 5 ♘c3 a6 6 g3 e6 7 ♗g2 ♗e7 8 0-0 0-0 9 ♗e3 ♗d7**

With this unusual move-order De Firmian renounces the opportunity of meeting g4-g5 with the standard plan of an exchange of knights on d4 followed by the retreat of the king's knight to d7. But he has a very novel stance in mind.

**10 g4 ♘c6 11 g5 ♘e8 12 f4 g6 13 ♘de2 ♘g7**

An unusual method of holding up the attack. The fianchetto of the knight works out well!

**14 ♘g3 ♖c8 15 ♕d2 f5! 16 ♖ad1 ♗e8 17 ♕f2 b5 18 ♖fe1 ♕c7 19 exf5 gxf5! 20 h4 20...b4 21 ♘a4 ♘e5!?**

A highly original tactic.

**22 fxe5 ♗xa4 23 ♗b6 ♕b8 24 ♗a7 ♕c7 25 ♗b6 ♕d7**

Playing to win, but Black might have been wiser to reconcile himself to a draw. As things go he sails very close to the wind.

**26 b3 ♗b5 27 exd6 ♗xd6 28 ♗d4 ♕c7 29 ♘f1 ♖fe8**

This looks like an error, but...

**30 ♗xg7 e5!**

Another unexpected twist.

**31 ♖xd6 ♕xd6 32 ♗f6 f4 33 ♗e4 ♗c6 34 ♗xc6 ♖xc6 35 ♘h2 e4 36 ♘g4 e3 37 ♘h6+ ♔f8 38 ♕f3 ♖xc2 39 ♘f5 ♕d2**

The game reaches boiling point. I imagine that there was a big time scramble here.

**40 ♗g7+ ♔g8 41 ♘h6+!**

Somehow a draw results.

**41...♔xg7 42 ♕b7+ ♔h8 43 ♘f7+ ♔g7 44 ♘h6+ ½-½**

## Game 10
## Timman-Ljubojevic
*Brussels (World Cup) 1988*

**1 e4 c5 2 ♘f3 e6 3 d4 cxd4 4 ♘xd4 ♘c6 5 ♘c3**

The immediate 5 g3 can be met by the freeing 5...d5! 6 ♗g2 dxe4! 7 ♘xc6 ♕xd1+ 8 ♔xd1 bxc6 9 ♗xe4 ♗b7 10 b3 0-0-0+ 11 ♔e2 ♗e7! 12 ♗b2 (12 ♗a3 ♗f6) 12...♗f6 with equality, Anand-Salov, Buenos Aires 1994.

**5...a6 6 g3 d6 7 ♗g2 ♗d7 8 0-0 ♖c8!?**

I believe this to be the first time that this move had been tried. 8...♘f6 is of course standard.

**9 ♘xc6 ♗xc6 10 a4 ♗e7 11 ♕g4 h5!? 12 ♕e2 h4 13 ♖d1 hxg3 14 hxg3 ♕c7 15 ♗f4 ♘f6 16 ♖d2 ♘d7 17 ♘b5**

This sort of elegant tactic is bound to appeal to someone of Timman's tastes.

**17...axb5 18 axb5 ♘e5 19 bxc6 ♕xc6 20 b3 g5!?**

'Ljubo' continues to go for it.

**21 ♗e3 g4 22 ♖ad1 ♖g8 23 ♗f4 ♕c5 24 ♗e3 ♕c6 25 c4 ♖g6 26**

**♖d4 ♔f8 27 ♗c1**

Heading for a3, from where the bishop will eye d6.

**27...♕c5 28 ♗e3 ♕a3 29 ♖b1 ♔g7**

Finally completing an unorthodox system of development.

**30 ♕d1 ♖h8 31 ♖a1 ♕c5 32 ♖d5!? ♕c7 33 ♖b5 ♘c6 34 ♖a2 ♗f6 35 ♗b6 ♕b8 36 ♖d2 ♗e5 37 c5**

After a great deal of manoeuvring, some engagement between the two sides finally occurs. Ljubojevic stays alert.

**37...♘a7! 38 ♖a5 ♘c6 39 ♖b5 ♘a7 40 ♖a5 ♘c6 41 ♖a4?**

It would have been better to repeat with 41 ♖b5 or sacrifice with 41 cxd6 ♘xa5 42 ♗xa5 ♕a7 43 ♗b4 ♕b6 44 ♗a3, with an unclear position.

**41...dxc5 42 ♗xc5 ♖h5**

Already intending ...♗xg3. Timman's now plays too optimistically failing to take the attack down the h-file seriously enough. Disaster results..

**43 ♗b6 ♕h8 44 ♖da2 ♖h2 45 ♗e3 ♖xg2+! 46 ♔xg2 ♕h3+ 47 ♔g1 ♗xg3! 48 fxg3 ♕xg3+ 49 ♔f1 ♕xe3 50 ♕e2 ♖f6+ 0-1**

White resigned. A highly creative game from Ljubo.

## Summary

In the lines with ...♕c7, providing he does not underestimate the latent attacking potential of the white position, Black should be able to reach either a stolid middlegame or at least one with just a marginal and not very significant structural inferiority. After 6...♘ge7 I am sure that the best policy is to retreat with 7 ♘b3, so 6...♘xd4 is worth serious consideration.

**1 e4 c5 2 ♘f3 e6 3 d4 cxd4 4 ♘xd4 ♘c6 5 ♘c3 a6 6 g3**

**6...♕c7**
>     6...♘ge7 *(D)*
>>         7 ♗g2 - *game 5*
>>         7 ♘b3 d6 8 ♗g2 ♗d7 9 0-0 ♘c8 10 a4 ♗e7 11 ♕e2 0-0
>>>             12 a5 - *game 6*
>>>             12 ♗e3 - *game 7*
>     6...♘xd4 - *game 8*
>     6...d6 7 ♗g2
>>         7...♗e7 - *game 9*
>>         7...♗d7 - *game 10*

**6...a6 7 ♗g2 ♘f6**
>     7...d6 - *game 4*

**8 0-0** *(D)* **♘xd4**
>     8...d6 - *game 3*

**9 ♕xd4 ♗c5 10 ♗f4 d6 11 ♕d2 h6 12 ♖ad1 e5 13 ♗e3 ♔e7** *(D)*
>     14 f4 - *game 1*
>     14 h3 - *game 2*

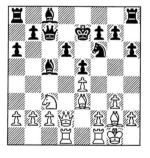

*6...♘ge7*　　　　　*8 0-0*　　　　　*13...♔e7*

# CHAPTER TWO

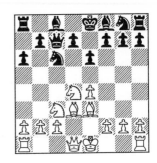

## 5 ♘c3 a6 6 ♗e3 ♛c7 7 ♗d3

**1 e4 c5 2 ♘f3 e6 3 d4 cxd4 4 ♘xd4 ♘c6 5 ♘c3 a6 6 ♗e3 ♛c7 7 ♗d3**

One of the features of the Taimanov move-order is that it does not present White with an obvious active method of deploying either of his bishops: 6 ♗g5, as in the Richter-Rauzer, is impossible, and 6 ♗c4, as in the Sozin, is also quite ineffectual. Nor can White make any dangerous pawn advances (nobody has ever ventured 6 g4!?). Accordingly the formation with 6 ♗e3 and 7 ♗d3 is probably as active as anything for White, as the d3-square is the most aggressive placing of the king's bishop.

If White lines up his pieces thus: pawn on e4, pawn on f4, queen on f3, bishop on e3, bishop on d3, knight on c3 and knight b3, with Black having something like: pawn on a6, pawn on b5, pawn on d6, pawn on e6, queen on c7, bishop on b7, bishop on e7, knight on f6 and knight on c6, then we have what has become known, for obvious reasons, as the 'three-line' set-up.

*see following diagram*

With 6 ♗e3 and 7 ♗d3 White heads towards just such a position, but this book is concerned with Taimanov formations, so the games in this chapter focus on ways in which Black can dodge that Scheveningen-style position. Black has tried four 'Taimanov' alternatives at move seven. I do not consider 7...♗b4?! to be trustworthy (one needs to show some respect for those weak dark squares). The rather drab 7...♘xd4 might be okay, but Black's most critical moves are 7...b5 and 7...♘f6, both of which are worthy of serious attention.

While 7...b5 (Games 11-12) is very much in keeping with the ethos of rapid queenside development, Portisch's 7...♘f6 8 0-0 ♗d6!? is something else: see how easily he equalised

with unconventional bishop move against the World Champion in Game 13. 7...♘f6 8 0-0 ♘e5 (Games 14-17) is one of the oldest treatments, but one that still allows nuances of interpretation, as demonstrated by Pia Cramling in Game 16. From e5 the knight has the flexibility to annoy White at d3, g4 or c4, or drop back to d7 or g6. The transfer of the queen's knight to g6 is a comparative rarity in the Sicilian, but Games 14 and 17 illustrate its viability. Lastly there is the outlandish 7...♘f6 8 0-0 h5!? (Games 18-20), which looks risky but has not yet suffered an outright refutation.

It is possible for great violence to occur very early on in these games, as you will soon gather.

---

### Game 11
### Khalifman-Salov
*Wijk aan Zee (4th match game) 1994*

---

**1 e4 c5 2 ♘f3 ♘c6 3 d4 cxd4 4 ♘xd4 e6 5 ♘c3 ♕c7 6 ♗e3 a6 7 ♗d3 b5 8 ♘xc6**

8 0-0 is considered in the next game.

**8...♕xc6**

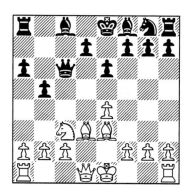

**9 0-0**

In Klovans-Budde, Germany 1995, White played the aggressive 9 e5 and, instead of the standard 9...♗b7, Black played 9...♗b4 10 0-0 ♗xc3 11 bxc3 ♗b7. However, after 12 ♕g4 the deficiencies in Black's dark squares began to show.

**9...♗b7 10 a3**

10 ♕e2 b4 11 ♘b1 ♘f6 12 ♘d2 d5 is obviously perfectly satisfactory for Black (Taimanov).

**10...♘f6**

Taimanov recommends 10...♘e7, to meet 11 ♕g4 ♘g6 12 f4 with 12...♗c5, as in Minic-Taimanov, Palma de Mallorca 1970.

**11 ♕e2 ♗e7 12 f4 0-0 13 ♕f3**

This was a new move at the time. Previously 13 e5 had been tried, when 13...♘d5 14 ♘xd5 ♕xd5 offers equal chances.

**13...♗c5! 14 ♔h1**

On 14 ♗xc5 ♕xc5+ 15 ♔h1, Black might even consider 15...e5!?

**14...♖ac8 15 ♗xc5 ♕xc5 16 ♕g3**

Planning e4-e5.

**16...d5! 17 e5 ♘e4 18 ♕h4 f5!**

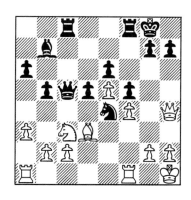

18...f6 looks tempting, but Salov thought White would be able to

---

generate some counterplay with 19 f5!
♘xc3 20 bxc3 fxe5 21 fxe6 e4 22 ♗e2.
He therefore tries for a more long-term, strategical advantage.

**19 ♘e2 d4**

Black has the upper hand: White
has no initiative and the knight on e4
is splendidly deployed.

**20 ♘g1 ♘d2 21 ♖f2 ♘c4 22 b4
♕d5**

22...♕b6! looks even better.

**23 ♘f3 ♘e3 24 h3 ♖c7 25 a4 ♖fc8
26 axb5 axb5 27 ♖a5 ♘c4 28 ♖a1
♘b2?**

The beginning of a miscalculated
tactical sequence, which ultimately
squanders some of Black's advantage.

**29 ♖d2! ♖d7**

Since the apparently devastating
coup 29...♘xd3 30 ♖xd3 ♖xc2 31
♖xd4 ♕xd4!? 32 ♘xd4 ♖xg2 is actually adequately countered by 33 ♕e7!
♗d5 34 ♕xe6+!, Salov changes direc-
tion.

**30 ♕f2?**

Not the best. White should have
played 30 ♗f1 d3 31 c3.

**30...♘c4 31 ♖e2 ♖cd8 32 ♔h2 ♕c6
33 ♕h4 ♘b2 34 ♕e1 ♘xd3 35 cxd3
♕c3 36 ♕b1 ♗d5**

After 36...♗xf3 37 gxf3 White has
compensation for his own weaknesses
in the form of the targets at b5 and e6,
plus the a-file.

**37 ♖a6 h6 38 ♖a5 ♖b7 39 ♖a1 ♖c8
40 ♘e1 ♖bc7 41 ♖a5 ♖b8 42 ♖a1**

Not 42 ♖c2?? ♕xe1! 43 ♕xe1 ♖xc2
and wins.

**42...♖bc8 43 ♖a5 ♖b8 44 ♖a1 ♕c6**

Black retains some positional advantage here.

**45 ♕b2 ♕b6 46 ♖c2 ♖bc8 47 ♖xc7
♖xc7 48 ♕f2 ♖c3 49 ♕h4 ♔b7 50
♕f2 ♕b6 51 ♕h4 ♕c7 52 ♖a5?!**

52 ♕f2 would have been better.

**52...♗c6 53 ♕f2 ♕d7 54 ♖a6 ♔h7
55 ♖a1 ♖b3 56 ♕d2 ♗b7 57 ♖c1
♗d5 58 ♖c5 ♖a3 59 ♕b2?**

Now, at last, Black succeeds in
achieving something along the diagonal.

**59...♖a2 60 ♕xd4 ♕b7! 61 ♖c2**

Conceding that it is all over, but after 61 ♕g1 Black would have been
able to give a spectacular demonstration of the power of his coordinated
major pieces by tying White up completely with the sacrifice 61...♗xg2! 62
♘xg2 ♕f3!

For example:

a) 63 ♖c1 ♖xg2+! 64 ♛xg2 ♛xf4+ and 65...♛xc1.

b) 63 ♖xb5 ♛xf4+ 64 ♔h1 ♛g3! 65 ♖a5 ♖b2 66 ♖a1 ♛xh3+ 67 ♛h2 ♛g4 68 ♖f1 f4!, and the pawn will march triumphantly on, for, clearly, it cannot be captured.

c) 63 d4 ♛xf4+ 64 ♔h1 ♛g3 65 ♖c1 ♛xh3+ 66 ♛h2 ♛g4 and Black can help himself to the pawns, for instance, 67 ♖g1 ♛xd4.

**61...♖xc2 62 ♘xc2 ♗xg2 63 ♛c5 ♗h1 64 ♘e1 ♗d5**

Excellent centralisation.

**65 ♔g3 ♛a6 66 ♛c1 ♛a2 67 ♛c2 ♛a1 68 ♛d2 g5! 69 ♛e3 ♔g6 70 ♘f3 ♛f1 71 fxg5 ♗xf3 72 ♛xf3 ♛g1+ 0-1**

**1 e4 c5 2 ♘f3 ♘c6 3 d4 cxd4 4 ♘xd4 ♛c7 5 ♘c3 e6 6 ♗e3 a6 7 ♗d3 b5 8 0-0!? ♗b7**

In J.Polgar-Ljubojevic, Buenos Aires 1994, play went instead 8...♘f6 9 ♛e2 ♗b7 10 a3 ♗e7 11 f4 d6 12 ♘f3 0-0 13 ♖ae1 b4! with level chances.

**9 ♘b3**

---

*see following diagram*

---

This is not the most ambitious formation for White, and now Black should really have gone into the three-line middlegame mentioned in the introduction to this chapter with 9...d6. Instead he embarks on a time-consuming manoeuvre that quickly rebounds on him.

**9...♘e5?! 10 f4 ♘c4 11 ♗d4!**

A novelty that was proposed by V.Sokolov some twenty-five years before this game! The weedy 11 ♗c1? merely justifies Black's escapade.

**11...d6**

11...♘xb2 12 ♘xb5! axb5 13 ♗xb2 is better for White.

**12 ♛e2**

Threatening a2-a4.

**12...e5?! 13 ♘d5!**

Already the black game is critical.

**13...♗xd5 14 exd5 ♗e7**

14...f6 was just about the only defence, but it is difficult to bring oneself to play such an ugly move.

**15 fxe5 dxe5**

15...♘xe5 16 a4 is also strong.

**16 &xc4 exd4 17 d6!**

Destroying the opposition.

**17...&xc4 18 &f3 &b8**

There is no defence: 18...&a7 19 &ae1 &f6 20 dxe7 and wins; or 18...&d8 19 &a5 &e6 20 dxe7 &xe7 21 &ae1 &d5 22 &c6 &xf3 23 &xe7+ &f8 24 &xf3, etc.

**19 &ae1!**

With the idea of &a5.

**19...&f6 20 &xe7+ &f8 21 &a5 &c5**

Black has had it, but the finale after 21...&b4 would have been highly attractive:

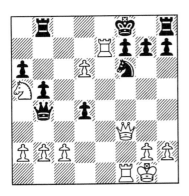

22 &d5!! &xd5 23 &fxf7+ &g8 24 &xg7+ &f8 25 &ef7+ &e8 26 d7+ &d8 27 &c6+ &c7 28 d8&+ &xc6 29 &f6+!! &xf6 (or 29...&c5 30 &c7+ &xc7 31 &xc7+ &d5 32 &c6+ &e5 33 &e6 mate) 30 &c7+ &d5 31 &g5+ and mate. King hunts can be fun!

**22 &b3 &h5 23 &c6 &c8 24 d7 &d8 25 &e8+! 1-0**

Black resigned because of 25...&xe8 26 &xd8 &f6 27 &c6 and wins, or 25...&xe8 26 &b4+ &g8 27 dxe8&+ &xe8 28 &e7+ &f8 29 &g6+ &f8 20 &f8 mate. Very much a Jonny Hector game.

---

**1 e4 c5 2 &f3 e6 3 d4 cxd4 4 &xd4 a6 5 &c3 &c7 6 &d3 &c6 7 &e3 &f6 8 0-0**

Here Black can meet 8 &xc6 with 8...bxc6 followed by ...d7-d5.

**8...&d6!?**

Theory currently regards this as an acceptable move. Black's alternatives here are considered in Games 14-20.

**9 &xc6**

There is also the razor-sharp 9 f4!? &xd4 10 e5!? with great complications, which are as yet unresolved, but look what happened to Bojan Kurajica when he played Black against Zurab Azmaiparashvili at Strumica 1995: 10...&c5 11 exf6 &xc2 12 fxg7 &xe3+ 13 &h1 &g8 14 &xc2 &xg7 15 &ae1 &xf4 16 &xf4! &xf4 17 &d5 &h4 18 &e4! and White is winning. Instead of 9...&xd4 Black can virtually force the win of material with 9...&c5, since 10 &e2 would allow an excellent trade of the queen for three minor pieces after 10...&b6 11 &a4

♗xd4 12 ♘xb6 ♗xe3+ 13 ♔h1 ♗xb6. White must therefore play 10 ♘f5, when 10...♘e7!? is critical: after 11 ♘xg7+ ♔f8 12 ♗xc5 ♕xc5+ 13 ♔h1 ♔xg7 14 e5 ♘e8 15 ♘e4 White has a strong attack, but there are many defensive resources for Black too. One of the latest games in this crucial line, Topalov-Hübner, Wijk aan Zee 1996, continued: 15...♕c7 16 ♕h5 ♘g6 17 ♘f6!? (a new move; Ma.Tseitlin-Faerman, Israel 1993, went 17 ♖f3 d5 18 ♘g5 with a strong attack. Play concluded 18...♔g8 19 ♕h6! ♘g7 20 ♖h3! ♗d7 21 ♘xh7 ♗e8 22 ♗xg6 fxg6 23 ♘f6+ 1-0) 17...♕d8 18 f5! exf5 19 ♕xf5 d5 20 ♕g5

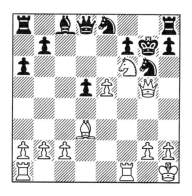

(White has just the one pawn for his knight but he retains a strong attack, in particular through the powerful knight at f6) 20...♗e6 21 ♖ae1 ♕a5?! 22 ♘h5+ ♔f8 23 ♗xg6 hxg6 24 ♘f4 ♗f5 25 e6! ♕c7 26 exf7 ♔xf7 27 g4! (winning the piece back with a good game) 27...♖xc2 28 ♖e2 ♕c6 29 gxf5 d4+ 30 ♔g1 d3 31 ♕e7+ ♔g8 32 ♖e6 ♖h7 33 ♘xg6 ♖xe7 34 ♘xe7+ ♔f7 35 ♘xc6 bxc6 36 ♖d1 ♖d8 37 ♖e3 and Black resigned. (This game goes some way to demonstrating why many people regard Veselin Topalov as a potential challenger for the World Championship.)

Of course White can also play the placid 9 g3 ♘xd4 10 ♗xd4 ♗e5 11 ♗xe5 ♕xe5 with equal chances or 9 h3, although after 9...♗h2+!? (9...♗f4 immediately is probably better) 10 ♔h1 ♗f4 11 ♕c1?! (11 ♗xf4! ♕xf4 12 ♘de2 ♕c7 13 f4 is perhaps a shade in White's favour) 11...♗xe3 12 ♕xe3 ♕b6 13 ♘f5 ♕xe3 14 ♘xe3 b5 Black enjoyed comfortable equality in Anand-Portisch, Brussels 1992. There was also a curious game between Marciano (not Rocky!) and Hjartarson in 1993 which went 9 ♔h1 h5!? (9...♗f4 is also perfectly playable) 10 ♘xc6 (not 10 ♗e2 ♗xh2 11 g3 h4!) 10...dxc6 11 f4 ♘g4 12 ♕e2 e5 13 f5 ♕e7 14 ♘a4 b5 15 ♘b6 ♖b8 16 ♘xc8 ♖xc8 17 a4 ♗c5 18 ♗xc5 ♕xc5 19 g3 ♔e7, when Black stood better.

**9...bxc6**

The alternative recapture 9...dxc6 is considered slightly too risky for Black due to Ivanchuk's 10 f4 e5 11 f5 b5 12 a4 ♖b8 13 ♕e2, intending g2-g4 once Black castles.

**10 f4 e5 11 f5 ♗e7 12 ♘a4**

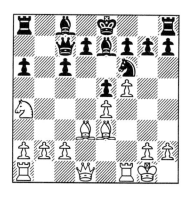

One of Kasparov's most fearsome weapons is his ability to surprise opponents with new moves in the opening. Many of these enrich or even alter the theory of established lines, but this is not always the case, and although 12 ♘a4 was new here, Kasparov did not repeat the experiment.

Black also manages to organise the ...d7-d5 break after 12 ♕f3 ♗b7. Emms-Sion Castro, Benidorm 1993, continued 13 g4!? h6! 14 ♗c4 d5! 15 exd5 cxd5 16 ♘xd5 ♕xc4 17 ♘xf6+ ♗xf6 18 ♕xb7 ♕xg4+ 19 ♕g2 ♕xg2+ 20 ♔xg2 ♖c8 with equality, while in Ma.Tseitlin-Kurajica, Benasque 1993, 13 ♘a4 was tried, although Black's reaction in the centre was once again sufficient after 13...d5 14 ♗b6 ♕b8 15 c4 (Black is also fine after 15 ♕g3 0-0 and 15 ♗c5 ♗xc5 16 ♘xc5 ♗c8!) 15...dxc4 16 ♗xc4 c5!? 17 ♗xc5 ♗xc5+ 18 ♘xc5 ♕a7 19 b4 ♗xe4 20 ♕f2 ♗b7 21 ♘xb7 ♕xb7 22 ♕c5 ♘d7 23 ♕d6 ♕b6+ 24 ♕xb6 ♘xb6, when the game was drawn in 37 moves.

**12...d5 13 ♗b6 ♕b8 14 ♕e2!? c5!**

A very ingenious twist; Portisch creates the threat of 15...♗d7.

**15 ♗xc5?!**

Perhaps this move does not warrant any question-marks, as it seems that White can still hang on, but 15 c4! ♘d7 (15...♗d7 16 ♗c2! dxc4 17 ♗a5 is a little better for White) 15 ♗a5 d4 would have led to an equal position.

**15...♗xc5+ 16 ♘xc5 ♕b6 17 ♕f2**

17 ♕e3 ♘g4 18 ♕g5 ♕xc5+ 19 ♔h1 fails to 19...h5! 20 h3 ♗b7!

**17...♘g4 18 ♘a4 ♕xf2+ 19 ♖xf2 ♘xf2 20 ♔xf2 d4 21 b4**

Kasparov sets about erecting a fortress. When selecting his fifteenth move the World Champion must have assessed this ending as tenable.

**21...♗d7 22 ♘c5 ♗b5 23 a4 ♗xd3 24 cxd3 ♔e7 25 ♖c1 ♖hc8 26 ♖c4 ♖c6 27 a5**

After this there is really very little that Portisch can undertake.

**27...♖b8 28 ♔e2 ♔d6 29 h4 h5 30 ♔f3 ♖b5 31 g4 g6 32 g5 ♖b8 33 f6 ♖b5 34 ♔e2 ♖cxc5 35 bxc5+ ♔c6 36 ♖a4 ♖xc5 37 ♖a2 ♖b5 ½-½**

*Game 14*
**Short-Ribli**
*Belfort (World Cup) 1988*

**1 e4 c5 2 ♘f3 e6 3 d4 cxd4 4 ♘xd4**

♘c6 5 ♘c3 ♕c7 6 ♗e3 a6 7 ♗d3
♘f6 8 0-0 ♘e5!?

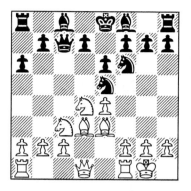

One of the oldest treatments, and still popular.

**9 h3**

To dissuade a knight from coming to g4.

**9...♗c5 10 ♕e2**

White can prepare f2-f4 either with this move or with 10 ♔h1, which is considered in Games 15 and 16. The pseudo-Maroczy Bind 10 ♘a4 ♗a7 11 c4 is much less effective here as Black's bishop is very well placed on a7.

**10...d6 11 f4 ♘g6**

11...♘ed7 is also playable, and I would imagine perhaps more harmonious.

**12 ♕f2**

The most critical move. 12 ♘b3 ♗xe3+ 13 ♕xe3 b5 14 a3 0-0 presents Black with few problems.

**12...0-0! 13 ♔h1**

This was the first time that this natural move had been played. 13 e5?! dxe5 14 ♘xe6 ♗xe6 15 ♗xc5 ♘xf4!? grants Black interesting compensation for the exchange.

**13...♗d7 14 ♖ae1 ♖ac8 15 ♘b3**

♗xe3 16 ♕xe3 h6!?

On 16...e5, White could effect a dangerous exchange sacrifice with 17 fxe5 dxe5 18 ♖xf6!? gxf6 19 ♘d5 ♕d6 20 ♕h6.

**17 e5 dxe5 18 fxe5 ♘h7 19 a4 ♖cd8**

A little inaccurate. 19...♗c6! would have held the balance, but now Short skilfully manoeuvres himself into a position of advantage.

**20 ♖f2 ♗c6 21 ♔g1 ♖fe8 22 ♘d2!**

Off to a better place.

**22...♘hf8 23 ♘c4 ♖e7 24 a5!**

Fixing the queenside dark-squared weaknesses.

**24...♗d5 25 ♘b6 ♗c6 26 ♖d2 ♖ee8?!**

Here, and again at move 30, Ribli himself claims that the waiting move ...♔h8 would have been better.

**27 ♘c4 ♖e7 28 ♖ed1 ♖ed7 29 ♕c5 ♕b8 30 b4 ♘f4? 31 ♘b6! ♘xd3 32 ♘xd7! ♘xd7 33 ♖xd3 ♖c8 34 ♕d6 ♕a7+ 35 ♕d4 ♕b8 36 ♖e1 b6**

**37 ♖g3?**

It would have been better to have captured on b6, preserving the integrity of his queenside, as the splitting of the white pawns helps Black in his efforts to draw the game.

**37...bxa5 38 bxa5 ♕c7 39 ♕f4 ♔f8 40 ♕g4 g6 41 ♕b4+ ♔g7 42 ♖ge3 ♗a8**

Black has counterplay down the c-file, but he should still lose this position. However, Short commits a series of second-rate moves and lets Ribli grab the very useful a-pawn.

**43 ♕d4 ♘c5**

Not 43...♘xe5 44 ♘a4! f6 45 ♘b6 and Black is struggling.

**44 ♕f4? ♕xa5**

Thank you.

**45 ♖f1 ♖f8 46 h4 ♘d7 47 ♘e2 ♕c5 48 ♘d4 a5?**

Dreadfully imprecise! Black should have played 48...♗d5 with equality.

**49 ♕xf7+! ♖xf7 50 ♘xe6+ ♔g8 51 ♘xc5 ♘xc5 52 ♖c3 ♖c7 53 ♖a1 ♘e6**

Now Black has nothing better.

**54 ♖xc7 ♘xc7 55 ♖xa5**

It is certainly a lot less drawn than it was!

**55...♗e4 56 ♔f2 ♔f8 57 ♖a4 ♗f5 58 ♖a7 ♘b5 59 ♖a8+ ♔e7 60 c4 ♘c7?!**

60...♘d4 61 ♔e3 ♘c6 62 ♔f4 ♗d3 63 c5 h5 would have been better.

**61 ♖h8 ♔e6 62 ♔e3?!**

62 ♖xh6 ♔xe5 63 g4! was more promising.

**62...♔xe5 63 ♖xh6 ♘e8! 64 g4 ♘f6!**

A clever defence.

**65 gxf5 ♘g4+ 66 ♔d3 ♘xh6 67 fxg6 ♘f5 68 h5 ♘e7!**

Although stretched to their limits, Black's defensive resources are sufficient to draw this ending.

**69 c5**

The variation 69 ♔c3 ♔f5 70 ♔d4 ♔g5 71 ♔e5 ♔xh5 72 g7 ♔g6 73 ♔e6 ♘g8 74 c5 ♔xg7 75 c6 ♔f8! 76 c7 ♘e7 shows just how close Black is to defeat.

**69...♔d5!**

The only move.

**70 ♔e3 ♔e5 71 ♔d3 ♔d5 72 g7 ♘g8 73 ♔e3 ♔xc5 74 ♔f4 ♔d6 75 ♔f5 ♔e7 76 ♔g6 ♔e6 77 h6 ♘e7+ ½-½**

---

*Game 15*
### Kasparov-Anand
*Tilburg 1991*

---

**1 e4 c5 2 ♘f3 ♘c6 3 d4 cxd4 4 ♘xd4 ♕c7 5 ♘c3 e6 6 ♗e3 a6 7 ♗d3 ♘f6 8 0-0 ♘e5!? 9 h3 ♗c5 10 ♔h1 d6 11 f4 ♘c6?**

This looks innocent enough, but this game shows why the knight ought to go to g6, d7 or d3, but definitely not back here. 11...♘xd3 is considered in the next game.

**12 e5!**

Already we find ourselves in the midst of a dark wood of complications.

**12...♘xe5**

There are many sub-variations, but they all favour White:

a) 12...dxe5 13 ♘db5! axb5 14 ♗xc5 and Kasparov assesses White's advantage as already decisive.

b) 12...♘d7 13 exd6 with advantage.

c) 12...♘d5 13 ♘xd5 exd5 14 ♘xc6!, e.g. 14...♗xe3 15 ♘b4, intending 16 ♕f3.

d) 12...♗xd4 13 ♗xd4 dxe5 14 fxe5 ♘d7 15 ♘e4! ♘cxe5 16 ♕h5 with dangerous threats.

**13 fxe5 dxe5**

Now Black must regain his piece, but it is a case of out of the frying pan and into the fire!

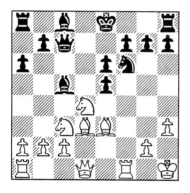

**14 ♗b5+?**

Even the best players sometimes get lost in the forest! The right move was 14 ♘db5!, viz. 14...axb5 15 ♗xb5+ ♗d7 (or 15...♔e7 16 ♗g5 with a strong attack) 16 ♗xd7+ ♘xd7 17 ♗xc5 ♕xc5 (after 17...♘xc5, 18 ♘b5-d6+ will win) 18 ♖xf7! and wins.

**14...axb5?**

Thud and blunder! Black should have played 14...♔f8!, when after 15 ♖xf6!? exd4! 16 ♗f4!? ♕e7 he is hanging on by the skin of his teeth in horrendous complications. Now a series

of punches puts him away

**15 ♘dxb5 ♕b6 16 ♗xc5 ♕xc5 17 ♘d6+ ♔e7 18 ♖xf6!**

The main point.

**18...gxf6**

Of course 18...♕xd6 fails to 19 ♖xf7+.

**19 ♘ce4 ♕d4**

Trying somehow to shield the soft spot at f6, but in a lost cause.

**20 ♕h5 ♖f8 21 ♖d1**

A useful gain of time.

**21...♕e3 22 ♕h4 ♕f4 23 ♕e1!**

Even this elliptical prosecution of the attack will do; Black's men do not cooperate in any way.

**23...♖a4 24 ♕c3 ♖d4 25 ♖xd4 ♕f1+ 26 ♔h2 exd4 27 ♕c5 ♔d7 28 ♘b5!**

A neat finish.

**28...♕f4+ 29 g3 1-0**

And since capturing the knight allows mate in three, Black resigned.

---

*Game 16*
## Kindermann-P.Cramling
*Germany 1995*

1 e4 c5 2 ♘f3 e6 3 d4 cxd4 4 ♘xd4 ♘c6 5 ♘c3 a6 6 ♗e3 ♕c7 7 ♗d3 ♘f6 8 0-0 ♘e5!? 9 h3 ♗c5 10 ♔h1 d6 11 f4 ♘xd3!?

Nobody had ever played this obvious move before Pia gave it a whirl.

**12 cxd3**

12 ♕xd3 b5 13 ♘b3 ♗xe3 14 ♕xe3 ♗b7 is equal.

**12...b5 13 ♖c1**

Threatening b2-b4.

**13...♕b6 14 ♘ce2 0-0!?**

It would be crazy for Black to try and win material with 14...e5?: after

15 fxe5 dxe5 16 ♖xc5! ♕xc5 17 ♘f5
White has a rampant initiative, e.g.
17...♕f8 18 b4!?

**15 ♗g1**

A critical juncture. 15 b4 was the
sharpest move, but it is by no means
clearly favourable for White after
15...♗xb4 16 ♘c2 ♕a5 (16...♗c5 17
d4 traps the bishop, but Black may
still be in the game with 17...♘xe4 18
dxc5 dxc5) 17 a3 ♗c5 18 d4 ♗xa3!? 19
♗d2 ♕a4!? 20 ♖a1 ♘xe4!? 21 ♖xa3
♕c4.

Black has three pawns and a sound
position for her bishop.

**15...b4!**

Stopping all the nonsense with b2-
b4.

16 e5 ♘d7!? 17 ♕e1 ♗b7 18 ♕g3
♖ac8 19 ♖fe1

Passing on 19 ♘xe6 fxe6 20 d4,
since this would have been fine for
Black after 20...♕b5! 21 dxc5 ♕xe2 22
cxd6.

**19...♗d5 20 ♘xe6!?**

But now White tries it.

**20...fxe6 21 d4 ♕b7**

There is nothing better.

**22 dxc5 dxc5 23 a3 ½-½**

---

*Game 17*
**Sax-Zso.Polgar**
*Aarhus 1993*

---

1 e4 c5 2 ♘f3 e6 3 d4 cxd4 4 ♘xd4
♘c6 5 ♘c3 ♕c7 6 ♗e3 a6 7 ♗d3
♘f6 8 0-0 ♘e5!? 9 h3 d6!?

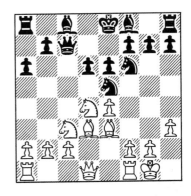

Zsofia has quite a different set-up in
mind to 9...♗c5: she keeps the dark-
squared bishop inside the pawn chain
and shifts her knight across to g6,
where it serves as something of a lure
for the aggressively minded Gyula
Sax.

10 ♕e2 ♗e7 11 f4 ♘g6 12 g4!? h6!
13 a4?! 0-0 14 ♘f3?! ♘d7!? 15
♕g2?!

A motley bunch of moves indeed!

**15...♗f6!?**

The lady poises herself.

**16 ♖a3?**

Sax is unrecognisable here as a former World Championship Candidate.

**16...d5!? 17 e5**

Or 17 exd5 ♘xf4 with good counterplay.

**17...♗e7 18 ♖aa1 ♗c5 19 ♘d4?**

White's last gaffe.

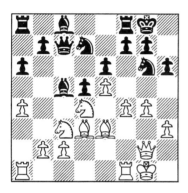

**19...♘xf4! 20 ♖xf4 ♘xe5**

Now Black threatens to take on d3 and then fork the rook and knight with ...e6-e5. White's uncoordinated pieces cannot prevent material loss.

**21 ♖f2 ♘xd3 22 cxd3 ♛e5 23 ♔h1 ♛xe3 0-1**

> ### Game 18
> ### Golubev-Zviaginsev
> *Loosdorf Open 1993*

**1 e4 c5 2 ♘f3 e6 3 ♘c3 ♘c6 4 d4 cxd4 5 ♘xd4 ♛c7 6 ♗e3 ♘f6 7 ♗d3 a6 8 0-0 h5!?**

Really avant-garde! The immediate 8...♘xd4 9 ♗xd4 ♗c5 leads to very similar play, but without the moves h2-h3 ...h7-h5, and this gives White the interesting additional possibility

of 10 ♗xf6 gxf6 11 ♛g4!?, when Black should play 11...♔f8! Note that 8...b5 transposes to the note to Black's eighth move in Game 12.

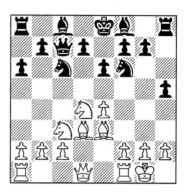

**9 h3 ♘xd4**

9...b5 is considered in Game 20.

**10 ♗xd4 ♗c5 11 ♗xc5**

See the next game for 11 ♗e2.

**11...♛xc5 12 ♛f3 d6**

This does not seem very precise. Golubev proposed 12...h4! 13 ♖ad1 d6 in order to keep a grip on the dark squares.

**13 ♛g3 g5?!**

Something of a shot in the dark.

**14 ♘a4!? ♛a5**

Black must stay on the g5-pawn.

**15 b3**

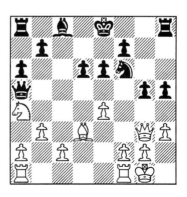

The upshot of White's surprising 14th move is that Black must somehow cover both d6 and g5.

**15...♗e7**

Hence this decision.

**16 f4**

Naturally White strives to open up lines to exploit the underdevelopment of his opponent's pieces, whilst also hoping to show that the early kingside advances have created weaknesses.

**16...♖g8 17 e5 ♘e8 18 ♖ad1 ♗d7 19 exd6+ ♘xd6 20 ♗h7!**

White proceeds in very active fashion.

**20...♗xa4 21 ♗xg8 ♕c5+ 22 ♕f2 ♕xf2+ 23 ♖xf2 ♘e4!? 24 ♗h7! ♘xf2 25 ♔xf2 ♗c6 26 fxg5 ♖h8 27 ♗d3 h4 28 g3 f6 29 gxf6+ ♔xf6 30 gxh4**

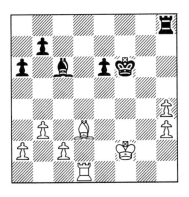

The smoke clears and we have an endgame in which the h-pawn leaves White clearly better.

**30...e5 31 ♗e2! ♖xh4 32 ♗g4**

The best post in the endgame for the bishop.

**32...♔e7 33 ♖d2 b5 34 c4 b4 35 c5 ♖h6 36 ♔e3**

Inexorably White makes progress.

**36...a5 37 ♖f2 ♔d8 38 ♖f8+ ♔c7 39 ♖f7+ ♔b8 40 ♖f8+ ♔c7 41 ♖f7+ ♔b8 42 ♖e7 ♗g2 43 ♖xe5 ♗xh3 44 ♗xh3 ♖xh3+ 45 ♔d4**

This position is an easy win. In addition to his extra pawn, which is already passed, White has an active king in comparison to the stranded and ineffectual black one.

**45...♖c3 46 ♔d5 ♔b7 47 ♖e7+ ♔a6 48 ♖e6+ ♔a7 49 ♔c6 a4 50 ♔b5 axb3 51 axb3 1-0**

---

*Game 19*
**Kulaots-Miezis**
*Riga Zonal 1995*

---

**1 e4 c5 2 ♘f3 e6 3 d4 cxd4 4 ♘xd4 a6 5 ♘c3 ♕c7 6 ♗d3 ♘c6 7 ♗e3 ♘f6 8 0-0 h5 9 h3 ♘xd4 10 ♗xd4 ♗c5 11 ♗e2**

I do not like this move. In principle, if White can get an advantage by retreating his bishop from d3 to e2 here, then Black's preceding moves must have been pretty grotty.

**11...♕d6**

Insisting upon the swap.

**12 ♗xc5 ♕xc5 13 ♕d3 b5 14 ♕g3 ♗b7!**

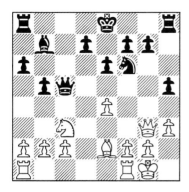

**15 e5**

The consequences of 15 ♕xg7 ♔e7 16 ♕g3 ♖ag8 are fine for Black: his activity constitutes full compensation.

**15...h4!**

With this zwischenzug Black takes over the initiative.

**16 ♕f4**

And not 16 ♕xg7? ♖g8.

**16...♘h5 17 ♗xh5**

17 ♕xh4 ♕xe5 18 ♖ae1 ♕f4! 19 ♕xf4 ♘xf4 is also better for Black.

**17...♖xh5 18 ♘e4 ♗xe4 19 ♕xe4 ♖c8**

White cannot cover both pawns.

**20 ♖ad1 ♕xe5 21 ♕b7 ♖c7 22 ♕a8+ ♔e7 23 c3**

Black is also on top after 23 ♕xa6 ♖xc2 24 ♕a3+ ♕c5.

**23...♕c5! 24 ♖d4**

Now 24 ♕xa6 would have been met by 24...♖a7.

**24...g6 25 ♖fd1 ♕c6 26 ♕xc6 dxc6 27 c4**

White has scant drawing chances unless he can manage to activate his rooks.

**27...c5 28 ♖d6 bxc4 29 ♖xa6 ♖d5 30 ♖c1 ♖b7 31 ♖c2 ♖d1+ 32 ♔h2 ♖b1 33 ♖xc4 ♖1xb2 34 f3 ♖c7?!**

A simpler idea would have been 34...♖f2!? 35 ♖xc5 ♖bb2 (doubled rooks on the seventh – rarely a bad scheme) 36 ♖g5 ♖xf3 37 ♖a4 ♖ff2 38 ♖xh4 ♖xa2, and although there is still a long road ahead, it might well have victory at the end of it.

**35 ♖xh4 c4 36 ♖a4!**

The only move.

**36...c3 37 ♖hc4 ♖bb7 38 ♖ab4 ♖a7**

Perhaps this was time pressure. The last winning try was 38...♔d8!?, e.g. 39 ♖xb7 ♖xc4 40 ♖b1 ♔c7 41 ♔g3 ♔c6 42 ♔f2 ♖a4! 43 ♖a1 ♔c5 44 ♔e3 ♔c4 45 h4 ♖a5, when Black still holds the upper hand.

**39 ♖a4! ♔f8? 40 ♖xc3 ♖xa4 41 ♖xc7 ♖xa2 42 ♔g3 e5 43 ♖c5 ♖e2 44 ♖c4 ♔g7 45 ♖e4 ♖xe4 46 fxe4 f5 47 exf5 gxf5 48 ♔f3 ♔f6 49 g4 fxg4+ 50 hxg4 ♔g5 51 ♔e4 ♔xg4 52 ♔xe5 ½-½**

---

*Game 20*
**Mainka-Miladinovic**
*Ano Liosia Open 1995*

---

1 e4 c5 2 ♘f3 ♘c6 3 d4 cxd4 4 ♘xd4 ♕c7 5 ♘c3 e6 6 ♗e3 ♘f6 7 ♗d3 a6 8 0-0 h5 9 h3 b5

Another way to start the day.

**10 a3**

White also has a slight edge after 10 ♘xc6 ♕xc6 11 a3 ♗b7 12 ♖e1, as Black does not have a safe haven for his king.

**10...♗b7 11 ♕e1 ♖c8 12 f4 ♘xd4 13 ♗xd4 ♗c5 14 ♗xc5 ♕xc5+ 15 ♔h1**

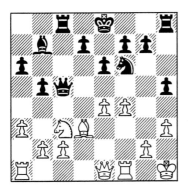

So we have a standard Taimanov middlegame in which Black's h-pawn has gone sailing away, which means that he can hardly contemplate castling. White is therefore always liable to stand better, particularly in the event of lines becoming open. But, for all that, Miladinovic, one of the world's most creative Taimanov players, makes a good show of it.

**15...d6 16 ♕h4 ♔f8 17 ♖ae1 b4 18 axb4 ♕xb4 19 ♖a1 ♕xb2 20 ♖ab1 ♕xc3 21 ♖xb7 a5**

Black's lack of coordination makes it hard for him to capitalise on his extra pawn in this complex position.

**22 ♕g5 e5 23 fxe5 dxe5 24 ♕e3 ♖h6!? 25 ♕a7 ♖g6 26 ♖xf7+ ♔g8**

**27 ♖b7 a4**

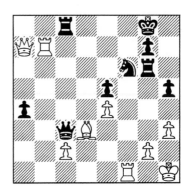

**28 ♕f2 ♖f8 29 ♕e2 a3 30 ♖a7 ♔h7 31 ♗c4 ♔h6 32 ♖a6 h4 33 ♖f5 ♔g5 34 ♖f3 ♕a1+ 35 ♖f1 ♕d4 36 ♖d1 ♕c5 37 ♖d5 ♕b4 38 ♖b5 ♕c3 39 ♖b3 ♕a1+**

Finally ending the funny chase between the rook and queen.

**40 ♔h2 ♕c1 41 ♖f3 ♔h7 42 ♕f2**

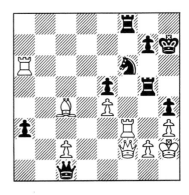

**42...♖g3?**

A gross oversight.

**43 ♖xg3 ♘g4+ 44 ♖xg4 1-0**

Realising that 44...♖xf2 loses to 45 ♖xh4+, Black resigned. A curious game altogether.

## Summary

The fact that such natural attackers as Kasparov and Topalov favour this variation for White should alert you to the fact that Black needs to exert extreme caution in this variation. I cannot really recommend 7...♘f6 8 0-0 h5 (much as I would like to!), but 7...b5, 7...♘f6 8 0-0 ♘e5!?, and 7...♘f6 8 0-0 ♗d6!? are all playable, but do please watch yourself in the last of these!

**1 e4 c5 2 ♘f3 e6 3 d4 cxd4 4 ♘xd4 ♘c6 5 ♘c3 a6 6 ♗e3 ♕c7 7 ♗d3**

**7...♘f6**
    7...b5
        8 ♘xc6 ♕xc6 9 0-0 - *game 11*
        8 0-0 ♗b7 9 ♘b3 - *game 12*
**8 0-0 *(D)* ♘e5**
    8...♗d6 - *game 13*
    8...h5 9 h3
        9...♘xd4 10 ♗xd4 ♗c5 *(D)*
            11 ♗xc5 - *game 18*
            11 ♗e2 - *game 19*
        9...b5 - *game 20*
**9 h3 ♗c5**
    9...d6 - *game 17*
**10 ♔h1**
    10 ♕e2 - *game 14*
**10...d6 11 f4 *(D)***
    11...♘c6 - *game 15*
    11...♘xd3 - *game 16*

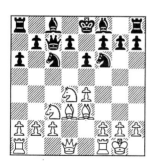
    *8 0-0*

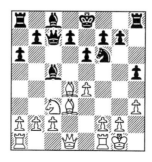
    *10...♗c5*

    *11 f4*

# CHAPTER THREE

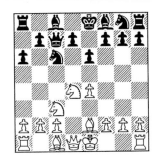

## 5 ♘c3 a6 6 ♗e2 ♕c7: Introduction

**1 e4 c5 2 ♘f3 e6 3 d4 cxd4 4 ♘xd4 ♘c6 5 ♘c3 a6 6 ♗e2 ♕c7**

The next three chapters examine systems that are distinguished by the placing of the white bishop at e2. Naturally this simple, classical formation has attracted the following of many strong grandmasters, and is also popular with club and tournament players. This chapter focuses on lines with an early f2-f4, and deals with 7 ♗e3 b5; Chapter 4 features the main line, 7 ♗e3 ♘f6 8 0-0 ♗b4 9 ♘a4; and Chapter 5 rounds off with 6...♘ge7.

The first four games in this chapter discuss 7 ♗e3 b5. In Games 21 and 22 Black reacts with a manoeuvre mentioned in the introduction: ...♘a5-c4. The presence of the bishop on e3 renders this transfer particularly efficacious, and the upshot of the opening in each case is fine for Black. Game 23 is a classic Taimanov: White's 10th move is too tame and Black swiftly rather more than just equalises. Shirov handles this variation more ambitiously in Game 24, where Adams fails to find the most precise moves in the early middlegame, and suffers a cramped and uncoordinated game.

Game 25 is intriguing. Pia Cram-

ling has introduced many new ideas in the Taimanov; here she unexpectedly captures on c6 with the d-pawn and rapidly expands on the queen's flank to seize the initiative and a memorable victory. In Game 26 Ian Rogers offers a very dangerous pawn sacrifice that was probably better declined. Viswanathan Anand preferred to hold Black up on the queenside with b2-b4 in Game 27, a manoeuvre that is most unusual in the Sicilian in general. Nobody has repeated the idea, despite Anand's impressive victory. Game 28 is one of the most theoretically significant. As befits his straightforward style Nunn adopts a very classical development in this critical game (he was desperately unfortunate not to qualify for the Candidates matches), but Anderson keeps the balance with a blend of themes, including the advance of the h-pawn. In the last game we see the hyper-aggressive strategy of queenside castling from White.

---

*Game 21*
**Rojo-Rajkovic**
*Madrid 1994*

**1 e4 c5 2 ♘f3 e6 3 d4 cxd4 4 ♘xd4**

♘c6 5 ♘c3 ♕c7 6 ♗e2 a6 7 ♗e3 b5 8 f4

White chooses the most direct response to Black's queenside advance, but one that has been found wanting. 8 ♘xc6 is dealt with in Games 23 and 24.

**8...♗b7**

A logical approach, immediately forcing White to protect his centre.

**9 ♗f3 ♘a5**

**10 0-0**

At first sight castling long seems more aggressive here, but in Lopez-Plaskett, Hastings 1988/89, a problem revealed itself: 10 ♕e2 ♘c4 11 0-0-0 ♘xb2! 12 ♔xb2 ♗a3+! 13 ♔xa3 ♕xc3+ 14 ♘b3 ♗c6 15 ♗c5 a5 and White resigned.

Berlovich-Eingorn, Berlin 1995, saw instead 10 ♕d3 ♗b4 11 a4 ♘c4! (this advance of the knight threatens to take on b2) 12 ♗c1 e5!? 13 ♘f5 g6 14 ♘e3 exf4 15 ♘xc4 bxc4 16 ♕d4 f6 17 ♔e2 ♗d6 and Black emerged with the better position.

**10...♘c4 11 ♗c1 ♗c5**

11...b4 is discussed in the next game.

**12 ♔h1 ♘e7 13 ♕d3**

**13...♕b6**

Black starts to become a little over-ambitious and takes away a natural retreat square for the c4-knight.

**14 ♘ce2 0-0 15 b3 ♘d6**

Whilst White regroups normally, Rajkovic conceives an exotic formation in the hope of deliberately unbalancing the struggle against a weaker opponent. But this is one of the best ways to beat yourself!

**16 ♗b2 f6 17 ♘g3 ♘f7 18 ♖ad1 ♖ad8 19 ♕e2 ♘g6 20 ♗h5 ♘fh8**

Not a good sign, however much Nimzowitsch you have read.

**21 ♕g4 ♗c8 22 ♗xg6! hxg6 23 ♘f3 d5 24 e5 f5 25 ♕h4**

Black is now clogged up, and White did not take long to finish him off.

**25...♘f7 26 ♘e2 ♕c7 27 ♘ed4 ♗e7 28 ♕g3 ♔h7 29 ♖d3 b4 30 ♕h3+ ♔g8 31 g4 g5 32 gxf5 exf5 33 fxg5 ♘xe5 34 ♘xe5 ♕xe5 35 g6 ♗h4 36 ♕xh4 ♕e4+ 37 ♘f3 1-0**

Game 22
**Minasian-Spassov**
*Munich Open 1993*

1 e4 c5 2 ♘c3 e6 3 f4 ♘c6 4 ♘f3

a6 5 d4 cxd4 6 ♘xd4 ♕c7 7 ♗e3
b5 8 ♗e2 ♗b7 9 ♗f3 ♘a5 10 0-0
♘c4 11 ♗c1 b4

This is also fine for Black.

12 ♘ce2 ♘f6 13 b3 ♘a5 14 ♕d3
♖c8 15 ♗b2 ♗c5 16 ♔h1 0-0 17 e5
♘e8 18 ♗xb7 ♕xb7 19 f5

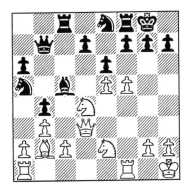

The initiative gathers momentum,
but Black can soak it all up.

19...♘c6 20 ♘xc6 ♕xc6 21 f6 gxf6
22 exf6 ♔h8 23 ♖f3 ♖g8 24 ♘f4

Now that g2 is covered, White actually threatens to crash through with
♖h3.

24...♗f8! 25 ♖h3 h6 26 ♖g1 ♘d6

Bouncing back to the centre.

27 ♗e5 ♘e4 28 ♕e3 ♘g5 29 ♖h4
♕e4 30 ♕xe4 ♘xe4 31 ♘d3 d5 32
♖c1 ♔h7 33 ♖f4 a5 34 ♖f3 ♗c5 35
♖e1 ♖c6 36 ♖e2 ♖gc8 37 ♖f4 ♗f8
38 ♘e1 ♔g6 39 g4 ♗d6 40 ♗xd6
♖xd6

Grandmaster Jonathan Mestel is of
the opinion that one of the indica-
tions of a very strong player, is the
ability to handle endings involving
both rooks and knights.

41 ♘d3 ♖c7 42 ♘e5+ ♔h7 43 ♖g2
♖d8 44 h4 ♘d6 45 g5 ♖g8 46 ♖fg4
h5 47 ♖f4 ♘f5 48 ♔g1 ♘e3 49 ♖e2

♘f5 50 ♔f2 ♖gc8 51 ♔e1 ♔g8

Now threatening the c-pawn.

52 ♔d1 ♖c3 53 ♔c1 ♖h3 54 ♔b2
♘xh4 55 a3 bxa3+ 56 ♔xa3 ♖f8 57
♖a4 ♔h7 58 ♖xa5 ♘g6 59 ♘d7 ♖d8
60 ♖a7 ♔g8 61 ♘c5 ♘f4 62 ♖f2 e5

A tense 'balance of assets' situation
has arisen.

63 g6!? ♘xg6 64 ♘e6!?

A wild idea.

64...♖h1! 65 ♘xd8 ♖a1+ 66 ♔b4
♖xa7 67 ♘c6 ♖d7 68 ♔c5 e4 69 b4
♘f8 70 ♖g2+ ♔h7 71 ♘e5 ♘e6+ 72
♔c6 ♖d8 73 ♘xf7 ♘d4+ 74 ♔b6
♖g8 75 ♘g5+ ♔h6 76 f7

Playing to win!

76...♖f8 77 ♔c5 ♘f3 78 ♘e6 ♖xf7
79 ♔xd5 h4 80 ♔xe4 h3 81 ♖g3 h2
82 ♖h3+ ♔g6 83 ♘f4+ ♔g5 84
♔xf3 ♖xf4+ 85 ♔g3 ♖xb4 86 ♖xh2
♖c4

A tough fight has burnt itself out.

87 ♖f2 ♖g4+ 88 ♔h3 ♖f4 89 ♖e2
♔f5 90 ♔g3 ♖e4 ½-½

*Game 23*
## Oll-Benjamin
*New York Open 1995*

1 e4 c5 2 ♘f3 ♘c6 3 d4 cxd4 4

♘xd4 e6 5 ♘c3 ♕c7 6 ♗e2 a6 7 ♗e3 b5 8 ♘xc6 ♕xc6

8...dxc6 has always been regarded as dubious in view of 9 f4, but this view of these types of position might have to be revised in view of Game 25.

**9 0-0**

9 f4 is discussed in Game 26.

**9...♗b7**

9...b4 does not win a pawn because of 10 ♗f3! with the threat of 11 e5, e.g. 10...♗b7 11 e5 ♕c7 12 ♘a4 with a clear plus for White.

**10 a3**

The more precise 10 ♗f3 is discussed in the next game.

**10...♖c8**

The usual Taimanov stuff from Black.

**11 ♕d2 ♗c5 12 ♖ad1 ♘f6 13 ♗f3 ♗xe3 14 ♕xe3 ♕c5**

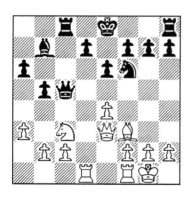

All problems solved.

**15 e5 ♗xf3! 16 gxf3 ♘d5 17 ♘xd5 exd5 18 c3 0-0 19 ♕d3 ♖fe8 20 ♕xd5**

Or 20 f4 d6 with an obvious advantage for Black.

**20...♖xe5 21 ♕xd7**

It would have been better to have exchanged queens, although there too

the doubled pawns mean that White has an uphill defensive task.

**21...♖ce8 22 ♕d6 ♕c8 23 ♖d5 ♖5e6 24 ♕f4 ♖f6 25 ♕g4 ♕c6 26 ♕d7 ♕xd7 27 ♖xd7**

This position should be tenable for White.

**27...h6 28 ♖fd1 ♖e2 29 ♖7d2 ♖xd2 30 ♖xd2 ♖xf3 31 ♖d6 a5 32 ♖d8+ ♔h7 33 ♖d5 b4 34 axb4 axb4 35 ♔g2 ♖f4 36 ♖d4?**

Dreadful! Instead, 36 cxb4 ♖xb4 37 f3! was one several drawing procedures.

**36...♖xd4 37 cxd4 ♔g6 38 ♔f3 ♔f5 39 ♔e3 ♔e6 40 ♔e4 f5+ 41 ♔f4 g5+ 42 ♔e3 ♔d5 43 f3 ♔c4 44 b3+ ♔d5 45 h3 h5 0-1**

---

*Game 24*
**Shirov-Adams**
*Chalkidiki 1993*

---

**1 e4 c5 2 ♘f3 ♘c6 3 d4 cxd4 4 ♘xd4 e6 5 ♘c3 ♕c7 6 ♗e2 a6 7 ♗e3 b5 8 ♘xc6 ♕xc6 9 0-0 ♗b7 10 ♗f3**

---

*see following diagram*

---

**10...♕c7 11 e5 ♘e7**

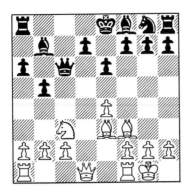

Back in 1963 Taimanov experimented with 11...♖d8 12 ♗xb7 ♛xb7 13 ♗g5 ♗e7 14 ♗xe7 ♘xe7 15 ♛d3 0-0 16 ♖ad1 ♘g6 with equal chances in Mukhitdinov-Taimanov, USSR Spartakiad 1963, an idea he later refined with 15...♛b8! in Petrosian-Taimanov, USSR Championship 1969.

**12 ♗xb7**

It is not clear why Shirov avoided 12 ♗c5!, a move that has been considered favourable for White ever since 1963!

**12...♛xb7 13 ♛d3 ♘f5 14 ♖ad1 ♗e7 15 ♗f4 ♖d8**

I prefer 15...h5, to secure the knight's future at f5.

**16 ♘e4 h6?!**

The same comment applies. White now easily and swiftly establishes a big plus by pushing Black back with tempo. This is especially bad against Alexei Shirov, who is one of the best tacticians in the world.

**17 g4 ♘h4 18 ♗g3 ♘g6 19 f4 ♛b6+ 20 ♔h1 ♘f8 21 f5 ♘h7 22 f6 gxf6 23 exf6 ♗f8 24 ♘d6+**

Simplest and best. White's advantage is already of decisive proportions.

**24...♗xd6 25 ♛xd6 ♛xd6 26 ♖xd6 ♖g8 27 ♖f4 ♖g6 28 ♖xa6 ♘xf6 29 ♗h4 ♘xg4**

Or 29...♔e7 30 ♖a3, heading for f3.

**30 ♗xd8 ♔xd8 31 ♖xf7 ♔e8 32 ♖f3 ♖g5 33 ♖g3 h5 34 h3 ♘f2+ 35 ♔g2 ♖f5 36 ♖f3 ♖xf3 37 ♔xf3 ♘xh3 38 ♖b6 ♘g5+ 39 ♔g2 d5 40 ♖xb5 ♔d7 41 a4 ♔c6 42 ♖b8 ♔c7 43 ♖b3 ♘e4 44 a5 ♘c5 45 ♖c3 ♔d6 46 b4 ♘a6 47 b5 ♘c7 48 b6 ♘a6 49 b7 1-0**

---

*Game 25*
### Forster-P.Cramling
*Biel 1994*

---

**1 e4 c5 2 ♘f3 e6 3 d4 cxd4 4 ♘xd4 ♘c6 5 ♘c3 ♛c7 6 ♗e2 a6 7 0-0**

**b5!?**

Theory used to say that this was mistimed, but perhaps it is not. The standard 7...♘f6 leads to Chapter 4 after 8 ♗e3 ♗b4 9 ♘a4. Although White may also try 8 ♔h1, I regard this as harmless after 8...♗b4 9 ♘xc6 (9 ♗g5 has been tried, but here I would recommend 9...♗xc3 10 ♗xf6 gxf6 11 bxc3 b6!?, as in the little-known struggle De Silva-Plaskett, London [Robert Silk] 1978) 9...bxc6 10 f4, when 10...d5 leads to typical play, or 8...♘xd4 9 ♕xd4 ♗c5 10 ♕d3 b5 (10...h5 11 e5 ♘g4 12 f4 leaves Black a choice between 12...d5 and 12...d6!?) 11 f4 ♗b7 12 ♗f3 h5 (12...0-0 is well met by 13 e5 ♘e8 14 ♘e4, with a slight but comfortable edge) 13 e5 ♘g4 14 ♗xb7 ♕xb7 15 ♘e4 ♗e7, leading to an unclear position in Anand-Ivanchuk, Buenos Aires 1994.

**8 ♘xc6 dxc6!?**

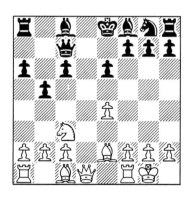

**9 f4 ♗b7 10 ♗e3 ♗e7**

Black cleverly delays the development of the king's knight, since the immediate 10...♘f6 is well met by 11 e5.

**11 ♕e1 c5 12 ♗f3 b4!? 13 ♘b1**

**♘f6 14 ♘d2 c4**

Highly creative play

**15 e5?!**

Under the circumstances I don't like this move: the black knight sits splendidly at d5.

**15...♘d5 16 ♗d4 ♖d8 17 c3 0-0**

Of course not 17...♘xf4? because of 18 ♗xb7 ♕xb7 19 ♖xf4.

**18 ♘e4?! ♘xf4!**

Correctly calculating that the complications favour Black.

**19 ♘f6+ gxf6 20 exf6 ♗d6 21 ♕e3 ♔h8 22 ♗xb7 e5!**

Winning.

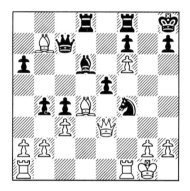

**23 ♖xf4 exf4 24 ♕f3 ♗c5 25 ♗e4 ♗xd4+ 26 cxd4 ♕d6 27 ♗xh7**

A last fling, but Black was not likely to fall for such a crude tactical tyr.

**27...♕xd4+! 28 ♔h1 ♕xf6!**

And Pia finished things off with accuracy.

**29 ♗c2 ♖fe8 30 ♖f1 ♖d2 31 ♕h5+ ♔g7 32 ♗f5 ♖e5 33 ♕g4+ ♔f8 34 ♗h7 ♖g5 35 ♕c8+ ♖d8 36 ♕xc4 f3! 37 ♕xb4+ ♔g7 38 ♗e4 ♖d4 39 ♕b7 f2 40 ♗f3 ♖d2 41 ♕a7 ♖xb2 42 a4 ♖a2 43 h3 ♕f4 44 ♕xa6 ♖e5 45 ♕d3 ♖e1 46 ♕c3+ ♕f6 0-1**

*Game 26*
**Rogers-Kudrin**
*Dutch League 1988*

**1 e4 c5 2 ♘f3 e6 3 d4 cxd4 4 ♘xd4 ♘c6 5 ♘c3 ♕c7 6 ♗e2 a6 7 f4 b5**

7...♘xd4 is considered in Games 27 and 28.

**8 ♘xc6 ♕xc6 9 ♗f3**

On 9 ♗e3, 9...♗a3! is regarded as an equaliser (9...♗b7 10 ♗f3 only transposes to the next note).

**9...♗b7 10 e5**

10 ♗e3 is also possible. In Anand-Timman, Novi Sad Olympiad 1990, play went 10...♕c4!? (previous games had seen 10...♖c8) 11 e5?! (11 ♕d3 was better, when in Berelovich-Poluliahov, Krasnodar 1995, play continued 11...♖c8 12 0-0-0 ♘f6 13 e5 ♗xf3 14 gxf3 b4 with equality) 11...♗xf3 12 ♕xf3 ♖c8 13 0-0-0 ♘e7 (or 13...b4 14 ♕b7 ♖c7 15 ♕b8+ ♖c8 16 ♕b7, etc.) 14 ♖d4 ♕c6 15 ♕xc6 dxc6!, and Black was better.

**10...♕c7 11 ♘e4 ♖c8**

Taimanov has suggested 11...♖d8 12 ♕e2 d5 13 ♘g3 g6 14 ♗e3 h5 15 ♕d3 ♘e7 with unclear play, while

11...♘h6 is also worthy of consideration.

**12 0-0!**

An enterprising pawn sacrifice.

**12...♕xc2**

In view of what now befalls Black, he might well be better off decline this sacrifice with 12...♘h6: chances were equal in Smith Hansen-G.Horvath, Berlin 1988, after 13 ♗e3 ♘f5 14 ♗f2 d5!? 15 exd6 ♗xd6 16 ♘xd6+ ♘xd6 17 ♗xb7 ♘xb7.

**13 ♕xc2 ♖xc2 14 ♘d6+ ♗xd6 15 ♗xb7 ♗c5+ 16 ♔h1 ♘h6**

Preferring development to trying to hang on to the pawn with 16...a5?!, when White can continue 17 ♗a6 b4 18 ♗d3! ♖f2 19 ♖xf2 ♗xf2 20 a3! with an advantage.

**17 ♗xa6 ♘g4 18 h3 ♘f2+**

On 18...♘e3, White keeps a slight pull after 19 ♗xe3 ♗xe3 20 ♖f3 ♗d4 21 ♗xb5 ♗xb2 22 ♖d1.

**19 ♔h2 b4**

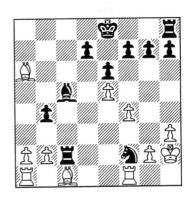

**20 ♖e1!**

Varying from Chandler-Wilder, London (Lloyds Bank) 1987, where White tried 20 ♗b5!? and stood better after 20...♔e7 21 ♗a4 ♖c4 22 ♗b3 ♖e4 23 ♔g3 ♘d3 24 ♔f3 ♖e1 (forced)

25 ♗d2 ♖xa1 26 ♖xa1, although it
finished as a draw at move 34.

**20...d5 21 exd6 ♗xd6 22 ♔g1!**

It appears that the knight may be in
trouble!

**22...♗c5**

On 22...♔e7, 23 ♗e3 ♘e4 24 ♗d3
wins.

**23 ♗e3 ♗xe3 24 ♖xe3 ♔e7 25
♗e2!**

The decisive move.

**25...♘xh3+ 26 gxh3 ♖xb2 27 f5 e5
28 ♗c4 ♔f6 29 ♖b3 ♖c2 30 ♖xb4
♖d8 31 ♗b3 ♖c3 32 ♖b7 ♔xf5 33
♖f1+ ♔g5 34 ♖bxf7 g6 35 ♖xh7 e4
36 ♗d1! 1-0**

Intending h2-h4 mate!

---

### Game 27
### Anand-Lautier
*Manila Interzonal 1990*

---

**1 e4 c5 2 ♘f3 e6 3 d4 cxd4 4 ♘xd4
♘c6 5 ♘c3 ♕c7 6 ♗e2 a6 7 f4
♘xd4**

As mentioned in the introduction,
this is a standard method of relieving
the pressure. Theory regards it as
quite acceptable here.

**8 ♕xd4 b5**

In this position 8...♘e7 can be met
by 9 ♕f2 ♘c6 10 ♗e3.

**9 a3!?**

The standard 9 ♗e3 is considered in
the Games 28 and 29.

**9...♗b7 10 b4!?**

---

*see following diagram*

---

A bit over the top. Nobody has
ever played this before or since.

**10...♖c8**

Perhaps 10...♗e7!? 11 0-0 d6, keep-

ing the possibility of ...♗f6 up his
sleeve, would have been even better.

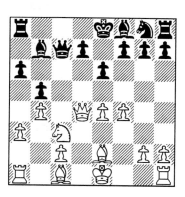

**11 ♗d2 ♗e7 12 0-0 d6 13 ♖ae1**

Just about forced, but still okay.

**13...♘f6**

On 13...♗f6, White has to play 14
e5!

**14 e5 dxe5**

It was better to play 14...♘d7! 15
exd6 ♕xd6 with full equality.

**15 fxe5 ♘d7 16 ♕f4! 0-0**

16...♘xe5?! would have been really
dicey, e.g. 17 ♘xb5 ♕c6 18 ♖f2 axb5
19 ♕xe5 0-0 20 ♗f3 ♕c7 21 ♗xb7
♕xb7 22 ♗c3! and wins.

**17 ♗d3 ♘b6**

The start of Black's troubles. Although this move is playable, there
was no need to remove an important
defender. 17...f5! was best, when after
18 exf6 ♕xf4 19 ♖xf4 ♗xf6 everything is fine.

**18 ♕g4 g6 19 ♘e4 ♘c4?!**

And here 19...♗xe4 20 ♖xe4 ♘d5
would have been a better defence.

**20 ♗xc4! ♗xe4**

On 20...♕xc4 21 ♗h6, the attack
forces decisive gains, e.g. 21...♗xe4 22
♗xf8 ♗xf8 23 ♖xe4 ♕xc2 24 ♖ef4
♖c7 25 ♕f3 and f7 falls.

**21 ♖xe4 bxc4 22 ♗h6 ♖fd8 23 ♕f4 ♗f8 24 ♗xf8 ♖xf8 25 ♕h6 ♖cd8 26 h3 ♖d5?**

Under pressure, Lautier fails to find the toughest defence: 26...♕a7+ 27 ♔h1 ♕c7. Now 28 ♖h4 can be met by 28...f5 29 exf6 ♖xf6!, so White should prefer 28 ♕f4 ♖c8 29 ♖d1 with an edge.

**27 ♖h4 f5 28 exf6 ♖f5 29 ♖xf5 exf5 30 ♕f4**

30 ♖xc4! would have been even better. After a complex middlegame the technical phase is handled badly by both sides.

**30...♕xf4 31 ♖xf4 ♖c8 32 ♖d4 ♔f7 33 ♖d6 ♖e8**

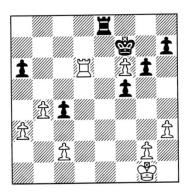

**34 ♖c6??**

Even top players sometimes forget about the old maxim: 'activate your king in the endgame'. Anand pointed out afterwards that 34 ♔f2! would have been much simpler, e.g. 34...f4 35 ♖xa6 ♖e3 36 a4 ♖c3 37 ♖c6 ♖xc2+ 38 ♔f3 c3 39 a5 ♖b2 40 ♖xc3 ♖xb4 41 ♖a3 ♖b7 42 a6 ♖a7 43 ♔xf4 with a trivial technical win. With the white rook at its optimum posting, behind the extra outside passed pawn, Black will soon be forced to give way with

his king and permit a winning penetration by the white monarch on one wing or the other.

**34...♖e3 35 ♖xa6**

White has squandered a whole tempo.

**35...♖c3 36 ♖c6 ♖xc2 37 a4 c3 38 b5?**

Another inaccuracy. It was better to keep the more remote a-pawn with 39 a5 ♖b2 40 ♖xc3 ♖xb4 41 ♖a3, but then Black has a pawn more than in the ending that White could have reached at move 34, and the win is not so easy.

**♖a2 39 ♖xc3 ♖xa4 40 ♖b3 ♖a7 41 b6 ♖b7 42 ♔f2 ♔xf6 43 ♔e3 ♔e5 44 h4 h6 45 h5?**

Again not the best. 45 g3 g5 46 h5 would have retained some winning chances.

**45...gxh5?**

And Lautier promptly blows it. 45...f4+! either seals the game up after 46 ♔f3 g5, or, on the superior 46 ♔d3, enables Black to just scrape together enough counterplay with 46...gxh5 47 ♔c4 f3! (without the diversionary play that this creates, Black's goose would have been well and truly cooked) 48 gxf3 ♔f4 49 ♔c5 ♔g3! 50 ♔c6 ♖b8 51 ♔c7 ♖h8 52 b7 h4. The general scenario now is that Black will be forced to give up his rook for the white b-pawn, but then White will have to give up his in return, e.g. 53 b8♕ ♖xb8 54 ♔xb8 h5! 55 ♔c7 h3 56 f4+ ♔xf4 57 ♖xh3 ♔g4, when Black draws by advancing his remaining unit.

**46 g3**

Now Black is soon pushed back.

**46...h4 47 gxh4 ♔f6 48 ♔f4 ♔g6 49 ♖b4 ♔f6 50 h5 ♖g7!? 51 ♖b1! ♖b7 52 ♖g1! ♔f7 53 ♖g6 ♖d7 54 ♖xh6 ♖d4+ 55 ♔xf5 ♖d5+ 56 ♔e4 ♖b5 57 ♖h7+ 1-0**

Rook and pawn endings are hard!

---

### Game 28
### Nunn-Andersson
*Szirak Interzonal 1987*

---

**1 e4 c5 2 ♘f3 e6 3 d4 cxd4 4 ♘xd4 ♘c6 5 ♘c3 a6 6 ♗e2 ♕c7 7 f4 ♘xd4 8 ♕xd4 b5 9 ♗e3 ♗b7 10 0-0**

The aggressive 10 0-0-0 is considered in the next game.

**10...♖c8**

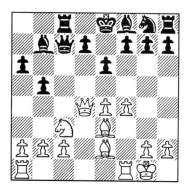

**11 ♖ad1**

Some players have put the other rook here, 11 ♖fd1. In Xie Jun-A.Maric, Germany 1991, play went 11...♗c5! 12 ♕xc5 (not 12 ♕xg7? ♗xe3+ 13 ♔h1 ♔e7! 14 ♕xh8 ♘f6 15 ♕g7 ♗xf4 and Black dominates the board) 12...♕xc5 13 ♗xc5 ♖xc5 14 ♖d4 ♘e7! 15 ♖ad1 ♗c6!? (a clever treatment; Black spots that she can get it together by advancing with ...e6-e5) 16 ♖1d3 a5 17 a3 e5! 18 fxe5 ♖xe5, and Black stood well. In fact after 19

♗f3?! (19 ♗g4 would have been better) 19...0-0 20 h3 h5 21 ♘d5 ♗xd5 22 exd5 ♘f5 23 ♖e4 ♖xe4 24 ♗xe4 ♘d6 25 ♗f3 ♖c8 Black had an edge due to her superior minor piece. 11...♗c5! definitely looks better than 11...♘f6, as in Illescas-J.Polgar, Amsterdam 1989, when Black struggled to demonstrate equality after 12 e5 ♘d5 13 ♘xd5 ♗xd5 14 a4!, and Illescas revealed the significance of leaving his queen's rook unmoved by opening up the a-file to his advantage.

**11...♘f6 12 ♗f3**

A few months prior to this game the same protagonists had disputed this position at Dortmund, but Nunn obtained no advantage with 12 e5 ♘d5 13 ♘xd5 ♗xd5 14 ♗f3 ♗c5! 15 ♕xc5 ♕xc5 16 ♗xc5 ♗xf3! 17 ♖xf3 ♖xc5, electing to 'cleanse' the position with 18 ♖fd3 ♖xc2 19 ♖xd7 0-0.

**12...h5!? 13 ♔h1**

The year before Ulf Andersson had had the same position against Velimirovic, who chose 13 h3, which has the virtue of taking away the g4-square. But Ulf sighted on g3 instead: 13...h4 14 e5 ♘h5 (note the use of this newly created square) 15 ♗xb7 ♕xb7 with equality. Instead of 14 e5, the recent game Anka-Landa, Hungary 1995, went 14 ♖f2!? ♗c5! 15 ♕xc5 ♕xc5 16 ♗xc5 ♖xc5 17 ♖d6 (17 e5 ♗xf3 18 exf6 ♗c6 19 fxg7 ♖g8 is not a worry for Black) 17...♔e7! 18 ♖b6 ♗c6! 19 ♖xa6 ♘h5!?, when Black's well coordinated pieces granted him splendid compensation for the pawn, and indeed it was White who had to play accurately to gain the draw after 20 ♗xh5 (not 20 e5 ♗xf3 21 ♖xf3 b4 and

22...♖xc2) 20...♖hxh5

21 a4 (in the face of Black's pressure, White decides to return the pawn; if 21 a3 then 21...f5! 22 exf5 [or 22 e5 g5! with rampant activity] 22...♖hxf5, intending ...♖c4. In all of these variations note how much the rook on a6 is out of it) 21...bxa4 22 ♘xa4 ♖c4 23 ♘c3 ♗xe4 24 ♘xe4 ♖xe4.

13 ♖d2!?, intending to triple along the d-file, may be best.

**13...♗e7 14 ♖d2 d6 15 a4?**

Almost certainly missing Black's reply. Taimanov proposed instead 15 f5.

**15...b4! 16 ♘d1**

The sorry truth is that 16 ♕xb4 is met by 16...d5, and 17 ♕d4 fails to 17...dxe4 18 ♘xe4 (or 18 ♗xe4 ♖d8 19 ♕a7 ♘xe4 20 ♘xe4 ♕c6 winning a piece) 18...♗xe4 19 ♗xe4 ♖d8, when the queen has no square from which it can hang on to the bishop.

**16...0-0 17 ♘f2 e5 18 ♕d3 ♖fd8**

The upshot of White's error at move 15 is that he has been routed in the opening struggle. All of Black's pieces coordinate well and he is about to take over the centre.

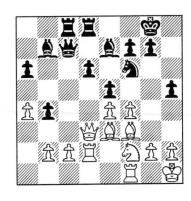

**19 ♕e2**

Hurrying out of the way.

**19...d5**

Of course.

**20 exd5 exf4 21 ♗d4 ♘xd5**

Not the best. 21...♗xd5 was a surer way to claim superiority after 22 ♗xf6 ♗xf3 23 ♕xe7 ♖xd2 or 23 ♖xd8+ ♗xd8! 24 ♕e8+ ♔h7.

**22 ♗e5! ♗d6 23 ♗xg7!**

Doing his best to create complications.

**23...♖e8 24 ♕d3?**

Missing the last chance to complicate: 24 ♗e4!, e.g. 24...♔xg7 25 ♕xh5 with obscurity.

**24...♔xg7**

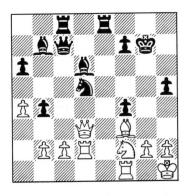

From now on in, Ulf makes no

mistake.

**25 ♗xd5 ♖e3!**

The lady is to be harassed out of squares: an unusual winning technique!

**26 ♕d4+ ♗e5! 27 ♕xb4 ♖b8! 28 ♕c4**

After 28 ♗xb7? ♖xb7 there is no hiding place.

**28...♕xc4 29 ♗xc4 f3 30 ♗d5?!**

30 gxf3, though insufficient, would have been a better try.

**30...♖e2 31 ♖d3 ♗xd5 32 ♖xd5 ♖xb2**

As Soltis once said 'the Taimanov Sicilian runs on active piece play', and here Black's men are uprooting the white position, which can hardly withstand it for long.

**33 gxf3 ♖bxc2 34 ♔g2 ♗f4 35 ♖xh5 ♗e3 36 ♖e5 ♖xf2+ 37 ♖xf2 ♗xf2 38 ♖d5 ♖a2 39 ♔f1 ♗e3 40 ♖a5 ♖f2+ 0-1**

> ### Game 29
> ### Kupreichik-Kotronias
> *Lvov 1988*

**1 e4 c5 2 ♘f3 e6 3 ♘c3 ♘c6 4 d4 cxd4 5 ♘xd4 ♕c7 6 f4 a6 7 ♗e2 ♘xd4 8 ♕xd4 b5 9 ♗e3 ♗b7 10 0-0-0!?**

This is the kind of variation that one might expect from Victor Kupreichik, who is one of the most dangerous and imaginative attacking players in the world.

**10...♖c8**

The standard Taimanov move; and this time with the threat of 10...b4, winning a piece.

**11 ♖d2 ♘f6 12 ♗f3**

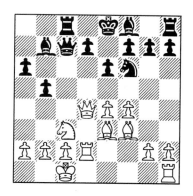

Here we reach a major parting of ways.

**12...b4?!**

Nobody has played this move since: as soon becomes apparent, the weaknesses it inflicts in the black queenside are severe, not withstanding the reduction in middlegame pressure which it brings about. Another idea that came and went was 12...♕a5, as ventured in Polihroniade-J.Polgar, Thessaloniki Women's Olympiad 1988, when Black notched up a pretty victory after 13 e5 ♗c5 14 ♕d3 ♗xe3 15 ♕xe3 b4! 16 ♗xb7 bxc3 17 ♖d3 (17 ♗xc8? cxd2+ 18 ♕xd2 ♕xa2 wins) 17...♘g4

18 ♖xc3? (stumbling amidst the

complications; either 18 ♕g3 ♕b5 19 ♗xc8 ♕xb2+ 20 ♔d1 ♕b1+ 21 ♔e2 ♕xc2+ 22 ♔e1 ♕b1+ 23 ♔e2 or possibly even 18 ♕d4 0-0! 19 ♗xc8 ♕xa2 20 ♖xc3 ♕a1+ 21 ♔d2 ♕xh1 would have been okay) 18...♘xe3 19 ♖xc8+ ♔e7 20 ♖xh8 ♕xa2 and the attack was decisive (0-1, 27 moves). But two years later Joe Gallagher played an improvement against Pia Cramling in Biel: 13 ♕a7! and Black back-pedalled with 13...♕c7, not liking either 13...♗a3 14 ♘b1! or 13...♖xc3 14 bxc3 ♕xc3 (14...♗a3+ 15 ♔d1) 15 ♖d3!, when Gallagher's idea was to meet 15...♕a1+ with 16 ♔d2 ♗b4+ 17 ♔e2 ♕xh1 18 ♖d1! ♕xh2 19 ♕b8+ ♔e7 20 ♕xb7!, when White has a big initiative and will aim to exploit the remote placing of the black queen either by a direct attack or just by gathering in the two black queenside pawns. The critical line after 13...♕c7 was 14 ♖e1, to meet 14...b4 with 15 ♘d5!, with a dangerous attack, but White played 14 e5, when after 14...♗xf3 15 ♕xc7 ♖xc7 16 gxf3 ♘g8 17 ♘e4 the game ended in a draw.

The best move is probably 12...♗e7!, after which Black appears to be able to complete development and negotiate all the tactical problems adequately. In Short-Kotronias, also at Thessaloniki 1988 (a good event from which to learn about this line), White played 13 ♔b1?! here, but this is hardly in keeping with the sharp character of the struggle and Black rapidly seized the upper hand. After 13...d6 Kotronias already assesses Black's chances as superior because of the 'misplaced' white queen: 14 g4 0-0

15 g5 ♘d7 16 h4 (a standard pawn storm, but here Black is getting in first) 16...♖fd8?! (not bad but 16...♕a5!, intending ...♖c4 and then doubling along the c-file, was better still) 17 ♖f1? ♘e5!

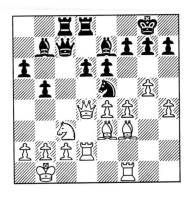

This clever tactic establishes Black's advantage. Taking on e5 is bad because of 18...dxe5 19 ♕a7 ♖xd2 20 ♗xd2 ♗c5 21 ♘xb5 ♕d7. Short defended well and managed to draw on move 55.

After 12...♗e7, another 13th move which does not work out well is 13 g4?!, as in Masserey-P.Cramling, Germany 1995. Pia spotted that after this advance Black has extra chances to get to work at softening up the kingside in the ending, so: 13...♗c5! 14 ♕xc5 ♕xc5 15 ♗xc5 ♖xc5 (Black has the positional threat of ...g7-g5) 16 g5 (16 ♖hd1 is an untried suggestion of Joe Gallagher) 16...♘g8 17 ♖hd1 ♖c7 18 ♖d4 (hoping to play a2-a4 without permitting ...b5-b4) 18...♘e7! 19 a4 ♘c6 20 ♖d6 b4 21 ♘e2 h6!

*see following diagram*

(an instructive move: Black starts to take advantage of the gaps in White's

kingside)

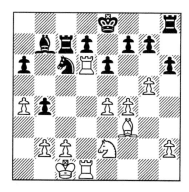

22 h4 hxg5 23 hxg5 ♖h3 24 ♖6d3 ♘a5! (threatening to capture on f3, and then on e4, and then on f3 or c2) 25 ♘d4 ♖h4 26 ♘e2 ♖h3 27 ♘d4 ♖h4 28 ♘e2 b3! (finally getting down to it) 29 c3 e5! 30 ♖h1 (if 30 fxe5, 30...♘c4!? or 30...♗xe4 with a big advantage in either instance) 30...♖xh1+ 31 ♗xh1 ♖c4 32 f5 ♖xa4 33 ♘g3 ♖a1+ and White resigned. The Hungarian grandmaster Zoltan Ribli was so impressed by this game that he commented 'That is an essential game: exactly how one should play the Taimanov variation.'

Instead of 13 ♔b1?! or 13 g4?!, 13 ♖hd1 looks better, when after 13...0-0 14 e5 Black should play 14...b4!, e.g. 15 exf6 bxc3 16 ♕xc3 ♕xc3 17 fxe7!? ♕xe3 18 exf8+ ♔xf8 19 ♗xb7 ♖b8 with a big advantage in Hector-P.Cramling, Sweden 1991, or 15 ♘a4 ♗xf3 16 gxf3 ♘d5 17 ♘b6 ♘xb6 18 ♕xb6 ♕c4 with unclear chances. Instead in Ehlvest-Andersson, Belfort 1988, Black chose the inferior 14...♗xf3 15 gxf3 b4? and was smashed by 16 exf6 bxc3 17 ♖g2! ♕b7 18 ♖xg7+ ♔h8

19 ♖g8+! and Black resigned because of 19...♖xg8 20 fxe7+ ♖g7 21 ♖g1 ♕xb2+ 22 ♔d1 ♕b1+ 23 ♗c1. This may well be the shortest game that Andersson has ever lost.

**13 ♘a4 ♕c4 14 b3 ♕xd4 15 ♖xd4**

Despite the queen exchange Black's problems persist.

**15...d5**

Almost forced. If 15...♗e7?, then 16 e5.

**16 exd5 ♗xd5**

16...♘xd5 is also strongly answered by 17 ♘b6.

**17 ♘b6 ♗xf3 18 ♘xc8 ♗xg2 19 ♖e1!**

Intending f4-f5.

**19...♘d5 20 ♖d2 ♗f3**

Probably better defensive chances were offered by 20...♗e4 21 ♘b6 ♘xe3! 22 ♖xe3 f5.

**21 f5! ♔d8 22 ♘b6 ♔c7 23 fxe6! fxe6**

Or 23...♘xb6 24 ♗xb6+ ♔xb6 25 e7 and wins.

**24 ♖f2 ♗h5 25 ♘xd5+ exd5 26 ♖f5**

Now White mops up.

**26...♗g6 27 ♖xd5 ♗d6 28 ♖ed1 ♗xh2 29 ♖c5+ ♔b8 30 ♖d4 ♔a8 31 ♖c6 ♖e8 32 ♖xb4 1-0**

## Summary

In the vast majority of these games the knights on d4 and c6 soon disappear. I am uncertain what the original thinking was behind White capturing on c6, but I suspect that it had more to do with the power of the manoeuvre ...♞a5-c4 than any great benefit to White. In any case Black's play in these classical lines seems to be sufficient.

**1 e4 c5 2 ♞f3 e6 3 d4 cxd4 4 ♞xd4 ♞c6 5 ♞c3 a6 6 ♗e2 ♛c7**

**7 ♗e3**
>     7 0-0 - *game 25*
>     7 f4 b5 - *game 26*
>     7...♞xd4 8 ♛xd4 b5 *(D)*
> >         9 a3 - *game 27*
> >         9 ♗e3 ♗b7
> > >             10 0-0 - *game 28*
> > >             10 0-0-0 - *game 29*

**7...b5 *(D)***
>     7...♞f6 - chapter 4

**8 f4**
>     8 ♞xc6 ♛xc6 9 0-0 ♗b7
> >         10 a3 - *game 23*
> >         10 ♗f3 - *game 24*

**8...♗b7 9 ♗f3 ♞a5 10 0-0 ♞c4 11 ♗c1 *(D)***
>     11...♗c5 - *game 21*
>     11...b4 - *game 22*

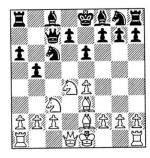
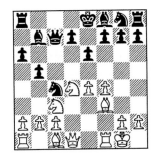

*8...b5*        *7...b5*        *11 ♗c1*

# CHAPTER FOUR

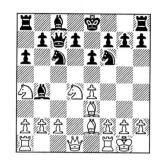

## 5 ♘c3 a6 6 ♗e2 ♛c7: Main Line

**1 e4 c5 2 ♘f3 e6 3 d4 cxd4 4 ♘xd4 ♘c6 5 ♘c3 a6 6 ♗e2 ♛c7 7 ♗e3 ♘f6 8 0-0 ♗b4 9 ♘a4**

This variation merits a chapter to itself because of its extraordinary popularity and significance to Taimanov theory: the stem position for this chapter is one of the oldest in the whole theory of this opening.

The earliest examples of 9 ♘a4 mostly continued with White going after the c8-bishop and the a6-pawn, i.e. 9...0-0 10 ♘xc6 bxc6 11 ♘b6 ♖b8 12 ♘xc8 ♖fxc8 13 ♗xa6.

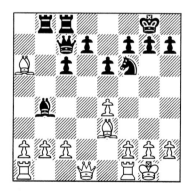

Then everyone started to haggle over where the rook should go to. One of the most important games at the Leningrad Interzonal of 1973 was the game Smejkal-Karpov, where An-

atoly chose 13...♖d8, which at the time was hailed as an important novelty. Play continued 14 ♗d3 (14 ♗g5!? remains untested) 14...♗d6 (ensuring the restoration of material parity) 15 ♔h1!? (another watershed; a completely different type of game results from 15 f4 e5 16 f5 ♖xb2 17 g4 ♛a5! 18 ♔h1 ♗c5, but theory regards Black's defensive chances as sufficient) 15...♗e5 16 c3 ♖xb2 17 ♛c1 ♘g4! 18 f4 (not of course 18 ♛xb2? ♗xc3!) 18...♘xe3 19 ♛xb2 ♗xf4! 20 ♛f2! (returning the exchange is best; if 20 ♖f3 ♘g4 21 h3? then 21...♗c1!) 20...♘xf1 21 ♖xf1.

Here Karpov played 21...e5 (21...g5! 22 g3 ♛d6 may be best here) 22 g3 ♛d6 23 ♗e2 ♗g5 24 ♛xf7+ ♔h8, and here the significance of playing 13...♖d8 instead of 13...♖e8 becomes apparent: in the former instance the rook would now have been en prise. Smejkal played 25 a4, when the a-pawn guarantees a small edge for White, although he later blundered and lost. That was rough for Smejkal, who deserved a Candidates place. Eighteen years later, in Game 35, Ehlvest preferred to put the rook back on f8, from where it had just come. Games 36-39 look at White alternatives after 9...0-0 10 ♘xc6 bxc6, such as the dangerous 11 f4 and 11 c4.

These days, however, 9...♗e7 is just as popular as 9...0-0. Now after 10 ♘xc6 bxc6 11 ♘b6 ♖b8 12 ♘xc8 Black will simply play 12...♕xc8, without sacrificing the a-pawn (Games 33 and 34). In Games 30-32 we see White pursuing a quite different approach of advancing c2-c4 and aiming for a bind/space advantage. To my mind this is a promising method, and there is scope for new ideas here.

---

### Game 30
### Shirov-Miladinovic
*Belgrade 1995*

---

**1 e4 c5 2 ♘f3 ♘c6 3 d4 cxd4 4 ♘xd4 ♕c7 5 ♘c3 e6 6 ♗e2 a6 7 ♗e3 ♘f6 8 0-0 ♗b4**

Of course 8...d6 transposes to a standard position of the Scheveningen, but that is outside the scope of this monograph.

**9 ♘a4!**

Certainly the strongest move. White temporarily abandons protection of the e-pawn in order to embar-

rass the bishop on b4.

**9...♗e7**

9...b5 should be met by 10 ♘xc6 dxc6 11 ♗c5!, e.g. 11...bxa4 12 ♗xb4 c5 13 ♗a3! ♘xe4 14 ♗f3 ♗b7 15 ♖e1 ♘d6 16 ♖e5 ♖d8 17 ♖xc5 with a clear advantage for White in Renet-Lautier, Lyon 1990. In the 12th round of the 1994 Buenos Aires tournament, Karpov experimented with 9...d5 10 ♘xc6 (Taimanov recommends 10 c3 to meet 10...♗d6 with 11 ♘b6) 10...bxc6 11 exd5 ♘xd5?! (Piket suggests 11...cxd5 12 c3 ♗d6 13 ♘b6 ♖b8 14 ♘xc8 ♕xc8 15 ♕a4+ ♔e7 16 ♗xa6 ♕c7) 12 ♗d4 c5?! 13 c3, when White was on top (Anand-Karpov). 9...0-0 is considered in Games 35-39.

**10 c4!**

A recently revitalised gambit that aims to establish a bind.

**10...♘xe4 11 c5!**

This new move, establishing a queenside grip, was introduced by Kamsky at Buenos Aires in 1994. Previously theory had focused on 11 ♘xc6 bxc6 12 ♕d4 ♘f6 13 ♘b6 ♖b8 14 c5 d6 15 cxd6 ♗xd6 16 ♘c4 ♗xh2+ 17 ♔h1 c5 18 ♕xc5 ♕xc5 19 ♗xc5, which was regarded as unclear.

## 11...0-0

On this and the next few moves Black has several different methods of wriggling against the bind, but they almost all result in White retaining substantial compensation. 11...♘xc5? loses instantly to 12 ♘xc6 ♕xc6 13 ♘xc5 ♗xc5 14 ♖c1 d6 15 b4, whilst 11...♘f6 is discussed in the next game.

## 12 ♖c1 f5

I suspect that this is a bit over the top, and prefer 12...♘f6 with a probable transposition to Game 31 after 13 ♗f3.

## 13 f4!

Surprisingly, this natural move was new. 13 g3 f4!? 14 ♗xf4 ♖xf4 15 gxf4 ♕xf4 is obscure.

## 13...♖b8

Again I doubt if this is best. In Igudesman-Maksyutov, Kazan 1995, White had strong compensation after 13...♖d8 14 ♗f3 ♘f6 15 a3 ♔h8 16 b4. Perhaps Black should play 13...d5!? 14 cxd6 ♗xd6 15 ♗d3 ♘f6 16 ♗c4 ♘g4!?, with the long variation 17 ♘xf5 ♘xe3 18 ♕xd6 ♕xd6 19 ♘xd6 ♘xf1 20 ♗xf1 ♖d8! 21 ♘b6 ♖xd6 22 ♘xa8 ♗d7, which is about equal, according to Shirov.

## 14 ♗f3 ♗f6 15 ♗xe4!

Simple and powerful.

## 15...fxe4 16 ♘xc6 bxc6 17 ♖c4 ♖d8

On 17...♗xb2 18 ♘xb2 ♖xb2 19 ♗d4 White has an enormous bind and can easily get back at least one pawn. Meantime the black bishop sleeps on.

## 18 ♖xe4 d5

Black has no chance unless he can become active, but now his pawn structure is dreadful.

## 19 cxd6 ♖xd6 20 ♕e2 ♗d7

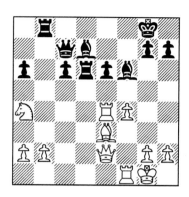

## 21 b4

To prevent the liberating ...c6-c5.

## 21...a5 22 a3 axb4 23 axb4 ♗e8

In a desperate search for activity, Black offers a pawn back.

## 24 ♗c5 ♖d5 25 ♖xe6 ♗f7 26 ♖xf6!

Now Shirov turns on the tactics.

## 26...gxf6 27 ♘c3

Re-centralising with a vengeance. On 27...♖f5 28 ♕g4+ ♔g6 29 ♘e4 or 27...♖h5 28 ♘e4 ♕d8 29 ♕b2 ♖h6 (29...♔g7 30 ♘xf6!) 30 ♗d4 ♔g7 31 ♖f3 White has a fierce initiative, so Miladinovic gives back the exchange, but this didn't help much either.

## 27...♖xc5 28 bxc5 f5 29 ♖f3

White has the superior minor piece and some dangerous threats.

## 29...♖e8 30 ♖e3 ♖a8 31 ♕f3 ♖a5?!

## 32 ♕g3+ ♔f8 33 ♕h4

Turning towards the king.

## 33...♖xc5 34 ♕xh7 ♕d6 35 ♕h8+ ♗g8 36 ♖g3 ♕e6 37 ♕g7+ 1-0

> *Game 31*
> **Kamsky-Karpov**
> *Buenos Aires (round 8) 1994*

(This and the following three games

are all from the same event, but not because the participants were unable to conceive of any other way of starting a chess game: the rules of this particular tournament specified that each game had to be an Open Sicilian, in tribute to that great Sicilian exponent Lev Polugayevsky.)

**1 e4 c5 2 ♘f3 e6 3 d4 cxd4 4 ♘xd4 ♘c6**

It is interesting that Karpov, who is not normally a Sicilian player nowadays, regularly opted for the Taimanov variation in this tournament. In fact he had a lot of experience with it in the 1970s, but then switched to 1...e5 and 1...c6 as his main defences to 1 e4.

**5 ♘c3 ♕c7 6 ♗e2 a6 7 0-0 ♘f6 8 ♗e3 ♗b4 9 ♘a4 ♗e7 10 c4**

As we have already noted, this is the latest fashion, although Karpov had faced this move before – against Larsen in 1977 (see the notes to the next game)!

**10...♘xe4**

Taking up the gauntlet. Earlier in the tournament Salov had declined this gambit (see the next game).

**11 c5!**

Kamsky's innovation.

**11...♘f6 12 ♗f3 0-0 13 ♖c1 ♖b8 14 g3**

Hardly a dynamic move. White wants to be able to drop the bishop to g2 should Black harry it with ...♘e5, but such manoeuvring is an indication that White cannot undertake much of an active nature yet, and in his search for an advantage must rely on some structural plus after Black has made

his breakout, most probably via ...d7-d5. Theory is undecided as to whether or not White's plan is justified.

**14...g6 15 ♘b6 ♖d8 16 ♕a4 e5 17 ♘b3 d5 18 cxd6 ♖xd6 19 ♘a5 ♗d7!?**

19...♗h3 led to unclear play in Korneev-Tunik, Elista 1995, while Piket analyses yet another move, 19...e4!?, in the tournament book, and concludes that Black has prospects after either 20 ♗xe4 ♘xe4 21 ♘xc6 ♖xc6 22 ♕xe4 ♗f5 or 20 ♗g2 ♗f5 21 ♘ac4 ♖d3 22 ♗f4 ♕d8 23 ♗xb8 ♕xb8 24 ♘e3 ♕e5 25 ♘bc4 ♕e6. Karpov opts for a more stolid defence.

**20 ♘xd7 ♕xd7 21 ♗xc6**

After 21 ♘xc6 bxc6 22 ♗xc6 ♕e6 23 b3 h5!? Black has counter-chances.

**21...bxc6 22 ♗c5! ♖e6 23 ♖fd1 ♕e8 24 ♗xe7 ♕xe7 25 ♘xc6 ♕e8 26 ♕xa6 ♔g7**

A strategically sharp situation, with each side possessing assets on opposite wings.

*see following diagram*

**27 ♘xb8?!**

When both sides have mobile pawns it is always dangerous to

generalise: one does best to rely on concrete calculation. Here 27 b4! would have set Black tougher problems, e.g. 27...♖xb4 28 ♕a3!, intending 29 ♖d8, or 27...♖c8 28 b5 ♖a8 29 ♕b6 e4 30 ♕e3!

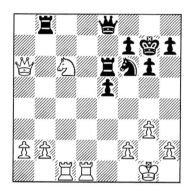

**27...♖xa6 28 ♘xa6 ♕b5 29 ♘c5 ♕xb2 30 a4**

White's pride and joy, but Karpov has enough going for him in other areas to hold the balance.

**30...♕a3**

Preventing ♖a1.

**31 ♖c2 h5! 32 ♖e1 h4 33 ♔g2 h3+!**

A persistent pest!

**34 ♔xh3 ♕f3 35 ♖xe5!**

Here care is called for. After 35 ♖e3 ♕d1 36 ♖ce2 ♕f1+ 37 ♔h4 g5+! 38 ♔xg5 ♕h3 White has had it.

**35...♘h5! 36 ♖e4 g5! 37 ♖d2**

Abandoning all hope of victory; instead preparing a fortress.

**37...♘f4+ 38 ♖xf4 gxf4 39 ♘d3 ♕h5+ 40 ♔g2 f3+ 41 ♔g1 ♕d5 42 ♔f1 ♕d4 43 ♔e1 ♕a1+ 44 ♖d1 ♕c3+ 45 ♖d2 ½-½**

And not 45 ♔f1??, 45...♕c2 winning, but now there are no more ideas left in the position. This is one of the most important games in the Taima-

nov over the past few years, and has led to a new fashion with 10 c4 ♘xe4 11 c5.

> ### Game 32
> ## Kamsky-Salov
> *Buenos Aires (round 5) 1994*

**1 e4 c5 2 ♘f3 ♘c6 3 d4 cxd4 4 ♘xd4 e6 5 ♘c3 ♕c7 6 ♗e2 ♘f6 7 0-0 a6 8 ♗e3 ♗b4 9 ♘a4 ♗e7 10 c4 0-0**

Salov declines the gambit, content to play a cramped but solid Maroczy Bind position, in which he stands slightly worse, but in the tournament book, entitled *Sicilian Love*, Kamsky states a preference for Karpov's recent choice of 10...♘xe4.

**11 ♘c3**

In the aforementioned Larsen-Karpov game (Las Palmas 1977), White captured on c6 immediately, leading to very similar play: 11 ♘xc6 dxc6 12 ♕c2 c5 13 f4 b6 14 ♖ad1 ♗b7 15 e5 ♘d7 16 ♘c3 ♖fd8 17 ♘e4 ♘f8 18 ♗f3 with a slight advantage for White.

**11...b6 12 ♘xc6! dxc6 13 f4 c5 14 e5 ♖d8 15 ♕c2**

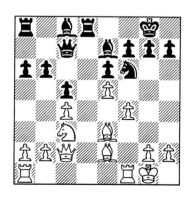

I would prefer an attack with 15 ♗d3 ♘d7 16 ♖f3, but that's me.

**15...♘d7 16 ♗d3 ♘f8 17 ♖f3 ♗b7 18 ♖h3 g6**

On 18...♘g6, 19 ♕e2 gives White a promising attack.

**19 ♖f1**

Certainly not 19 ♘e4? ♖xd3! 20 ♕xd3 ♕c6 and Black wins, but Kamsky criticises this decision, preferring 19 a4 with the threat of a4-a5.

**19...♖d7 20 ♗e4 ♖ad8?**

It was probably better to break out now with 20...f5 21 exf6 ♗xf6 22 ♗xb7 ♕xb7 23 ♘e4, than to suffer the bind that follows.

**21 ♗xb7 ♕xb7 22 ♘e4 ♕c6 23 ♗f2 ♔g7 24 ♕e2 b5 25 b3 bxc4 26 bxc4 ♖b7 27 ♖b3 ♖db8 28 ♖fb1 ♘d7 29 ♗e1 ♖xb3**

Every exchange eases the cramp.

**30 axb3 h5 31 ♕e3 ♔g8 32 ♖d1 ♘f8 33 ♗a5 ♘d7**

White has ideas of attack as well as those of squeeze. If 33...♖b7 34 ♗d8!

**34 ♖d3 ♘f8 35 h3 ♔g7 36 ♘f6 ♘h7 37 ♘e4 ♘f8 38 ♔h2**

Planning g2-g4.

**38...♖b7 39 ♗d8 ♗xd8 40 ♖xd8 ♖xb3!**

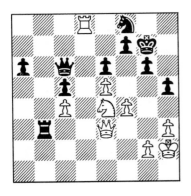

Correctly surmising that his best chances lie in the ending with one pawn for the exchange, since White's attacking pressure was mounting. But here White misses a golden chance.

**41 ♕xb3?**

41 ♕xc5 would have given White a winning position: 41...♕xc5 42 ♘xc5 ♖c3 43 ♖c8 followed by ♘e4-g5 or ♘e4-d6 and ♖c7, as pointed out in the bulletin.

**41...♕xe4 42 ♕g3 a5**

Or 42...♕xc4 43 ♖a8 with an advantage.

**43 ♕h4! ♘h7! 44 ♕f2 a4 45 ♖c8 ♕xc4 46 ♖xc5 ♕e4 47 ♖a5?**

Imprecise. 47 h4! would have made life very tough for Salov.

**47...g5! 48 fxg5 h4!! 49 ♕f3 ♕d4 50 ♕g4**

Since Black can hold the ending, it might have been better to punt 50 g6!?

**50...♕xg4 51 hxg4 ♘xg5 52 ♖xa4**

A body of theory exists on such rook against knight endings in which all the pawns are on the same wing. With a pristine set of f-, g- and h-pawns, a three against three ending is easily won, but here the pawns are split and mangled, which enormously complicates the winning attempt.

**52...♘h7 53 ♔h3 ♘f8 54 ♖e4 ♘g6 55 g5 ♔g8 56 ♔g4 ♔h7 57 ♔f3 ♔g8 58 ♔e3 ♔f8 59 ♔d4 ♔e7 60 ♔c5 ♔d7 61 ♔b6 ♔e7 62 ♔c6 ♔f8 63 ♔d6 ♔g7 64 ♖e2 ♔f8 65 ♖f2 ♔g8 66 ♖f6 ♔g7 67 ♖f1 ♔f8 68 ♖f2 ♔g8 69 ♖a2 ♔g7 70 ♖a4 ♔f8 71 ♖e4 ♔e8 72 ♔c6 ♔e7 73 ♔c7 ♔f8 74 ♔d7 ♔g7 75 ♔e8**

White has gone all the way in, but

the weakness of his e-pawn deprives him of victory.

**75...♔g8 76 ♖e1 ♔g7 77 ♖e2 ♔g8 78 ♖f2 ♘xe5 79 ♖f4 ♔g7 80 ♖xh4 ♔g6 81 ♖e4 ♘d3 82 ♔e7 ♔xg5 83 ♖e3 ♘f4 84 ♖g3+ ♔f5 85 ♔xf7 e5 86 ♖g8 ♘xg2!**

**87 ♖xg2 e4 ½-½**

This is now a book draw. A dour defence from Valery Salov.

### Game 33
### Salov-Karpov
*Buenos Aires (round 2) 1994*

**1 e4 c5 2 ♘f3 e6 3 d4 cxd4 4 ♘xd4 ♘c6 5 ♘c3 ♕c7 6 ♗e2 ♘f6 7 ♗e3 a6 8 0-0 ♗b4 9 ♘a4 ♗e7 10 ♘xc6**

As White Salov avoids the Maroczy Bind 10 c4, preferring a more direct strategy.

**10...bxc6 11 ♘b6**

11 ♕d4 is easily countered by 11...♖b8 12 c4 c5! 13 ♕d3 (13 ♘xc5 e5) 13...d6 with equal chances.

**11...♖b8 12 ♘xc8 ♕xc8 13 e5 ♘d5 14 ♗c1**

Note the important difference between 9...♗e7 and 9...0-0: here the white b-pawn is attacked, so White

has no time for 14 ♗a7 to deflect the black rook.

**14...♗c5! 15 ♕d3**

15 c4 is considered in the next game, while in the tournament book Piket suggests 15 a3 a5 16 ♗d3, when he prefers White.

**15...0-0 16 ♕g3**

An active stationing, but it will not lead to mate. 16 b3 ♕c7 17 ♗b2 is a more conservative set-up, when the situation is still very unclear.

**16...♖e8!?**

Another Karpov novelty.

**17 ♖d1 a5! 18 b3?!**

Piket recommends 18 a3 followed by 19 b3, preventing Black from exchanging his weak a-pawn (18...a4?! 19 ♗h6 ♗f8 20 ♖d4!).

**18...a4 19 ♗h6?!**

A blow in the air, and on the wrong side of the board to boot. In his notes Salov recommends 19 a3!, assessing 19...axb3 20 cxb3 as equal.

**19...♗f8 20 h4**

Here 20 ♖d4 can be met by 20...♖b4!

**20...♕c7! 21 ♗g5**

21 h5? f6! 22 ♗xg7 ♗xg7 23 h6 ♖e7 would have been to Black's advantage.

**21...axb3 22 axb3 ♖a8 23 c4 ♘b4 24 ♕c3 c5 25 ♗f3 ♖xa1 26 ♖xa1 d6 27 ♗f4 ♖d8 28 h5 h6 29 ♖d1 dxe5 30 ♖xd8 ♕xd8 31 ♗xe5 ♕d7**

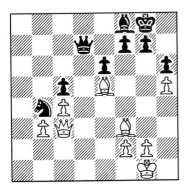

The upshot of it all is equality, White's pawn majority being completely suppressed...or so you might be forgiven for thinking!?

**32 g3 ♘d3 33 ♗c6!? ♕d8!? 34 ♕d2 ♗e7 35 ♗c3 ♗g5 36 ♕d1 ♘c1 37 ♕c2 ♕d3 38 ♕xd3 ♘xd3 39 ♔f1 ♘c1 40 ♗a4 ♗f6?**

Move forty, and Anatoly mucks things up big time! 40...♘a2! was quite okay, or even 40...♔f8 (Piket).

**41 ♗xf6 gxf6**

**42 b4! ♔f8**

Sadly necessary. After 42...cxb4 43

c5 b3 44 c6 b2 45 ♗c2 we see why bishops are supposed to be better than knights.

**43 b5! ♔e7 44 ♗c2!**

44 b6 would fail to capitalise on the distracting effect of the passed pawn: after 44...♔d6 45 ♗e8 ♘b3 46 ♗xf7 ♘d2+ 47 ♔e2 ♘xc4 48 ♗xe6 ♘xd6 Black can hold.

**44...f5!**

Practically forced, otherwise a visitor would come via h7 to g8.

**45 ♔e1 ♘a2 46 ♔d2 ♘b4 47 ♗b1 ♔d6?**

47...♔f6! would have been better.

**48 ♔e2! ♔e5**

48...f4 is met by 49 g4.

**49 ♔e3 ♔f6?**

A war is being waged for an entry point for the white king. Here 49...f6 was a better way of keeping it out.

**50 ♔f4 ♔e7**

Or 50...e5+ 51 ♔e3 ♔g5 52 f4+ and wins.

**51 ♔e5 f6+ 52 ♔f4 ♔f7 53 b6**

Now the power of the pawn, dragging Black's defenders away, comes to the fore.

**53...♘c6 54 b7 ♔e7**

**55 ♗xf5! ♔d6**

Equivalent to resignation, but taking the piece was also hopeless, e.g. 55...exf5 56 ♔xf5 ♔f7 57 g4 ♞b8 58 f3! ♞a6 59 f4 ♞b8 60 g5 fxg5 61 fxg5 hxg5 62 ♔xg5 ♔g7 63 ♔f5 ♔h6 64 ♔e6 ♔xh5 65 ♔d6 ♔g6 66 ♔xc5 ♔f7 67 ♔d6 ♔e8 68 c5 ♔d8 69 c6 and wins.

**56 ♝e4 ♞b8 57 ♝g6 ♔c7 58 ♝f7 ♔d6 59 ♝e8 ♔e7 60 ♝b5 ♔d6 61 ♔e4 ♔c7 62 g4 1-0**

---

### Game 34
### Shirov-Karpov
*Buenos Aires (round 8) 1994*

---

**1 e4 c5 2 ♞f3 e6 3 d4 cxd4 4 ♞xd4 ♞c6 5 ♞c3 ♛c7 6 ♝e2 a6 7 0-0 ♞f6 8 ♝e3 ♝b4 9 ♞a4 ♝e7 10 ♞xc6 bxc6 11 ♞b6 ♖b8 12 ♞xc8 ♛xc8 13 e5 ♞d5 14 ♝c1 ♝c5! 15 c4**

Another approach. Evidently Karpov was content to repeat his game against Salov from the second round.

**15...♞e7 16 b3 ♛c7 17 ♝b2 0-0**

It is slightly risky for Black to open up the position before he has castled. After 17...d6 18 exd6 ♝xd6 19 ♛d4! ♞f5 20 ♛e4 White stood clearly bet-

ter in Matulovic-Portisch, Sousse Interzonal 1967, but Miladinovic has experimented with 19...c5, intending to meet 20 ♛xg7 with 20...♝xh2+ 21 ♔h1 ♖g8.

**18 ♔h1**

To permit the advance of the f-pawn. After 18 ♝d3 ♞g6 19 ♛h5 Black can also play 19...a5!?

**18...♖fd8!**

A new move. 18...♞g6 19 f4 or 19 ♝d3 is regarded as marginally in White's favour.

**19 ♛c2**

In the tournament book Piket suggests the more active 19 ♝d3 d6 20 ♛e2.

**19...a5!**

A by now familiar strategic theme that not only rids Black of a weak pawn, but will also inflict one upon his opponent (see also the previous game).

**20 ♖ad1 a4 21 ♖d3 axb3 22 axb3 ♞g6!**

Karpov defends with great precision. After 22...d6 23 ♖fd1! White keeps the upper hand.

**23 f4 d6 24 exd6 ♖xd6 25 g3 ♖xd3 26 ♛xd3 ♝f8 27 ♛c3 c5! 28 ♖f3**

♘e7 29 ♕e5 ♕c8 30 ♖d3 ♘c6 31 ♕e3 ♕a6 32 ♗f3 ♘d4!

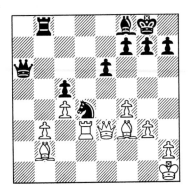

A neat device which, in view of the opposite-coloured bishops and Black's clamp on the queenside pawns, speedily brings proceedings to a close.

**33 ♗xd4 cxd4 34 ♕xd4 g6 35 ♔g2 ♕a2+ 36 ♖d2 ♕a5 37 ♖d3 ½-½**

An instructive defensive performance from Karpov.

---

*Game 35*
**Kamsky-Ehlvest**
*Linares 1991*

---

**1 e4 c5 2 ♘f3 e6 3 d4 cxd4 4 ♘xd4 ♘c6 5 ♘c3 ♕c7 6 ♗e2 a6 7 0-0 ♘f6 8 ♗e3 ♗b4 9 ♘a4 0-0**

Obviously this is a very rational move, but it does involve a pawn sacrifice.

**10 ♘xc6 bxc6 11 ♘b6**

White's alternatives to this knight sortie, 11 f4 and 11 c4, are considered in Games 36-39.

**11...♖b8 12 ♘xc8 ♖fxc8**

The attempt to hang on to the pawn with 12...♕xc8 is well met by 13 e5 ♘d5 14 ♗a7 (after 14 ♗c1?! ♗c5 White is a whole tempo down

on Games 33 and 34, as Black has already castled!) 14...♖a8 15 ♗d4 c5 16 c4 cxd4 17 cxd5 with a clear advantage to White according to Taimanov.

**13 ♗xa6 ♖f8**

This is the modern refinement. Twenty years ago 13...♖d8 was commonly played, and before that 13...♖e8 (see the introduction to this chapter).

**14 ♗d3 ♗d6 15 g3!?**

This is Kamsky's attempt to improve on the well-known 15 f4 e5 16 f5 ♖xb2 17 g4 ♕a5 18 g5 ♗c5, when Black appears to have sufficient defensive resources.

**15...♗e5**

Ehlvest opts to regain his pawn this way. Kamsky has offered some long analysis of 15...♖xb2: 16 ♗d4 ♖b4 17 ♗xf6 gxf6 18 ♕g4+ ♔h8 19 ♕h4 ♗e5 20 ♖ad1 c5 21 f4 ♗d4+ 22 ♔h1 (22 ♔g2 c4 23 e5 cxd3 24 ♕xf6+ leads to a perpetual check) 22...c4 23 ♗e2 ♗c3 24 ♖f3 ♗b2 25 g4, intending ♖h3 with attacking operations, but clearly this is far from forced.

**16 a4!? ♗xb2 17 ♖a2 d5**

The character of the middlegame is set: White has the pair of bishops and a passed a-pawn, while Black hopes to make the most of his central pawn majority and dark-square control. In Sanchez Almeyra-Pogorelov, Zaragoza 1993, Black tried 17...♗c3, and after 18 ♖a3 ♕a5 19 ♕e2 d5 20 ♗f4 ♕c5 chances were balanced.

**18 exd5 ♘xd5?**

Rather inconsistent. 18...cxd5 would have given equal chances.

**19 ♗d2 ♖fd8**

Not 19...♘c3? 20 ♗xc3 bxc3 21 ♗xh7+!

**20 a5?!**

20 c4 would have been better.

**20...♗c3**

20...♘c3! 21 ♗xc3 ♗xc3 would have offered more chances of a successful defence.

**21 ♖a4**

Shoving the pawn on with 21 a6 was sensible too. Gata has dreams of ♖h4.

**21...♖b4 22 ♖a3!? ♗xd2 23 ♕xd2 ♖db8 24 a6 ♕a7 25 ♕e2 h6 26 ♕e5 ♖4b6 27 c4!**

With the big a-pawn and the more active pieces, Kamsky now sets about increasing his grip.

**27...♘f6 28 c5 ♖b2 29 ♕d6 ♘d5 30 ♖e1 ♖c8 31 ♖a4 ♖bb8 32 ♕e5 ♘f6 33 ♖f4**

Tacking around, looking for a way in.

**33...♖d8 34 ♖d4 ♖xd4 35 ♕xd4 ♘d5 36 ♕e4 g6 37 ♕e5 ♘b4?!**

A time pressure inaccuracy that eases White's task.

**38 ♗f1 ♖d8 39 ♕f4 ♘d5 40 ♕xh6 ♖b8 41 h4 ♖b2 42 h5 ♘f6 43 ♖d1 ♕e7 44 hxg6 ♖xf2 45 g7! ♖h2**

He's a hard case, this Ehlvest.

**46 ♕xh2 1-0**

---

### Game 36
### Shirov-Hjartarson
*Lucerne 1993*

---

**1 e4 c5 2 ♘f3 e6 3 d4 cxd4 4 ♘xd4 ♘c6 5 ♘c3 ♕c7 6 ♗e2 a6 7 ♗e3 ♘f6 8 0-0 ♗b4 9 ♘a4 0-0 10 ♘xc6 bxc6 11 f4**

An aggressive alternative to 11 ♘b6.

**11...♖b8**

11...♗e7 looks slightly safer – see Game 38.

**12 ♗d3 ♗e7 13 c4**

On 13 e5, 13...♘d5 and 14...f6 or 14...f5 generates counterplay.

**13...d6**

Tregubov's 13...e5 is considered in the next game.

**14 g4!?**

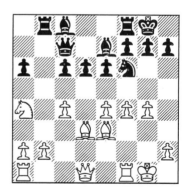

A radically different interpretation to that of the known 14 c5 dxc5 15 ♖c1, which is also promising for White. Shirov goes straight for the jugular.

**14...c5**

Black could also have tried 14...♘d7, when White presumably

ploughs on with 15 g5. Another set-up entirely is 14...e5 15 f5 h6.

**15 g5 ♘d7 16 ♖f2 g6 17 h4 f5!?**

A logical defence, but Black might instead have erected a different barrier with 18...h5!?

**18 h5 ♖f7!**

Ready to swing across when the h-file opens.

**19 hxg6 hxg6 20 ♖h2 ♘f8 21 exf5 gxf5 22 ♘c3 ♗d8 23 ♖c1! ♖h7 24 ♖cc2 ♗b7 25 ♖xh7 ♕xh7 26 ♖h2 ♕g7**

From this square the queen keeps an eye on the central goings on, as well as serving as a defender.

**27 ♘e2 ♗f3!**

Rightly ignoring the bait and preferring to coordinate his pieces for the defence. After 27...♕xb2 28 ♗d2 there are some nasty tricks.

**28 b3 ♗a5!**

Getting the most from this bishop.

**29 ♔f2 ♗g4 30 ♕h1 ♘g6 31 ♖h6!**

Threatening an invasion with ♕c6.

**31...♘f8!**

Hjartarson conducts an excellently coordinated defence. Now 32 ♕c6 ♕b7 is fine.

**32 ♖h4 ♘g6 33 ♖xg4!?**

The powerful and practical sacrifice allows White to retain a sound structure for minimal material investment plus several threats.

**33...fxg4 34 ♕h5 ♘f8**

34...♔f7 would also have left White with good compensation after 35 f5 exf5 36 ♗xf5 ♖h8 37 ♕xg4, when 37...♘e5 is met by 38 ♕g2!

**35 ♕xg4 ♖b7 36 ♘g3 ♖f7 37 ♘h5 ♕b2+ 38 ♔f3 ♕h2?**

Hjartarson cracks in time pressure. Instead 38...♗d8! 39 ♘f6+ ♗xf6 40 gxf6+ ♔h8 41 ♕h5+ ♔g8 is a draw.

**39 g6 ♕h1+ 40 ♔f2 ♕h2+ 1-0**

Time control reached...and Black resigned, because of 41 ♔f1 ♕h1+ 42 ♗g1 ♖g7 43 ♘xg7 ♔xg7 44 f5 etc.; 42...♖c7 43 g7; or 42...♖f5 43 ♗xf5 exf5 44 ♕xf5 ♕f3+ 45 ♗f2 and wins.

---

### Game 37
### A.Sokolov-Tregubov
*Alushta 1993*

**1 e4 c5 2 ♘f3 e6 3 d4 cxd4 4 ♘xd4 ♘c6 5 ♘c3 ♕c7 6 ♗e3 a6 7 ♗e2 ♘f6 8 0-0 ♗b4 9 ♘a4 0-0 10 ♘xc6 bxc6 11 f4 ♖b8 12 ♗d3 ♗e7 13 c4**

**13...e5!?**

Tregubov liked this innovation, but I have my doubts.

**14 fxe5**

14 c5 ♖b4!? 15 a3? ♖xa4 16 ♕xa4 ♘g4 is good for Black, Stirling-Plaskett, British rapidplay, Leeds 1996.

**14...♕xe5 15 ♖f5**

An odd square for a rook. I prefer 15 ♗f4 ♕d4+ 16 ♔h1, when no clear route to equality exists, e.g. 16...♖b4 17 e5 ♘e4 18 ♕c2! ♖xa4 19 b3!, when 19...♘f2+! 20 ♕xf2 ♕xf2 21 ♖xf2 ♖b4 22 ♖d1 is obviously in White's favour as he has superiority in both development and structure.

**15...♕e6 16 ♕f3**

Not 16 e5? g6!

**16...d6 17 ♘b6 ♘d7! 18 ♘xd7 ♗xd7 19 ♗d4?**

Now White's pieces start tripping over one another's feet. 19 ♕f2 would have been better.

**19...c5 20 ♗c3 ♕g6 21 ♕h3**

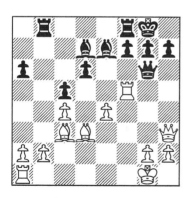

**21...♗g5!**

White has more compensation after 21...♗xf5 22 exf5 ♕h6 23 ♕xh6 gxh6 24 f6.

**22 e5 ♗xf5 23 ♗xf5 ♕h6 24 exd6 ♕xh3 25 ♗xh3 ♖bd8 26 ♖d1 ♗e3+ 27 ♔f1 ♗d4 28 ♖xd4!**

The only hope. On 28 d7, 28...f5 decides.

**28...cxd4 29 ♗b4 a5 30 ♗a3**

It would have been better to play 30 ♗c5, when Black should continue 30...f5! with a clear advantage.

**30...♖fe8 31 c5 d3**

Now the win is clear.

**32 c6 d2 33 ♗g4 ♖e1+ 34 ♔f2 d1♕ 35 ♗xd1 ♖xd1 36 d7**

Or 36 c7 ♖e8 with the plan of ...f7-f6, ...♔f7, ...♔e6, ...♔d7, etc.

**36...f5 37 b4 axb4 38 ♗xb4 ♔f7 39 a4 ♔e6?!**

39...♖a8, intending ...♔e6, would have been quicker.

**40 c7 ♖1xd7 41 cxd8♕ ♖xd8 42 a5 g6 43 ♗c5 ♖d2+ 44 ♔f3 ♖a2 45 ♗b6 ♖a3+ 46 ♔f4 ♖a4+ 47 ♔f3 g5 48 ♗d8 h6 0-1**

---

> ### Game 38
> ### Ye Jiang Chuan-Timman
> *Moscow Olympiad 1994*

---

**1 e4 c5 2 ♘f3 e6 3 d4 cxd4 4 ♘xd4 ♘c6 5 ♘c3 a6 6 ♗e2 ♕c7 7 0-0 ♘f6 8 ♗e3 ♗b4 9 ♘a4 0-0 10 ♘xc6 bxc6 11 f4 ♗e7 12 ♗f3**

Here 12 ♗d3 can be met by 12...c5 13 c4 d6 14 ♘c3 ♗b7 and 12 ♘b6 ♖b8 13 ♘xc8 by 13...♕xc8 14 e5 ♘d5 15 ♗c1 f6 16 c4 ♗c5+ 17 ♔h1 ♘e3 18 ♗xe3 ♗xe3 19 ♕d3 ♗c5 with equality (Taimanov).

**12...d5!?**

A very unusual way to play such a position. In the second game of the 1994 Candidates match between Khalifman and Salov there occurred 12...♖b8 (now that the white bishop has gone to f3 instead of d3, but of

course 12...d6 was also possible) 13 c4
d6 14 ♕d2 c5 15 ♖ad1 ♗b7 16 ♘c3
♖bd8 17 ♕f2 ♘d7 with equality.
Later Salov executed a classic manoeuvre to get his knight into an outpost at d4, viz. ...g7-g6, ...♗f6, ...♘b8
and ...♘c6.

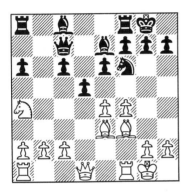

**13 e5**
Automatic.
**13...♘d7 14 c4**
White's space advantage simply
guarantees him a positional advantage.
**14...♖b8 15 a3!**
The immediate 15 ♖c1 would have
been met by 15...♕a5 (16 a3 ♘c5)
with equal chances, according to
Timman.
**15...a5**
Naturally.
**16 ♖c1 ♕b7 17 ♖c3**
On 17 ♖f2 ♕b3! 18 ♕xb3 ♖xb3 19
♗d2 ♘c5 Black has counterplay.
**17...♕a8 18 ♖f2 ♗a6**
Timman contorts ingeniously to
create activity.
**19 ♖d2 ♖fd8**
Not 19...f6? 20 cxd5 cxd5 21 ♖xd5!
**20 ♗e2 ♕b7 21 ♕c2 ♕a8 22 h3 g6**
An approximately equal has arisen.
**23 ♔h2**

This innocent move in fact sets up
some crucial tactical possibilities for
Timman later on. 23 ♔h1 would have
been a significant improvement.
**23...♗f8 24 ♕c1 ♗h6!**
A double over-fianchetto!
**25 ♕g1?!**
The Chinaman is oblivious to
Black's tricks. 25 ♕f1 would have
been an improvement.

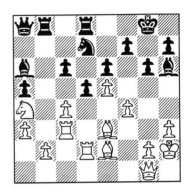

**25...c5!**
Seizing the chance to stir things up.
**26 cxd5 exd5 27 ♗f3**
Or 27 ♘xc5 ♘xc5 28 ♖xc5 d4! 29
♗xa6 dxe3 30 ♖xd8+ ♖xd8 31 ♗e2
♗xf4+ 32 g3 ♗h6 and Black is on top.
Alternatively 27 ♗xa6 is strongly met
by 27...d4!
**27...♗b7 28 ♘xc5 ♘xc5 29 ♖xc5
d4!**
You can bet Ye wished that his
king was on h1 now.
**30 ♗xb7 ♕xb7 31 ♕d1?**
The decisive error. Instead 31 ♖xd4
♖xd4 32 ♗xd4 ♗xf4+ 33 g3 ♗h6
would have left everything to play
for.
**31...♕e4**
Into the thick of things.
**32 ♖xd4**

Forced.

**32...♗xf4+ 33 ♔h1**

Not 33 ♗xf4 ♖xd4 or 33 g3 ♗xg3+ 34 ♔xg3 ♕xe3+ and wins.

**33...♖xd4 34 ♗xd4 ♖d8 35 ♖c4 ♗xe5 36 ♗g1**

Forced.

**36...♖xd1 37 ♖xe4 ♗c7! 0-1**

Heading for b6. White resigned, but I still doubt whether Jan will repeat his experiment with 12...d5.

> ## Game 39
> ## Rogers-Van Mil
> *Wijk aan Zee 1993*

**1 e4 c5 2 ♘f3 e6 3 d4 cxd4 4 ♘xd4 ♘c6 5 ♘c3 ♕c7 6 ♗e2 a6 7 0-0 ♘f6 8 ♗e3 ♗b4 9 ♘a4 0-0 10 ♘xc6 bxc6 11 c4**

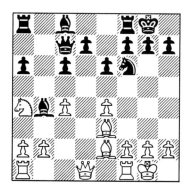

Perhaps the most consistent move if one is hoping to maintain a bind.

**11...♗d6!?**

Guaranteeing the win of a pawn, since White cannot cover everything, but 11...♗e7 is a perfectly solid alternative.

**12 f4 ♘xe4 13 ♗d3 ♘f6**

On 13...f5 White can keep material equality and the bind with 14 c5 ♗e7

15 ♗xe4 fxe4 16 ♕d4.

**14 ♗b6!**

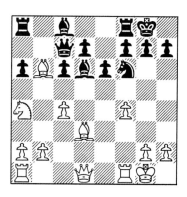

This was a new twist, as previously 14 c5 had been played, when Black can wriggle after 14...♗e7 15 ♗d4 ♖d8 16 ♖f3 d6 or 16...♖b8. Rogers intends to train his guns on the black king, but first shunts the queen into the corner.

**14...♕b8 15 ♗d4 e5?**

This did not work out well at all. Suggested improvements are:

a) 15...♗e7 16 ♘b6 (or 16 c5!? ♖d8 17 ♘b6 d6 18 ♘xa8 dxc5 19 ♗xf6 ♗xf6 20 ♕e2 ♕xa8 21 f5 with a dreadful mess in Thipsay-Al Modiakhi, Calcutta 1995) 16...c5!? 17 ♗xf6 ♗xf6 18 ♘xa8 ♕xa8, when Black, with the bishop pair, a sound structure and one pawn for the exchange, is not doing badly.

b) 15...♘e8!? 16 c5!? ♗c7 (after 16...♗xf4 17 ♘b6 Black is hopelessly overstretched, e.g. 17...e5 18 ♖xf4! exf4 19 ♕h5 h6 20 ♗f5, when he is almost move-bound) 17 ♘b6, which, I suppose is not 100% clear, although I prefer White.

**16 ♗c3 c5**

Black may already be lost. On

16...♖e8 17 c5 ♗c7 18 fxe5 ♗xe5 19 ♘b6! ♖a7, it is time to start enjoying yourself with 20 ♖xf6! gxf6 21 ♕h5 ♔f8 22 ♕h6+ ♔e7 23 ♖e1 ♔d8 24 ♕xf6+!! ♗xf6 25 ♗xf6+ ♔c7 26 ♖xe8 and wins.

**17 fxe5 ♗xe5 18 ♖xf6! ♗xf6 19 ♗xf6**

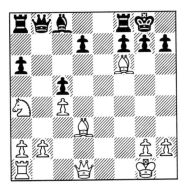

**19...♕f4**

Just about the only move.

**20 ♗c3 ♗b7 21 ♕d2**

Rogers decides to cash in for a technical position in which Black has little chance of holding out.

**21...♕xd2 22 ♗xd2 d6 23 ♘b6 ♖ad8 24 ♗g5 f6 25 ♗f4 ♖fe8 26 b3 ♗e4 27 ♗f1 g5 28 ♗d2 ♔g7 29 ♖d1 d5 30 cxd5?**

30 ♘xd5 ♗xd5 31 ♗a5! was the most accurate way.

**30...♗xd5 31 ♗a5 ♗b7 32 ♖c1 ♔g6 33 ♘a4 ♖d6 34 ♘xc5 ♗c8 35 a4 h5 36 b4 h4 37 h3 ♖e3 38 b5 axb5 39 axb5 ♖a3 40 ♗c7 ♖d2 41 ♘e4 ♖b2 42 ♘d6 ♗e6 43 b6 ♗d5 44 ♘c4 ♗xc4 45 ♗xc4 f5 46 ♗d5 ♖d3 47 ♗f3 g4 48 hxg4 h3 49 b7! ♖db3**

Or 49...hxg2 50 ♖c6+ ♔g5 41 ♖b6, etc.

**50 gxf5+ ♔xf5 51 g4+ ♔f6 52 b8♕ ♖xb8 53 ♗xb8 ♖xb8 54 ♔f2 1-0**

It is all over.

## Summary

In my view, in the lines where White exchanges on c8 and grabs the a-pawn, Black's active pieces and central pawns offset the passed white a-pawn. In contrast, where he prefers to try to establish a bind with an early c2-c4, even should this necessitates the sacrifice of his e4-pawn, White is more likely to emerge with an advantage.

**1 e4 c5 2 ♘f3 e6 3 d4 cxd4 4 ♘xd4 ♘c6 5 ♘c3 a6 6 ♗e2 ♛c7 7 ♗e3 ♘f6 8 0-0 ♗b4 9 ♘a4**

**9...♗e7**
>9...0-0 10 ♘xc6 bxc6
>>11 ♘b6 - *game 35*
>>11 f4 *(D)*
>>>11...♖b8 12 ♗d3 ♗e7 13 c4
>>>>13...d6 - *game 36*
>>>>13...e5 - *game 37*
>>>11...♗e7 - *game 38*
>>11 c4 - *game 39*

**10 c4**
>10 ♘xc6 bxc6 11 ♘b6 ♖b8 12 ♘xc8 ♛xc8 13 e5 ♘d5 14 ♗c1 ♗c5 *(D)*
>>15 ♛d3 - *game 33*
>>15 c4 - *game 34*

**10...♘xe4**
>10...0-0 - *game 32*

**11 c5** *(D)*
>11...0-0 - *game 30*
>11...♘f6 - *game 31*

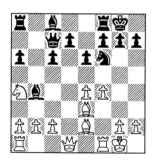
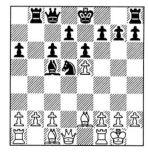
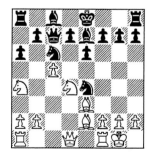

*11 f4*          *14...♗c5*          *11 c5*

# CHAPTER FIVE

## 5 ♘c3 a6 6 ♗e2 ♘ge7

**1 e4 c5 2 ♘f3 e6 3 d4 cxd4 4 ♘xd4 ♘c6 5 ♘c3 a6 6 ♗e2 ♘ge7**

This is the way the creator himself interprets his brainchild. Taimanov, who is still extraordinarily active in view of his years and alternative career as a pianist, hardly ever puts his king's knight on f6. The material here includes references to several of his recent games, illustrating how he continues to deepen and improve the theory of his legacy to chess.

In Game 40 Black exchanges knights and follows up with a strange knight sortie (of Taimanov's!) that I succeeded in refuting at the board. The cluster of references around Game 41 show how the more circumspect 9...♕c7 is a far better choice.

In Games 42 and 44 White permits the exchange on d4 and then seeks the advantage through probing the black queenside. Ulf Andersson (whose interpretations of this defence are well worth studying) shows what to do about it. The position after the thirteenth move of Game 43 is almost exactly what Black aims for in this system: a standard Sicilian middlegame but where the reduction in material lessens the danger of White commencing a successful attack.

The move 7 ♗f4 is perhaps the one more than any other that aims to punish Black by occupying the dark squares in his camp. This plan worked a treat in Game 45 as Psakhis took possession of d6 and did not relinquish it, even being prepared to give up the exchange to retain it, until his advantage was already decisive. Again Taimanov shows a superior reply for Black, as shown in the notes.

Game 47 is curious. Kuijf's idea of retreating the knight to f3 with his f-pawn unmoved should lead nowhere.

*Game 40*
**Plaskett-Hartston**
*Westergate (ARC Masters) 1986*

**1 e4 c5 2 ♘f3 e6 3 d4 cxd4 4 ♘xd4 ♘c6 5 ♘c3 a6 6 ♗e2 ♘ge7**

Hartston's preferred interpretation of the Taimanov, and indeed he once wrote 'all true Taimanov players should aim to be playing ...♘ge7.'
**7 0-0 ♘xd4 8 ♕xd4 ♘c6 9 ♕d3**

In Kontic-Damljanovic, Podgorica 1993, White tried an extraordinary escapade with 9 ♕e3 ♕c7 (9...♗e7 can be met by 10 ♕g3 0-0 11 ♗h6 ♗f6 12

♖ad1 b5 13 ♗f3, as in Kaplan-Taimanov, Hastings 1975/76, and, according to Taimanov himself, 9...♗d6!? should be met by 10 f4 0-0 11 ♕f2 ♗c7 12 ♗e3, when White retains the better prospects) 10 ♕g5!? b5 11 ♗f4 d6 12 ♖ad1 b4 13 ♘a4 ♘e5 14 ♗e3 ♗b7 15 ♘b6 ♖d8 16 f4 ♘d7 17 ♘xd7 ♖xd7, and chances were equal.

**9...♘b4**

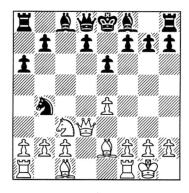

An odd idea which Taimanov himself had ventured a couple of times before against Kiril Georgiev and Karpov, but without success. Perhaps the idea was to shift the queen from the third rank, thus hampering her involvement in a later attack, for in the aforementioned games White dropped back with 10 ♕d2. Over the board I spotted a much more vigorous idea.

**10 ♕g3!**

A powerful innovation (there has been no subsequent master game with 9...♘b4).

**10...♘xc2**

Since Black cannot develop his kingside, he might as well take this pawn.

**11 ♗g5! f6**

11...♗e7 12 ♗xe7 and 13 ♕xg7 is very good for White, while after 11...♕b6 or 11...♕a5 I had nothing more definite in mind than 12 ♖ad1 with a large development lead for the pawn.

**12 ♗f4!**

The point being that 12...♘xa1 fails to 13 ♗h5+ g6 (13...♔e7 14 ♗d6 mate) 14 ♗xg6+ hxg6 15 ♕xg6+ ♔e7 16 e5! and Black has nothing better than 16...d5 17 ♕xf6+ ♔d7 18 ♕xh8 ♘c2 19 ♕h7+! (the final point), when he ends up two pawns down.

**12 ♔f7 13 ♗c7 ♕e8**

After 13...♕e7 14 ♖ad1 White would also have great pressure for his pawn.

**14 ♖ad1**

Intending ♘a4-b6.

**14...b5 15 e5!**

This advance reveals the extent of Black's disorganisation: his position is indefensible.

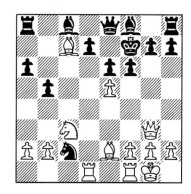

**15...♗b7**

Or 15...fxe5 16 ♗f3 ♖a7 17 ♗b6 ♖b7 18 ♗xb7 ♗xb7 19 ♕d3 and wins.

**16 exf6 ♔g8**

There is no way out: 16...gxf6 17 ♗h5+ ♔e7 18 ♕d6 mate; 16...♔xf6 17

♗e5+ ♔f7 18 ♗h5+ g6 19 ♕f4+ ♔g8 20 ♕f6 and wins; or 16...g6 17 ♕d3 and wins.

**17 fxg7 ♗xg7 18 ♗e5 1-0**

For if 18...♕xg6 19 ♕xg6 hxg6 20 ♗xg7 ♔xg7 21 ♖xd7+ wins the bishop on b7.

Imagine my surprise when a fortnight later Nigel Davies told me that he had also discovered 10 ♕g3!, *during home analysis*, and that he had intended to use it against Mark Taimanov at a tournament in Lisbon, but the Russian grandmaster had varied with 6...♕c7.

> ### Game 41
> ### Benjamin-Christiansen
> *USA Championship 1993*

**1 e4 c5 2 ♘f3 e6 3 d4 cxd4 4 ♘xd4 ♘c6 5 ♘c3 a6 6 ♗e2 ♘ge7 7 0-0 ♘xd4 8 ♕xd4 ♘c6 9 ♕d3 ♕c7**

Far more consistent than 9...♘b4.

**10 ♗g5!?**

Sailing into space. I prefer 10 ♗e3.

**10...♗d6!? 11 ♔h1 h6**

11...b5 was played in Kuijf-Van Mil, Wijk aan Zee (Sonnevanck) 1992, where White continued in imaginative fashion: 12 ♖ad1 ♗e5 13 f4 f6 14 fxe5 fxg5 15 ♗h5+ g6 16 ♕f3 ♕xe5 (16...♘xe5 17 ♕f6 is dangerous) 17 ♗g4 ♘d8 18 ♘d5!?

---
*see following diagram*

---

In another Van Mil game, against Nijboer, he played 11...f6 12 ♗e3 b5 13 f4 ♗e7 14 e5 0-0 15 exf6 ♖xf6 16 f5 ♗b7 17 ♗g5 ♖ff8 18 ♗xe7 ♘xe7. White retreated the bishop to h4 in Burnazovic-Krnic, Yugoslavia 1986,

and after 12...♘e5 13 ♕d2 ♘g6!? 14 ♗h5?! ♔e7! 15 ♗g3 ♘f4 16 ♖ad1 ♗e5 Black was doing very well.

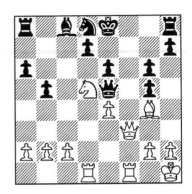

In Lukin-Taimanov, St Petersburg 1995, yet another 11th move cropped up in 11...♘e5!?, and play continued 12 ♕d2 f6 13 ♗h4 ♘g6 14 ♗g3 ♗xg3 15 hxg3 b5 16 f4 ♗b7 17 ♗d3 0-0 with equality (drawn in 34 moves).

**12 ♗e3 b5 13 f4 ♗b7**

**14 ♗b6**

A clever little tactic to exchange dark-squared bishops.

**14...♕xb6 15 ♕xd6 ♖c8 16 ♖ad1 ♕c7 17 ♕d2 0-0!?**

Christiansen is one of the most creative of the American players. Although this pawn sacrifice was not strictly necessary, it works well.

**18 ♕xd7 ♕b6**

Threatening to trap White's queen.

**19 ♕d2 ♘a5! 20 f5 ♘c4 21 ♗xc4 ♖xc4 22 fxe6**

22 f6!? might have been White's last chance to try for something.

**22...♕xe6**

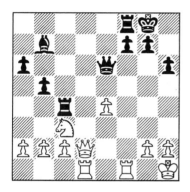

Black's piece activity and the weakness of the opponent's pawns mean that he does not stand worse.

**23 b3 ♖c5 24 ♕d4 ♖e5 25 ♕d7 ♗a8 26 ♕xe6 ♖xe6 27 ♖d4 ♖c8 28 ♖f3 ♖ec6 29 h3 ♖xc3 30 ♖xc3 ♖xc3 31 ♖d8+ ♔h7 32 ♖xa8 ♖c6**

The peace treaty could now have been signed.

**33 a4 bxa4 34 bxa4 h5 35 ♖a7 f6 36 ♔h2 h4 37 a5 ♔h6 38 ♔g1 g6 39 ♖b7 ♖xc2 40 ♖b6 ♔g5 41 ♖xa6 ♖a2 ½-½**

> ### Game 42
> ## Van der Wiel-Andersson
> *Wijk aan Zee 1987*

**1 e4 c5 2 ♘f3 e6 3 d4 cxd4 4 ♘xd4 ♘c6 5 ♘c3 a6 6 ♗e2 ♘ge7 7 f4 ♘xd4 8 ♕xd4 b5**

The immediate 8...♘c6 is consid-

ered in the next game.

**9 a4**

Trying to stir things up on the queenside, but the great Sicilian specialist Andersson comes up with an adequate counter.

**9...♘c6 10 ♕f2 b4 11 ♘b1 ♗e7 12 ♗e3 ♖b8 13 ♘d2 0-0 14 0-0 ♕c7 15 ♗d3 d6 16 ♕g3 f5!?**

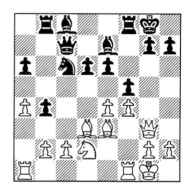

An interesting idea. Andersson stops the white attack before it starts.

**17 exf5 exf5 18 ♘f3 ♗f6 19 ♖ab1 ♘e7 20 ♖fe1 ♗b7 21 ♘d4 ♕d7 22 ♗f2 ♕xa4 23 ♘xf5 ♘xf5 24 ♗xf5 ♖be8 25 ♕d3 ♕c6!**

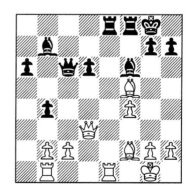

Accurate calculation. Ulf steers towards the drawing haven.

**26 ♗xh7+ ♔h8 27 ♕h3**

Forced.

**27...♖xe1+ 28 ♗xe1 ♗d4+ 29 ♔h1 ♕xg2+ 30 ♕xg2 ♗xg2+ 31 ♔xg2 ♔xh7 32 ♗xb4 ½-½**

---

### Game 43
### Wittmann-Klinger
*Austrian Championship 1993*

---

**1 e4 c5 2 ♘f3 e6 3 d4 cxd4 4 ♘xd4 ♘c6 5 ♘c3 a6 6 f4 ♘ge7 7 ♗e2 ♘xd4 8 ♕xd4 ♘c6 9 ♕f2 d6 10 ♗e3 b5 11 0-0 ♗e7 12 ♖ad1 ♕c7 13 ♗f3 0-0**

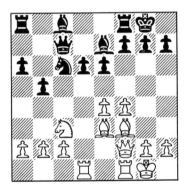

In this very standard position Black can face the future with total confidence.

**14 e5!? d5!**

Certainly preferable to 14...dxe5 15 ♗b6 ♕b7 16 fxe5 with a dominating bind.

**15 ♗b6 ♕b7 16 ♖fe1 ♗d7 17 ♗c5 ♗xc5 18 ♕xc5 ♖fc8 19 ♕f2 ♕a7**

If White could transfer the knight to d4, his control of the dark squares would leave him clearly better, but such is Black's activity that he is unable to do this, e.g. 20 ♘e2? ♘b4 21 c3 (or 21 ♘d4 ♘xc2!) 21...♘c2 and ...♘e3 wins the exchange.

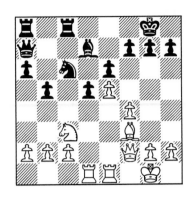

**20 ♖d2 ♘a5 21 ♘d1 ♘c4 22 ♖d4 b4!**

Staking out some more queenside space. The chances are about equal.

**23 f5?! ♘a5!**

So as to be able to take part in a defence, if necessary.

**24 fxe6 fxe6 25 ♖xb4 ♕xf2+ 26 ♘xf2 ♖xc2 27 ♘g4 ♖ac8 28 ♖b6 ♖8c6 29 ♖b8+ ♖c8 30 ♖b6 ♖2c6**

Klinger hopes to demonstrate that the isolation of White's e-pawn will cause him a headache for him.

**31 ♖b4 ♖c1 32 ♔f2 ♗b5 33 ♖xc1 ♖xc1 34 ♔e3 ♘c6 35 ♖b3 ♖c2**

Now Black is well on top.

**36 ♔f4 ♖c4+ 37 ♔g3 ♖a4 38 a3 h5 39 ♘f2 h4+ 40 ♔h3 ♘xe5 41 ♘g4 ♘g6 42 ♖c3 ♖c4 43 ♖xc4 ♗xc4 44 ♘e3 ♗b3 45 ♔g4 ♔f7 46 ♔g5 ♘e5 47 ♗d1 ♗xd1 48 ♘xd1 h3! 49 gxh3 ♘c4 50 h4 e5 51 h5 e4 52 ♔f4 ♔e6 53 h3 ♘e5! 54 b4 ♘d3+ 55 ♔e3 ♔e5 56 ♔d2 d4 57 ♔c2 ♔d5 0-1**

---

### Game 44
### Ricardi-Dorin
*Argentine Championship 1995*

---

**1 e4 c5 2 ♘f3 e6 3 d4 cxd4 4 ♘xd4**

♘c6 5 ♘c3 a6 6 ♗e2 ♘ge7 7 ♗e3 ♘xd4 8 ♕xd4 b5

It is important to note that 8...♘c6 is well met by 9 ♕b6!

**9 a4**

This direct attempt should not be sufficient for an advantage, but Black is also fine after 9 0-0 ♘c6 10 ♕d2 ♗e7 11 f4 ♗b7, as has occurred in several of Taimanov's own games, while the aggressive 9 0-0-0 can be neutralised by Taimanov's 9...♘c6 10 ♕d2 ♗b4! 11 a3 ♗e7, intending ...b5-b4.

**9...♘c6 10 ♕b6 ♕xb6 11 ♗xb6 b4?!**

I prefer 11...♖b8.

**12 ♘b1 ♗b7 13 ♘d2**

About to hop into the holes created by Black's 11th.

**13...♗e7 14 0-0-0!? ♘e5**

There is no longer any route to a genuine equality, so Dorin fishes around.

**15 f4 ♘g6 16 g3 0-0 17 ♗f3 ♖fc8 18 b3 ♖c3 19 ♗d4 ♖c7 20 ♘c4 ♘f8 21 ♖hf1! d6 22 ♗b6!**

Off to round up the b-pawn with 23 ♗a5, hence Black tries a standard Sicilian exchange sacrifice, but this is

also insufficient.

**22...♖xc4 23 bxc4 ♖c8 24 e5 ♗xf3 25 ♖xf3 dxe5 26 fxe5 ♖xc4 27 ♗d8! ♗c5 28 ♔b2 ♘g6 29 ♔b3 ♖e4 30 ♗c7 ♗e7 31 ♖d7 f6 32 ♗d6 ♗xd6 33 exd6**

There is no hope of resistance against such a monster pawn.

**33...♘e5 34 ♖d8+ ♔f7 35 ♖f4 ♖e3+ 36 ♔b2 b3 37 ♖b4 bxc2 38 ♔xc2 ♖d3 39 ♖b7+ ♔g6 40 ♖a7 ♖d4 41 ♖xa6 h5 42 a5 h4 43 ♖b6 ♖a4 44 a6 hxg3 45 hxg3 ♔f5 46 d7 g5 47 ♖d6 g4 48 ♖a8 1-0**

### Game 45
### Psakhis-Romanishin
*Irkutsk 1986*

**1 e4 c5 2 ♘f3 e6 3 d4 cxd4 4 ♘xd4 ♘c6 5 ♘c3 a6 6 ♗e2 ♘ge7 7 ♗f4 ♘g6 8 ♘xc6**

8 ♗e3 is considered in the next game.

**8...bxc6 9 ♗d6**

Establishing hegemony over the dark squares. Personally I find this plan so strong that I would deny White the chance to play it by interposing 7...♘xd4.

**9...♗xd6**

In Furhoff -Taimanov, Stockholm 1994, the creator showed us another way: 9...f6!? 10 0-0 ♗xd6 11 ♕xd6 ♕e7 12 ♖ad1 ♕xd6 13 ♖xd6 ♔e7 14 ♖fd1 ♖b8 and play now took an unlikely twist 15 g3!? ♖xb2 16 ♗xa6!? ♖xc2 17 ♗xc8 ♖xc8 18 ♖xd7+ ♔f8 19 ♘a4 ♘e5 20 ♖b7 ♖e8 21 ♘b6 ♖e7, and was drawn in 42 moves. Another try is 9...♕b6, but in Efimov-Shestoperov, USSR 1987, Black was soon in trouble after 10 ♗xf8! ♘xf8 11 0-0 ♘g6 12 ♘a4 ♕c7 13 ♕d4 0-0 14 ♖fd1!

**10 ♕xd6 ♕e7 11 0-0-0 ♕xd6 12 ♖xd6 ♔e7 13 ♖hd1 ♖a7**

This was a new move at the time, but it did nothing to alter the theoretical assessment of 'better for White'. Previously 13...♘f4 14 ♗f3 ♖a7 or 14...♖b8 (14...♘d5? 15 exd5! ♔xd6 16 dxc6+ and 17 cxd7) had occurred.

**14 g3 f6 15 f4 ♖d8 16 ♘a4 ♘h8**

Intending to boot the rook out, but Lev has other ideas.

**17 c4 ♘f7**

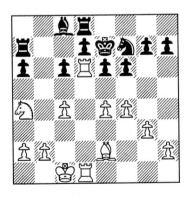

**18 c5! a5**

After 18...♘xd6 19 cxd6+ ♔f7 20 ♘c5 a5 21 b3!, and then the progressive advance of his queenside, Black is virtually move-bound.

**19 ♖6d4 e5**

Or 19...♗a6 20 ♗xa6 ♖xa6 21 ♖a4 and b2-b4 follows.

**20 ♖4d2 ♗a6**

There was nowhere else it could have gone to.

**21 ♗g4 d6 22 fxe5 dxe5 23 ♖xd8 ♘xd8 24 ♘b6**

White's crushing bind persists, hence Black's prospects are bleak.

**24...♖c7 25 ♔c2 g6 26 ♔c3 h5 27 ♖d7+!**

A much more accurate continuation than the lax 27 ♗h3, when the bishop slips into the game via 27...♗e2!

**27...♖xd7 28 ♗xd7 ♘e6**

The ending is lost. If 28...♗f1 then 29 b4! axb4+ 30 ♔xb4 ♗xg2 31 a4 ♗xe4 32 a5 ♗d3 33 ♗c8! and wins.

**29 ♗xc6 ♘xc5 30 ♘c4 ♗b7 31 ♗xb7 ♘xb7 32 b4 axb4+ 33 ♔xb4 ♔e6 34 a4**

This guy is the killer. Outside passed pawns are especially powerful in knight endgames.

**34...f5 35 a5 ♘xa5**

Or 35...♘d8 36 ♔c5 wins.

**36 ♔xa5 f4 37 ♔b5 g5 38 ♘d2 g4 39 ♘f1 ♔f6 40 ♔c5 ♔g5 41 ♔d5 ♔f6 42 ♔d6 1-0**

A game very much in the active and pragmatic style of Lev Psakhis.

> *Game 46*
> **Yemelin-Kochiev**
> *St Petersburg 1995*

**1 e4 c5 2 ♘f3 e6 3 d4 cxd4 4 ♘xd4**

a6 5 ♘c3 ♘c6 6 ♗e2 ♘ge7 7 ♗f4 ♘g6 8 ♗e3

This is not so testing for Black as 8 ♘xc6.

**8...♕c7**

In later round of the same tournament, Yemelin-Taimanov varied with 8...♗e7 9 0-0 0-0 10 ♘a4 ♘xd4 11 ♗xd4 b5 12 ♘b6 ♖b8 13 ♘xc8 ♕xc8 with equal chances.

**9 0-0 ♗d6!? 10 g3 ♗b4**

A quite different treatment to the ...♗e7 formations. As mentioned, very often when ...♗b4 comes it is in association with a threat to the e-pawn, but here the knight is on g6, so the 'threat' is merely to damage the white pawns.

**11 ♘xc6!? ♕xc6 12 ♕d4!**

This centralisation of the queen is a good plan.

**12...♗xc3 13 ♕xc3 ♕xc3 14 bxc3 b5!? 15 a4 ♗b7**

A common interchange.

**16 axb5 axb5 17 ♖xa8+ ♗xa8 18 ♗c5!?**

White could have won a pawn with 18 f3 ♗c6 19 ♖b1 ♔e7 20 ♗xb5 ♗xb5 21 ♖xb5, but he probably thought that, because of the doubled c-pawns,

his winning chances would not be good. He therefore prefers to keep the pawns equal but retain the pair of bishops.

**18...♗xe4 19 ♗xb5 f5! 20 f4 ♘e7 21 ♖a1 ♖g8 22 ♖a7 ♘c6 23 ♖c7 g5!**

A bid for some air.

**24 ♖c8+ ♔f7 25 ♖xg8 ♔xg8 26 fxg5 ♗xc2**

White does not have enough to win this.

**27 ♔f2 ♗d1 28 ♗d6 ♔f7 29 ♔e3 ♔g6 30 h4 h6 31 gxh6 ♔xh6 32 ♔f4 ♗h5 33 ♗a6 ♗e8 34 ♗d3 ♗h5 35 ♗a6 ♗e8 36 ♗d3 ♗h5 37 c4 ♔g6 38 ♗e5 ♗d1 39 ♗b2 ♘b4 40 ♗f1 ♘c6 41 c5 ♗h5 42 ♗a6 ♔h6 43 ♗c8 ♗e8 44 g4 ♘e7!? 45 ♗a6**

Or 45 g5+? ♔h5 46 ♔g3 ♘g6 wins the h-pawn, and probably the g-pawn soon after too.

**45...♘d5+ 46 ♔g3 fxg4 47 ♔xg4 ♗h5+ 48 ♔g3 ♘e7 49 ♗f6 ♘c6 50 ♗g5+ ♔g7 51 ♗c1 ♔f6 52 ♗c8 ♗e8 53 ♔f4 e5+ 54 ♔g4 ♘d4 55 h5 ♘e6 56 ♗e3 ♘f4! 57 h6 ♘d5 58 ♗g5+ ♔g6 59 ♗b7 ♗f7 60 ♔h4 ♗e6 61 ♗c8 ♘b4 62 ♗d2 ♘c6 63 ♗b7 ♘d4 64 ♗e4+ ♗f5 ½-½**

**1 e4 c5 2 ♘f3 e6 3 d4 cxd4 4 ♘xd4 ♘c6 5 ♘c3 a6 6 ♗e2 ♘ge7 7 ♘f3?!**

Hardly natural. By refraining from the advance of his f-pawn White deprives himself of any effective plan. In Orlov-Taimanov, St Petersburg 1995, White chose the retreat 7 ♘b3 b5 8 0-0 ♘g6 9 f4 ♗e7 10 ♗e3 0-0 11 ♗d3 ♘b4! 12 ♕h5 ♘xd3 13 cxd3 f5! (an excellent and consequent way of stopping any white offensive) 14 ♘d5 (this was an attempted improvement on a game Arnason-Romanishin, Lone Pine 1981, where 14 ♘d4 had been played, but after 14...♗c5! 15 exf5 ♗xd4 16 ♗xd4 ♖xf5 17 ♕g4 ♗b7 Black stood well) 14...♗b7! (this is superior to 14...exd5 15 exf5 ♘h8 16 f6!) 15 ♘xe7+ ♘xe7 16 ♘c5 ♗c6 17 ♗d4 ♕e8 (another important defensive theme to remember) 18 ♕g5 ♕f7, and Black had a good position.

**7...b5 8 0-0 ♘g6**

Now that White has castled, and can thus no longer create trouble by advancing the h-pawn, this move is perfectly safe.

**9 ♖e1 d6 10 a4 b4 11 ♘a2 ♖b8 12 ♗d2 ♗e7 13 c3 bxc3 14 ♗xc3 0-0 15 b4 ♗b7 16 b5 axb5 17 ♗xb5**

Rather remarkably, White has engineered a passed pawn.

**17...♗a8**

We are taught the best reaction to a wing thrust is a reaction in the centre, but here it is not clear how Black is to set about it since 17...d5 just leads to

the isolation of his d-pawn.

**18 ♕d2 ♕b6 19 ♘b4 ♘xb4 20 ♗xb4 ♖fc8**

Here also 20...♖fd8, aiming for ...d6-d5, is possible.

**21 ♖ad1 ♗c6 22 ♘d4 ♗xb5 23 ♘xb5 ♖c4?!**

23...♘e5 24 ♗xd6 ♘c4 would still have held the balance.

**24 ♗xd6 ♗xd6 25 ♘xd6 ♖b4**

Hereabouts I imagine that Van Mil, must have twigged that 25...♖xa4 fails to 26 ♘xf7! ♔xf7 27 ♕d7+.

**26 ♕c3!**

Now 26...♖xa4 allows the highly disruptive 27 ♘c8!, when Black's vulnerability on the back rank causes his downfall, e.g. 27...♕b7 28 ♖d8+ ♘f8 29 ♕c5.

**26...♖b2 27 ♖f1 ♖b3 28 ♕c1**

Even here the activity of Black's pieces is such that he has excellent chances to hold. Maybe now 28...h5!?

**28...♕b4?! 29 ♕c7! ♖f8 30 a5**

A simple and highly effective plan.

**30...♖a3 31 ♖a1 ♘f4 32 a6 ♖c3 33 ♕e7 ♕c5 34 a7 ♖h3 35 ♕xf8+ ♔xf8 36 a8♕+ ♔e7 37 ♕a7+ ♕xa7 38 ♖xa7+ ♔xd6 39 gxh3 ♘xh3+ 40 ♔h1 1-0**

## Summary

You will have noticed how right up to the present day Taimanov himself has been refining the ...♘ge7 systems. Even after decades of experimentation, theory still regards the idea of developing the king's knight in this manner as perfectly viable. Perhaps the most testing set-ups for White after ...♘ge7, as in the fianchetto variation, are those that involve the withdrawal of the knight from d4 to b3, but that is a comparative rarity.

**1 e4 c5 2 ♘f3 e6 3 d4 cxd4 4 ♘xd4 ♘c6 5 ♘c3 a6 6 ♗e2 ♘ge7**

**7 0-0**
  7 f4 ♘xd4 8 ♕xd4 *(D)*
    8...b5 - *game 42*
    8...♘c6 - *game 43*
  7 ♗e3 - *game 44*
  7 ♗f4 ♘g6 *(D)*
    8 ♘xc6 - *game 45*
    8 ♗e3 - *game 46*
  7 ♘f3 - *game 47*
**7...♘xd4 8 ♕xd4 ♘c6 9 ♕d3 *(D)***
  9...♘b4 - *game 40*
  9...♕c7 - *game 41*

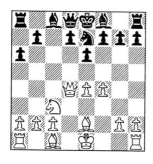

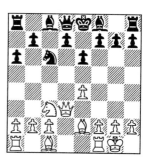

8 ♕xd4          7...♘g6          9 ♕d3

# CHAPTER SIX

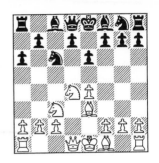

## 5 ♘c3 a6 6 ♗e3
## followed by f2-f3 and ♕d2

**1 e4 c5 2 ♘f3 e6 3 d4 cxd4 4 ♘xd4 ♘c6 5 ♘c3 a6 6 ♗e3**

All of the theoretical references in this chapter are very recent, because it is only since the mid-1980s that anybody thought of adopting this set-up against the Taimanov. No doubt people were most probably inspired by the successes recorded by English Grandmasters who played f2-f3, ♗e3, ♕d2 formations against sundry other Sicilians. Once again we are only concerned with pure Taimanov play, and so do not examine move-orders which veer back towards the Scheveningen with an early ...d7-d6.

Games 48-50 all feature the familiar Taimanov manoeuvre ...♘e5. Normally Black intends to meet a subsequent f3-f4 by moving the knight on, of course, but Portisch had quite another idea in mind in Game 49!

Games 49-52 see Black resorting to the pin ...♗b4. This is more because of the move's inhibiting and irritant effect than through any serious intention to double the c-pawns, as ...♗xc3 is particularly unlikely with the white queen stationed on d2.

In Games 49, 50 and 52 Black also makes the interesting decision to defer castling, possibly because White's projected g2-g4 makes him think that he would be running 'into it'. Indeed I found Game 52 altogether wonderfully original and inspiring, and Game 50, for all its brevity, is in many ways a classic Taimanov game, well worthy of close study.

In Game 53 Zviaginsev tried the far less common theme, in a Taimanov, of ...d7-d5. He may not have been satisfied with the dynamic potential of the middlegame that resulted, which may explain his frankly dubious choice in Game 56, but objectively this could well be a sound equaliser.

The standard plan of exchanging on d4 and bringing the king knight to c6 is seen in Game 54, and should have brought Gobet a major scalp.

In Game 55 Lautier, one of the big names amongst today's Taimanov exponents, who has used it to take the scalp of Garry Kasparov, opts to fianchetto his queen's bishop early on, and, perhaps through consequent fears of sacrifices on b5, follows up with an exchange on d4. Although I am not entirely convinced that his play was viable, it worked against one of the world's strongest grandmasters.

## Game 48
## Anand-Plaskett
### British Championship 1988

1 e4 c5 2 ♘f3 e6 3 d4 cxd4 4 ♘xd4
♘c6 5 ♘c3 a6 6 ♗e3 ♕c7 7 ♕d2!?

This move came as a surprise to me: I was unaware of the formation that Anand was about to reveal.

**7...♘f6 8 f3!?**

Perhaps White was inspired by the success which Short, Nunn and Chandler had had with the 'English Attack' against the Najdorf and Scheveningen Sicilians, i.e. 1 e4 c5 2 ♘f3 d6 3 d4 cxd4 4 ♘xd4 ♘f6 5 ♘c3 a6 (or 5...e6) 6 ♗e3 intending ♕d2, f2-f3, g2-g4, 0-0-0, etc. At any rate, had he castled immediately, the reply 8...♘g4 9 ♗f4 e5 10 ♘xc6 dxc6 equalises at once.

**8...b5**

Insisting upon a Taimanov character to the play, but we shall see that Black has other options apart from turning it into an Scheveningen.

**9 0-0-0**

9 g4 is also to be considered, when 9...d6 is simplest. In Saltaev-Ishevsky,

Bulgaria 1988, Black insisted upon the Taimanov flavour with 9...b4 10 ♘a4 ♘xd4 (10...d6!?) 11 ♗xd4 ♖b8 12 g5 ♘h5 13 ♗e3 ♗d6 14 0-0-0 ♗f4 15 ♗xf4 ♕xf4 16 ♕xf4 ♘xf4 17 ♘c5 a5, and White was a little better. Alternatively 9 ♘xc6 dxc6 10 0-0-0 e5 11 g4 ♗e6, as in Frolov-Miladinovic, Moscow 1994, is fine for Black.

**9...b4!? 10 ♘a4 ♘e5**

Once again choosing the consistent 'Taimanov' continuation.

**11 ♘b3**

Pretty much forcing Black's response. I was still surprised by Anand's system. After the game 11 g4 was proposed.

**11...♖b8 12 ♗c5**

Now I started to get it, but was unimpressed. It all seems a bit artificial.

**12...♗xc5 13 ♘axc5**

13 ♘bxc5 d5 14 exd5 ♘xd5 is no improvement for White.

**13...d5!**

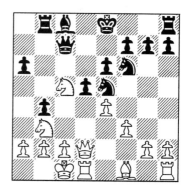

**14 exd5 ♘xd5**

Here Anand refrained from grabbing the a-pawn, since this would automatically grant Black an attack down the newly opened file.

**15 f4 ♘d7 16 ♘xd7 ♗xd7 17 f5 0-0**

Black emerges from the opening with rather more than just equality, due to his development lead and attacking chances.

**18 ♗e2 ♖fd8 19 ♗f3 ♗a4!**

Already the white game is critical.

**20 fxe6 ♗xb3 21 exf7+ ♔f8! 22 axb3 ♘c3! 23 ♕xd8+**

Hoping to bail out into an ending where the reduced material gives hope of constructing an unassailable fortress. However this is not possible.

**23...♖xd8 24 bxc3 bxc3 25 ♔b1 ♖xd1+ 26 ♖xd1 ♕a5 27 ♖d3**

Forced.

**27...♔xf7 28 h3 ♔f6 29 ♗a8 h5 30 ♗f3 g6 31 ♗a8 g5 32 ♗f3 h4 33 ♗a8 ♔e6 34 ♗f3 ♔e5**

**35 ♗a8**

The king and pawn endgame is lost for White after 35 ♖d5+ ♕xd5 36 ♗xd5 ♔xd5, because he cannot stop the black king penetrating on one or the other side of his position, e.g. 37 ♔c1 ♔e4 38 ♔d1 ♔e3 39 ♔e1 a5 with a zugzwang.

**35...♕c5 36 ♗f3 ♕a5 37 ♗a8 ♕b4 38 ♔a2 ♕a5+ 39 ♔b1 ♕c5 40 ♔a2 ♔e6 41 ♗f3 a5!**

After some fiddling around Black gets on with the correct plan.

**42 ♗h5 a4 43 ♗g4+ ♔e5 44 ♗f3 ♔f4**

By combining the threat of mate with the penetration of his king, Black is also able to create situations where he may sacrifice the queen for the rook and thus promote a pawn. White cannot cope with all of these problems.

**45 ♗d5**

Or 45 bxa4? ♕b4.

**45...a3 46 ♗f3 ♔g3 47 ♗a8+ ♔f2 48 ♗f3 ♕f5!**

Threatening to take the rook.

**49 ♗d1**

Of course 49 ♖xc3 is met by 49...♕e5.

**49...♔e1**

And again.

**50 ♖d8 ♕f6 51 ♖d5 ♕f2 52 ♖d3**

The fortress collapses.

**52...♕xg2 53 ♔xa3 ♕e4**

Once more intending to capture.

**54 ♖d7 ♕a8+ 55 ♔b4 ♕f8+ 56 ♔a4 ♕f5 0-1**

---

*Game 49*
### Anand-Portisch
*Biel Interzonal 1993*

---

**1 e4 c5 2 ♘f3 e6 3 d4 cxd4 4 ♘xd4 a6 5 ♘c3 ♕c7 6 ♗e3 ♘c6 7 ♕d2 ♘f6 8 f3 ♘e5!?**

A standard Taimanov theme but here with a particular sting. If now White kicks the knight with 9 f4 there comes 9...♗b4! 10 fxe5 ♘xe4 with great obscurity. Yet another way was shown in Zagrabelny-Landa, Noyabirsk 1995, with 8...♘xd4 9 ♕xd4 ♗d6!? 10 0-0-0 ♗e5 11 ♕b4! b5 12 a4! bxa4 13 ♘xa4 ♖b8 14 ♕a3, when White was a little better (0-1 in 41 moves).

**9 0-0-0 ♗b4 10 ♘b3 b5**

10...♗xc3 11 bxc3 d5 is strongly met by 12 ♗d4!, when 12...dxe4??

allows 13 ♗xe5 ♕xe5 14 ♕d8 mate.

**11 ♗d4!?**

With 12 ♕g5 in mind.

**11...h6 12 ♔b1**

So that ♘xb5 becomes a threat. 12 a3 is dealt with in the next game.

**12...♘c4 13 ♕f2 0-0 14 ♕g3**

The consequences of 14 ♗xf6 gxf6 are not so bad for Black. He dominates the black squares and has his own initiative, whilst White is a long way from getting the attack off the ground.

**14...♗d6!? 15 ♕e1 ♗e5**

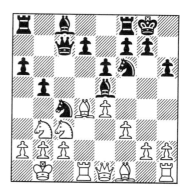

This leads to a queenless middlegame in which Black suffers through his lag in development. A better idea was 15...e5, intending to establish a centre with pawns on e5 and d6. Portisch may have feared White's kingside build-up, but after 16 ♗f2 ♗e7 17 g4 d6 18 h4 ♗e6 19 g5 ♘h5! 20 gxh6 g6 play is unclear.

**16 ♗xe5 ♕xe5 17 ♕g3! ♕xg3 18 hxg3 ♘e3 19 ♖d6 ♘e8 20 ♖d3 ♘c4 21 a4 ♘e5 22 ♖d2 b4 23 ♘a2 ♘c6 24 ♘d4 ♘xd4 25 ♖xd4 a5 26 ♗b5 ♘f6 27 ♖hd1 ♖d8 28 c3 bxc3 29 ♘xc3 ♖a7 30 e5 ♘e8 31 ♘e4 ♔f8 32 ♔a2**

White will seek to create a passed pawn on the queenside.

**32...♔e7?!**

32...f6 would have been better.

**33 ♘d6! ♘xd6 34 exd6+ ♔e8 35 ♖c4**

35 ♖g4! was even stronger.

**35...♗a6 36 ♖c7 ♖aa8 37 ♖dc1?**

A major inaccuracy. He should have played 37 ♔a3! ♗xb5 38 axb5 ♖db8 39 ♔a4 ♖b6, and now White can maintain his bind with 40 g4 ♖ab8 41 ♖c5 ♔d8 42 f4.

**37...♗xb5 38 axb5 ♖ab8 39 ♖1c5 ♖b6 40 ♔a3 ♖xd6**

A big achievement for the defender.

**41 ♔a4 ♔e7 42 ♖c8 ♖d2 43 ♖c2 ♖xc2 44 ♖xc2 d5!**

Hastening to utilise his one asset.

**45 b6 d4 46 ♔b5 d3! 47 ♖d2 e5 48 b7 f5**

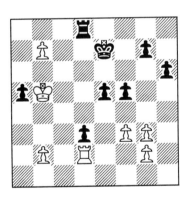

Dynamic equality has arisen. No variation now seems to afford White a winning opportunity, e.g. 49 b4 (not only getting another pawn running but also talking away Black's tricks with ...♖b3+; hence the protection of the d-pawn is necessitated) 49...e4 50 bxa5? e3 and wins, or 50 g4 (attempting an undermining opera-

tion) 50...axb4 51 gxf5 (51 ♔xb4? ♖b8 is greatly in Black's favour) 51...b3 52 fxe4 b2 53 ♖d1! d2, and Black, by taking all of his chances for counterplay, hangs in there with:

(a) 54 ♔c6 ♔f6 55 ♖xd2 (55 ♔c7? ♖f8 56 b8♕ ♖xb8 57 ♔xb8 ♔e5 is actually better for Black) 55...b1♕ 56 ♖xd8 ♕xe4+ 57 ♔c7 is a draw.

(b) 54 ♔b6 b1♕+ 55 ♖xb1 d1♕ 56 ♖xd1 ♖xd1 57 b8♕ ♖b1+ 58 ♔c7 ♖xb8 59 ♔xb8 and the pawn ending is drawn after 59...♔d6 60 ♔c8 ♔e5 61 ♔d7 ♔xe4 62 ♔e6.

**49 ♖xd3!? ♖xd3 50 b4!**

The only move, which now threatens promotion.

**50...♖d5+ 51 ♔c6 ♖d6+ 52 ♔c5 ♖d8 53 bxa5 e4 54 fxe4 fxe4 55 a6 e3 56 a7 e2 57 b8♕ ½-½**

A terrific struggle.

---

## Game 50
## Zagrebelny-Saltaev
*Moscow 1995*

---

**1 e4 c5 2 ♘f3 e6 3 ♘c3 ♘c6 4 d4 cxd4 5 ♘xd4 ♕c7 6 ♗e3 ♘f6 7 f3 a6 8 ♕d2 ♘e5!? 9 0-0-0 ♗b4 10 ♘b3 b5 11 ♗d4 h6 12 a3**

An attempt at improvement that Black counters successfully.

**12...♗e7 13 ♗xe5 ♕xe5 14 f4 ♕c7 15 e5 ♘g4!**

*see following diagram*

**16 ♕e2**

Certainly not 16 h3? ♘xe5!

**16...h5! 17 ♘e4**

On 17 h3 ♘h6 18 ♕xh5 Black has the more than satisfactory riposte, 18...♗xa3.

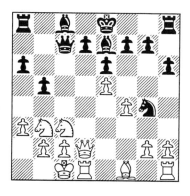

17...♗b7 18 h3 ♘h6 19 g4 ♕c4! 20 ♖d4 ♕xe2 21 ♗xe2 f5! 22 exf6 gxf6 ½-½

A short but instructive game, illustrating many of the themes of this opening.

---

### Game 51
### Pribyl-Christiansen
*Bundesliga 1993/94*

---

1 e4 c5 2 ♘f3 ♘c6 3 d4 cxd4 4 ♘xd4 e6 5 ♘c3 a6 6 ♗e3 ♕c7 7 ♕d2 ♘f6 8 f3 ♗b4!?

This is certainly quite logical after White plays f2-f3, because Black may go ...d7-d5 if he is allowed.

9 a3

The direct 9 g4 is considered in the next game.

9...♗e7

Now the insertion of a2-a3 could well help Black when the rival attacks kick off.

10 g4 0-0

10...h6!? transposes to the next game, but 10...d6 is another opening, another story.

11 0-0-0 b5 12 h4! ♖b8 13 h5 ♘xd4 14 ♗xd4 b4 15 axb4 ♖xb4 16 g5 ♘e8 17 f4 ♗b7 18 ♔b1

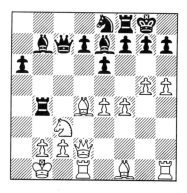

Black's opening does not quite seem to have worked. Retreating the knight to e8, rather than d7, has resulted in his rooks being unconnected and as a consequence he cannot coordinate fully.

18...♗c6 19 ♖g1 ♘d6

The only natural way to connect the rooks, but it runs into a tactic that nets the exchange. Christiansen realised that, of course, but must have hoped to generate attacking counterplay. However, Pribyl finds a novel method of suppressing him.

20 ♘d5! ♗xd5 21 ♕xb4 ♗xe4 22 ♕c5! ♕b7 23 ♕b6!

With the threat of exchanging,

White chases the black queen out of action.

**23...♕c8 24 ♖d2 ♘f5 25 ♗xa6 ♕a8 26 ♗c3 ♖b8 27 ♕c7! ♖f8 28 ♗d3 ♗d6**

Tantamount to resignation, but 28...♗xd3 29 ♖xd3 d5 was also insufficient.

**29 ♗xe4 ♗xc7 30 ♗xa8 ♖xa8 31 ♖xd7 ♗xf4 32 g6 fxg6 33 hxg6 h5 34 ♖f1 ♗h6 35 ♖e1 h4 36 ♖xe6 h3 37 ♗e5 ♘h4 38 ♖ed6 ♖f8 39 ♖d8 ♘f3 40 ♗g3 h2 41 ♖d1 ♗e3 42 ♖xf8+ ♔xf8 43 ♖h1 ♔e7 44 ♗xh2 ♘d2+ 45 ♔a2 ♔f6 46 ♖e1 ♗g5 47 ♖g1 ♗e3 48 ♖g2 ♔f5 49 ♗g1 ♗h6 50 ♗d4 ♘e4 51 b4 ♘d6 52 ♔b3 ♔e4 53 ♗b2 ♔d5 54 ♖h2 ♘c8 55 c4+ ♔d6 56 c5+ 1-0**

An excellent game from Pribyl against a strong opponent.

---

## Game 52
## Zagrebelny-Khatanbaatar
*Asian Team Championship 1995*

---

**1 e4 c5 2 ♘f3 ♘c6 3 d4 cxd4 4 ♘xd4 ♕c7 5 ♘c3 e6 6 ♗e3 a6 7 ♕d2 ♘f6 8 f3 ♗b4 9 g4 h6!? 10 a3 ♗e7 11 0-0-0 b5**

After White has announced his intentions of advancing the kingside pawns, delaying (or even dispensing with castling) is an interesting idea

**12 ♘xc6**

Perhaps 12 h4 or 12 ♔b1.

**12...dxc6!? 13 h4 b4**

Now on 14 axb4 ♗xb4 Black is doing fine, so Zagrebelny fishes around for something better. I doubt whether he found it.

**14 ♘a4?! bxa3 15 b3 c5 16 ♗c4 ♗d7 17 ♘c3 ♗c6 18 g5 ♖d8! 19 ♕g2 ♖xd1+ 20 ♖xd1 hxg5 21 hxg5 ♖h2! 22 ♕g1 ♕e5! 23 ♖d3**

Not 23 gxf6 ♕xc3 and mate.

**23...♘h5 24 ♔b1 ♖h4**

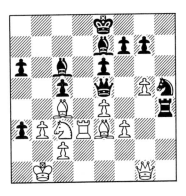

Black intends to round up the g-pawn with ...♘f4, so White pushes it on, but this cedes the wonderful f6-square to the bishop.

**25 g6 ♗b5! 26 gxf7+ ♔xf7 27 ♔a2 ♗xc4 28 bxc4 ♘f4 29 ♗xf4**

Forced.

**29...♕xf4 30 ♘b1 ♖h3 31 ♕d1 ♗f6 32 ♘xa3**

At last he rids himself of the pest, but all of the black pieces are now better placed than their opposite numbers and the white king is also under threat.

**32...♕e5 33 c3 ♖h2+ 34 ♘c2 ♔g8!
35 ♕b1 ♕g3 36 ♕b3 ♕f2 37 ♔b2
♔h7!**

Tucking the king away and emphasising White's helplessness.

**38 ♕a4 ♕e2 39 ♖d7**

It all falls down.

**39...♕xf3 40 ♕b3 ♕xe4 41 ♖f7
♖h3 0-1**

A highly original and dynamic game, and a splendid example of play over the whole board.

> ### Game 53
> ### Short-Zviaginsev
> *Moscow Olympiad 1994*

**1 e4 c5 2 ♘f3 e6 3 d4 cxd4 4 ♘xd4
♘c6 5 ♘c3 ♕c7 6 ♗e3 ♘f6 7 f3 a6
8 ♕d2 d5!?**

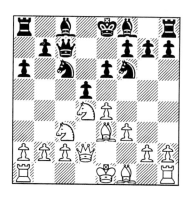

Theoretically this is quite an important move. If it works then Black can claim to have a simple way of solving his opening problems. Its main drawback may be that it leads to rather colourless positions.

**9 exd5 ♘xd5 10 ♘xd5 exd5 11
0-0-0 ♗d6 12 ♔b1 0-0 13 h4 ♖e8!
14 h5 h6**

Black could also have ignored it: 14...♗d7 15 h6 g6 is okay.

**15 ♗d3 ♗e5 16 c3 ♘xd4 17 cxd4
♗g3!**

An excellent method of slowing White down.

**18 ♗c2 ♗d7 19 ♕d3 f5**

White is now a little better; Black must play accurately.

**20 ♗b3 ♗b5!**

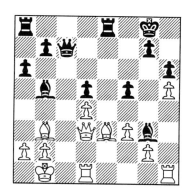

**21 ♗xd5+ ♔h8 22 ♕b3**

A more complex line was 22 ♕xf5 ♖xe3 23 ♗e4, when the position is unclear after 23...♖xe4 24 fxe4 ♕e7.

**22...♕d7 23 ♗f7! ♖e7**

After 23...♖xe3 24 ♕xe3 ♕xf7 25 f4 the bishop is trapped.

**24 ♗g6 ♗a4 25 ♕d3 ♗xd1 26 ♖xd1**

The solidity of White's game means that is very hard for Black to play for a win.

**26...♕d5 27 ♗d2 ♖d8 28 ♗b4 ♗d6
29 ♗xd6 ♕xd6 30 ♗xf5 ♕f4 31
♗e4**

Solid as a rock. Predictably, the game ends up drawn.

**31...♖c7 32 a3 b5 33 g4 ♖dc8 34
♕d2 ♕xd2 35 ♖xd2 ♖d8 36 d5 ♔g8
37 ♗f5 ♖d6 38 ♗e6+ ♔f8 39 ♖c2
♖c4 40 b4 ♖f4 41 ♖c3 ♔e7 42 ♔c2**

♔f6 43 ♔d2 a5 44 bxa5 ♖a6 45
♖b3 ♖xa5 46 ♔c2 ♖aa4 47 ♗f5
♖fc4+ 48 ♔b2 b4 49 axb4 ♖axb4
50 ♖xb4 ♖xb4+ 51 ♔c3 ♖a4 52
♗e4 ♔e5 53 ♔b3 ♖d4 ½-½

**1 e4 c5 2 ♘f3 e6 3 d4 cxd4 4 ♘xd4
♘c6 5 ♘c3 ♕c7 6 ♗e3 a6 7 ♕d2
♘xd4!?**

Perhaps the simplest treatment of
all.

**8 ♗xd4 ♘e7 9 ♕g5!?**

A move that would have been met
with serious censure had it been
played at club level. Perhaps Anand's
idea was to meet 9...♘c6? with 10
♗xg7! ♖g8 11 ♗e5!

**9...h6**

I prefer 10...d6 straightaway.

**10 ♕e3 d6?!**

But now this is wrong, as Anand
pins Black back. 10...b5 was correct.

**11 ♗b6!**

A probe to the right, a probe to the
left.

**11...♕b8 12 f4 ♗d7 13 f5**

Anand thought that castling would
have been even better here.

**13...♘c8 14 fxe6 fxe6 15 ♗e2?**

But this spoils everything. 15 ♗d4
e5 16 ♗b6 ♘xb6 17 ♕xb6 ♕a7 18
♘d5 with a slight advantage was correct.

**15...♘xb6 16 ♕xb6 ♕a7 17 ♗h5+
♔e7**

The king is quite happy here.

**18 ♕b3**

It would have been better to have
swapped queens and castled, as with
the bishop pair and a central pawn
majority, the future is rosy for Black.

**18...g6! 19 ♗g4**

Obviously 19 ♗xg6 ♖g8 is splendid
for Black.

**19...h5 20 ♗e2 ♗h6**

I can't castle? Right; neither can
you! But I observe in passing that
20...♗g7 21 0-0-0 ♗e5 would also
have left Black dominating the board.

**21 e5**

The only way to complicate matters.

**21...d5 22 ♕b4+ ♔e8 23 ♘d1 ♖f8
24 ♗d3 ♖f4! 25 ♗xg6+ ♔d8 26
♕a5+!**

A useful interpolation to shut
down the queen's influence. Anand
defends gamely.

**26...b6 27 ♕c3 ♖g4! 28 ♗xh5 ♖e4+
29 ♔f1 ♗b5+**

29...♖c8! was even stronger, after
which even the most dogged defence
would not have sufficed.

**30 ♔g1 ♖c8 31 ♕g3 ♕g7?**

There was no need for this: Black
should have kept queens on with
31...♕e7.

**32 ♕xg7 ♗xg7 33 ♘c3 ♖xe5 34**

♗f3 ♖e1+?!

Spectacular, but not the best. 34...♗c4 or 34...♗d7 would have left him with massive pressure for the pawn. Now Anand scrambles out of trouble.

**35 ♔f2! ♖xh1 36 ♖xh1 ♗xc3 37 bxc3 ♖xc3 38 ♗d1 e5 39 ♖e1 e4 40 h4 ♔e7 41 ♖e3 ♖c8 42 h5 ♔f6 43 ♖g3 d4 44 ♖g6+ ♔e5 45 ♖e6+!** ½-½

**1 e4 c5 2 ♘f3 e6 3 d4 cxd4 4 ♘xd4 ♘c6 5 ♘c3 ♕c7 6 ♗e3 a6 7 f3 b5 8 ♕d2 ♗b7 9 0-0-0 ♘xd4**

No b5-sacrifice nonsense for him.

**10 ♗xd4 ♖c8**

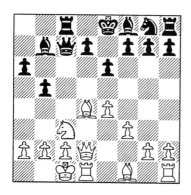

**11 g4 d6**

Much as I, and perhaps Joel Lautier too, have tried to keep ...d7-d6 off the board, here Black feels constrained to play it.

**12 ♔b1 ♘f6 13 a3 ♘d7!? 14 h4 ♘e5!?**

A manoeuvre to remember.

**15 ♕e3 ♘c4 16 ♗xc4 ♕xc4 17 ♖h2**

e5 **18 ♗a7**

Short's favourite move.

**18...♗e7 19 h5 h6 20 ♕b6**

Uncharacteristically Topalov prefers to try to exploit a small structural edge rather than go for an attack.

**20...♕c7 21 ♕xc7 ♖xc7 22 ♗b6 ♖c6 23 ♗a5 ♗g5 24 a4 bxa4 25 ♘xa4 ♔e7 26 b3 ♖b8 27 ♘c3 ♗a8 28 ♘d5+ ♔d7 29 ♗d2 f6 30 ♔b2 ♖f8 31 ♖a1 ♗b7 32 ♗e3 ♔e6 33 ♖d2 ♖f7 34 ♖d3 ♗xe3 35 ♘xe3**

With weaknesses at d6 and a5 to probe plus a much superior minor piece, White's chances look very good.

**35...♗c8 36 ♖ad1 ♖fc7 37 c4 a5 38 ♘f5 ♖d7 39 ♖a1 ♖a6 40 ♔c3 ♖c7 41 ♖d5 ♖ca7 42 ♖ad1 ♖d7 43 ♖b5 ♖c7 44 ♖b8 a4!?**

An inspired and opportunistic defence, but still not really good enough.

**45 bxa4 ♖xa4 46 ♘xd6**

46 ♖xd6+ ♔f7 47 ♘e3 might have been easier.

**46...♗d7 47 ♖b6 ♔e7 48 ♖db1?!**

Starting to lose his way.

**48...♗e6! 49 ♔b3 ♖ca7 50 ♔c3 ♖c7 51 ♖1b4 ♖a3+ 52 ♖b3 ♖a4 53**

♔b2

Acknowledging the impasse.

**53...♗xc4 54 ♖c3 ♖a2+ 55 ♔c1 ♖a1+ 56 ♔d2 ♖d7 57 ♖xc4 ½-½**

A fortunate escape for Black.

---

### Game 56
### Zagrebelny-Zviaginsev
*St Petersburg Open 1994*

---

**1 e4 c5 2 ♘f3 ♘c6 3 d4 cxd4 4 ♘xd4 ♕c7 5 ♘c3 e6 6 ♗e3 ♘f6 7 f3 b6!?**

It could be that Zviaginsev was dissatisfied with the type of middlegame that he got against Short in Game 53, perhaps because it yielded Black few winning chances.

**8 ♕d2 ♘xd4 9 ♗xd4 e5!?**

Original certainly.

**10 ♘b5 ♕b8 11 ♗f2 a6 12 ♘c3 ♕c7 13 0-0-0 ♗b7 14 ♔b1 ♖c8 15 ♘a4!**

An astute move. Unexpectedly White starts an action in the sector where Black is the one supposed to be making things happen.

**15...b5 16 ♘b6 ♖b8 17 c4 bxc4 18 ♗xc4 ♗c6 19 ♕e3 ♗e7 20 ♖c1 0-0 21 ♗d5**

Totally refuting Black's opening experiment.

**21...♖b7 22 ♘xd7! ♘xd7 23 ♗xc6 ♖b4 24 ♕a7**

The remaining moves are inexplicable. White passes over several wins before permitting Black a perpetual check.

**24...♕a5 25 b3 ♖fb8 26 ♗d5 ♕a3 27 ♖c3 ♘f6 28 ♖hc1 ♘xd5 29 exd5 ♖xb3+ ½-½**

A very strange game!

## Summary

Black is currently doing well against this newest of anti-Taimanov ideas. Both my treatment against Anand and that of Khatanbaatar versus Zagrebelny are looking good, and the simple idea of swapping on d4, as used by Gobet versus Anand, is worthy of future outings. However, there are obviously still new move-orders and nuances for White awaiting investigation, because of the system's novelty.

**1 e4 c5 2 ♘f3 e6 3 d4 cxd4 4 ♘xd4 ♘c6 5 ♘c3 a6 6 ♗e3 ♕c7**

**7 ♕d2 (D)**
> 7 f3 - *game 56*

**7...♘f6**
> 7...♘xd4 - *game 54*
> 7...b5 - *game 55*

**8 f3 (D) ♘e5**
> 8...b5 - *game 48*
> 8...♗b4
> > 9 a3 - *game 51*
> > 9 g4 - *game 52*
> 8...d5 - *game 53*

**9 0-0-0 ♗b4 10 ♘b3 b5 11 ♗d4 h6 (D)**
> 12 ♔b1 - *game 49*
> 12 a3 - *game 50*

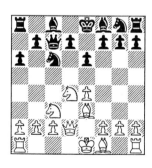
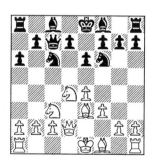

| *7 ♕d2* | *8 f3* | *11...h6* |

# CHAPTER SEVEN

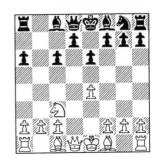

## 5 ♘c3 a6 6 ♘xc6 bxc6 and 6 f4 ♕c7 7 ♘xc6

**1 e4 c5 2 ♘f3 e6 3 d4 cxd4 4 ♘xd4 ♘c6 5 ♘c3 a6 6 ♘xc6 bxc6 and 6 f4 ♕c7 7 ♘xc6**

By exchanging knights on c6 White strengthens Black's centre, but reasons that the attacking chances that he hopes to gain will offset that. If you are going to make this exchange, it looks especially tempting after Black has played ...a7-a6, because in the ensuing middlegame that move is almost irrelevant. This being so you may vary your move-order with Black and obviate this opportunity for White by choosing 5...♕c7. The structures that we shall consider are radically different from the rest of the book, and indeed from the Sicilian in general.

White invariably points his weaponry towards the black kingside in this line, and, as in other menacing situations, attempts to castle can run into trouble, as we see in Game 59. In Games 60-63, we see Black deferring or even dispensing with castling and yet, or even because of it, emerging successfully into the middlegame. Despite White's quick win in Game 61 the opening is okay for Black and is further substantiation for 9...♗b7!? as the best choice in that line. Jansa had

several promising continuations early on. Game 62 though brief is weird and wonderful, and noteworthy.

After Black plays ...c6-c5 there are obvious comparisons with a French Defence structure. In Game 58 Benjamin smartly equalises with ...c6-c5 and then goes on to utilise a pair of hanging pawns which Patrick Wolff unwisely gifted him with, to swiftly overwhelm the opponent. In the next example though Curt Hansen is too slow in organising counterplay and the ex-World Champion scores a splendid victory with White. Likewise in Game 63 Krnic does not get his act together in time and reaches a prospectless middlegame.

The last two games illustrate the capture on c6 one move later, after 5 ♘c3 ♕c7 6 f4. Game 65 is a textbook example of a counterattack.

---

*Game 57*
### Smyslov-C.Hansen
*Biel Interzonal 1993*

**1 e4 c5 2 ♘f3 e6 3 d4 cxd4 4 ♘xd4 ♘c6 5 ♘c3 a6 6 ♘xc6 bxc6 7 ♗d3 d5**

7...d6 8 0-0 ♘f6 9 f4 ♕c7 10 ♔h1

---

♗e7 11 ♕e2 ♘d7 12 ♗d2 ♗f6?! 13 e5!? dxe5 14 ♘e4 gave White a dangerous initiative in Bezold-Plaskett, Hastings 1996/97.

**8 0-0 ♘f6**

8...♗b7 is dealt with in Game 63.

**9 ♕e2**

In Lutz-Einersen, Copenhagen Open 1995, White played 9 ♗g5 ♗e7 10 e5 (not 10 ♕e2 ♘xe4! 11 ♗xe7 ♘xc3 12 ♕e5 ♔xe7! 13 ♕xc3 f6 14 ♕xc6 ♖b8 15 ♗xa6 ♕d6 16 ♕xd6+ ♔xd6, when Black took control in Janosevic-Taimanov, Skopje 1970) 10...♘d7 11 ♗xe7 ♕xe7 12 ♕h5 ♖b8 13 b3 ♘c5 14 ♔h1 a5 15 f4 g6 16 ♕h6 ♗a6 17 ♗xa6 ♘xa6 18 ♘d1 ♘c5 19 ♘f2 ♕f8, and chances were equal. The aggressive 9 ♖e1 is considered in Games 59-62.

**9...♗e7 10 b3 0-0 11 ♗b2**

Remarkably, this was the first occasion on which this most natural of moves was played, and on the available evidence this certainly looks a wiser choice than 11 ♘a4, which is considered in the next game.

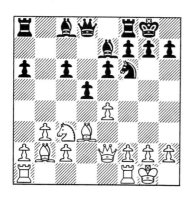

**11...a5**

It might have been better to advance in the centre with 11...c5 12

♖ad1 ♗b7 13 ♖fe1 ♖e8 14 ♘a4 ♗c6 15 16 ♘xc5 ♕a5 17 e5 ♗e7 18 ♘xa6 ♖ec8 19 ♖b1 ♕a2 20 b4 g6, when Black went on to win in Chomet-Taimanov, Paris-St Petersburg 1996.

**12 ♖ad1 ♕c7 13 ♘a4!?**

Preparing the advance of the c-pawn.

**13...♗b7 14 c4 ♖fd8**

Black would be clearly worse after 14...♘xe4 15 ♗xe4 dxe4 16 ♕xe4 c5, but this is better than the structure that he now has to try to work with.

**15 e5! ♘d7 16 cxd5 cxd5 17 ♖c1 ♕b8 18 ♗d4**

A powerful blockader.

**18...♗a3 19 ♖c3**

Already with ideas of the Greek gift: ♗xh7+.

**19...h6 20 ♗b5!**

Dominating both sides of the board.

**20...♘f8 21 ♖g3!**

Planning ♕h5 and ♗d3.

**21...♘g6 22 ♘b6! ♖a7 23 ♘d7! ♕a8**

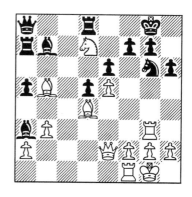

**24 ♖xg6!**

On the obvious 24 ♗xa7 ♕xa7 the knight on d7 has trouble getting out.

**24...fxg6 25 ♕g4 ♗a6**

An admission that Black's position is hopeless. On 25...♔f7, 26 ♘b6 ♕b8 27 ♗d3 g5 28 f4 is devastating.

**26 ♕xe6+ ♔h7 27 ♗xa6 ♖xa6**

Or 27...♖axd7 28 ♗d3 wins.

**28 ♕f7**

Intending to advance the e-pawn.

**28...♖xd7 29 ♕xd7 ♕c6 30 ♕f7 ♕e6 31 ♕xe6 ♖xe6 32 f4**

And the rest is easy.

**32...♖c6 33 g4 ♗c5 34 ♖d1 h5 35 gxh5 gxh5 36 f5 ♗xd4+ 37 ♖xd4 ♖c1+ 38 ♔f2 ♖c2+ 39 ♔f3 ♖xa2 40 ♖xd5 ♖a3 41 ♔f4 ♖xb3 42 ♖xa5 1-0**

---

> ## Game 58
> ### Wolff-Benjamin
> *Groningen (PCA) 1993*

**1 e4 c5 2 ♘f3 ♘c6 3 d4 cxd4 4 ♘xd4 e6 5 ♘c3 a6 6 ♘xc6 bxc6 7 ♗d3 d5 8 0-0 ♘f6 9 ♕e2 ♗e7 10 b3 0-0 11 ♘a4 c5**

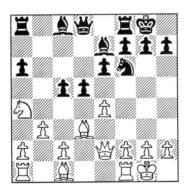

**12 e5**

Patrick Wolff had had this position earlier that same year against Larry Christiansen in the USA Championship. In that game he tried 12 c4, but after 12...dxe4 13 ♗xe4 ♘xe4 14

♕xe4 ♗d7 15 ♘b2 ♗f6 Black stood better.

**12...♘d7 13 c4 ♗b7 14 cxd5 exd5 15 ♗f4 ♘b6 16 ♘c3**

On 16 ♘c3 ♕d7 Black is fine.

**16...c4!? 17 bxc4 dxc4 18 ♗c2**

Of course not 18 ♗xc4? ♕d4 winning a bishop.

**18...♕d4 19 ♘e4 ♘d5**

The black pieces are rampant and defence is already difficult for White.

**20 ♗g3 ♘b4 21 ♖ad1 ♘d3! 22 ♘d2**

Or 22 ♗xd3? cxd3 and the knight falls.

**22...♘b2**

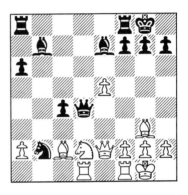

Really putting in the legwork! Black concentrates his hopes around the c-pawn.

**23 ♖b1 c3 24 ♘c4?**

Better was 24 ♘f3, keeping Black's advantage to a minimum.

**24...♗xg2! 25 ♔xg2 ♘xc4 26 ♗b3 ♘d2 27 ♖fd1 ♖ad8 28 ♖bc1 ♕b4 29 ♗c2 ♕b7+ 30 f3 ♗a3 0-1**

---

> ## Game 59
> ### Eismont-Romanishin
> *Biel Open 1995*

**1 e4 c5 2 ♘c3 e6 3 ♘f3 ♘c6 4 d4**

cxd4 5 ♘xd4 a6 6 ♘xc6 bxc6 7 ♗d3 d5 8 0-0 ♘f6 9 ♖e1

This prepares a more aggressive set-up for White than 9 ♕e2.

**9...♗e7 10 e5 ♘d7 11 ♕g4**

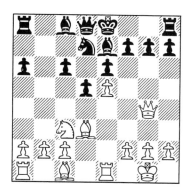

**11...g6**

Nine years earlier Romanishin had chosen 11...♔f8 against Jadoul at the SWIFT tournament in Brussels, and play went 12 ♕h5 ♖b8 13 a3 ♔g8 14 b3 ♘c5 15 ♗f1 a5 16 ♗e3 ♘d7 17 ♗f4 g6 18 ♕h6 ♗f8, whereupon White irrationally proposed a queen exchange with 19 ♕g5, and Black won in 42 moves. In J.Horvath-Van Mil, Budapest 1989, the superior 12 ♗d2 was played, and following 12...h5 13 ♕f3 ♔g8 14 ♘a4 ♗g5 15 ♕e2 ♗xd2 16 ♕xd2 g6 17 ♖ac1 White was clearly better. In principle, if you give up castling and the connection of your rooks then you had better proceed with care.

**12 ♘a4?!**

In Sax-Ost Hansen, Lucerne Olympiad 1982, White had attacking chances after 12 ♗h6 ♖b8 13 ♕h3!? (threatening 14 ♗g7, followed by taking Black's h-pawn) 13...♖g8 14 b3 ♕c7 15 ♘a4 c5 16 c4 d4 17 ♕g3 ♗b7

18 f4, but in the extraordinary game Martinez Socorro-Lebredo, Cabaiguan 1990, Black ignored the threat with 13...♖xb2!? 14 ♗g7 ♖g8 15 ♕xh7 ♖xg7 16 ♕xg7 ♗b4.

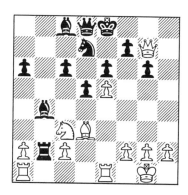

Not wanting to be a bad sport, Martinez Socorro threw some more wood on the fire by 17 ♖e3 ♗xc3 18 ♗xg6, when the fun continued: 18...♘xe5! 19 ♖xe5 fxg6 20 ♕xg6+, although in the end Black rode out the storm to emerge victorious.

Interestingly, the maestro himself chose to meet 12 ♗h6 with 12...♗f8 13 ♗xf8 ♔xf8 in the recent game Arakhamia-Taimanov, London (Foxtrot) 1996, but after 14 ♘a4 a5 15 b3 ♗a6 16 c4 ♔g7 17 ♖ac1 White was on top. Taimanov proposed 12...♖b8 as an improvement after the game, and in fact he had already played this move himself – against Kaiumov way back in 1972!

**12...♕a5!?**

Crossing White's plans.

**13 c3**

It was not too late for 13 ♗h6, although now Black can exchange queens with 13...♕b4.

**13...c5 14 ♗c2 ♗b7 15 ♗h6 ♗c6**

**16 ♕d1**

If White has to retreat like this then Black is unlikely to be troubled by a middlegame attack.

**16...♖b8 17 ♖b1 ♕c7 18 c4 d4 19 ♗e4 ♗xe4 20 ♖xe4 ♕c6 21 ♖e1 f5 22 exf6 ♗xf6**

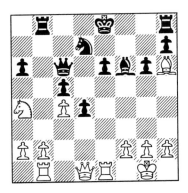

Now Black has slightly weakened his structure, but the time that it will take White to re-centralise his knight means that it is unlikely that serious problems will ensue.

**23 b3 ♔f7 24 ♕d2 ♖he8 25 ♘b2 e5 26 f3 e4 27 fxe4 ♖xe4 28 ♖xe4 ♕xe4 29 ♖e1 ♕g4 30 ♗f4 ♖e8 31 ♖xe8 ♔xe8 32 ♘d3 ♔f7 33 h3 ♕e6 34 ♕e1 ♕xe1+ 35 ♘xe1 ♗e5 36 ♗d2 ♘f6 37 ♘d3 ♗d6 38 ♔f2 ♘e4+ 39 ♔e2 ♔e6 40 a3 h5 41 ♗e1 ♔f5 42 ♔f3 ♘g5+ 43 ♔e2 ♘e4 44 ♔f3 ½-½**

---

*Game 60*
**Adams-Morovic**
*Las Palmas 1994*

---

**1 e4 c5 2 ♘f3 ♘c6 3 d4 cxd4 4 ♘xd4 e6 5 ♘c3 a6 6 ♘xc6 bxc6 7 ♗d3 d5 8 0-0 ♘f6 9 ♖e1 ♗b7!?**

Sensibly holding back ...♗e7 to avoid the immediate e5 ♘d7, ♕g4.

**10 ♗d2**

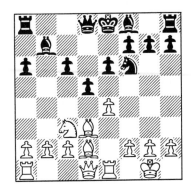

In Sax-Zapata, Subotica Interzonal 1987, 10 e5 was played. After 10...♘d7 11 ♘a4 ♕h4 12 b3 ♘c5 13 ♖b1!? there were interesting complications (1-0, 62 moves). In a game from Cannes two years later Ulf Andersson chose 11...♕c7 in this line against Michael Adams, and after 12 ♗f4 c5 13 c4 dxc4 14 ♗e4 ♗e7 15 ♖c1 0-0 16 ♖xc4 ♗xe4 17 ♖cxe4 ♖fd8 Black had equalised. White chose the alternative 10 ♗g5 in Hazai-Suetin, Leipzig 1986, but this led to somewhat less than nothing: after 10...♗e7 11 e5 ♘d7 12 ♗xe7 ♕xe7 13 ♕g4 0-0 14 ♘a4 f5! Black was better. However, 10 b3 is a flexible alternative to 10 ♗d2 (see the next game).

**10...♗e7 11 e5 ♘d7 12 ♕g4 g6 13 ♘a4**

Here 13 ♗h6 would have transposed to the previous game, except that Black has already placed his bishop on the very useful b7-square!

**13...c5**

Almost always a healthy move for Black in this quasi-French Defence structure.

**14 b3**

14 c4 dxc4 15 ♕xc4 was equal.

**14...♕c7 15 ♕g3 c4!? 16 bxc4 dxc4 17 ♗f1 h5**

Planning to make a go of it without castling.

**18 ♕f4 ♖c8 19 a3**

This is not very functional. White could and should have occupied the b-file.

**19...h4 20 h3 ♖h5 21 ♖ab1 ♗g5**

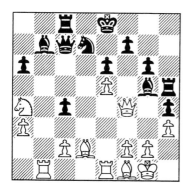

Playing to win!? 21...♖f5 22 ♕h6 ♖h5 would be sufficient to demonstrate that Black's opening has worked, yet Morovic goes for more. However, because of the loosening of both sides of his position, plus his king still in the centre, this is a double-edged policy.

**22 ♕d4 ♗xd2 23 ♕xd2 ♘xe5 24 ♗e2 ♖f5 25 ♕h6!**

Naturally the queen hops back in in order to cause as much mischief as possible

**25...g5 26 ♘b6 ♖d8 27 ♘xc4!**

Hereabouts I imagine that Morovic was experiencing doubts about the wisdom of his 21st move; the board starts to erupt.

**27...♘xc4 28 ♗xc4 ♖xf2!**

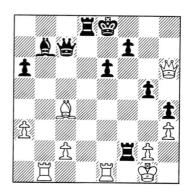

Almost forced. If 28...♕xc4 then 29 ♖xb7 is lethal, and 28...♗d5 is crushingly met by 29 ♗d3, so rather than just soak up White's attacking punches Morovic prefers to return a few.

**29 ♖xe6+!**

A big improvement on 29 ♔xf2 ♕g3+ 30 ♔e2 ♕xg2+ 31 ♔e3 ♕f3 mate.

**29...♔d7**

After 29...fxe6? 30 ♕xe6+ ♔f8 31 ♕g8+ ♔e7 32 ♕xg5+! ♔d6 33 ♖d1+ ♔c6 34 ♖xd8 and wins.

**30 ♖e7+?**

White would have had a slight edge after 30 ♖d1+! ♔c8 31 ♖xd8+ ♕xd8 32 ♔xf2 ♕d2+ 33 ♗e2 fxe6 34 ♕xe6+, but now the party carries on.

**30...♔xe7 31 ♕xg5+ ♖f6 32 ♖e1+ ♔d7 33 ♕xf6 ♕xc4?**

Now it is Black's turn to blunder. The correct way was 33...♕c5+! 34 ♔h1 (or 34 ♔h2 ♕xc4 35 ♖d1+ ♗d5 36 ♖d4 ♕c7+ and Black remains a piece up) 34...♕xc4 35 ♖d1+ ♗d5 36 ♖d4 ♕c6 and wins.

**34 ♖d1+ ♗d5 35 ♖d4**

Thus White regains the piece.

**35...♕c5?**

Another inaccuracy, when 35...♕c6! 36 ♕xc6+ ♚xc6 37 c4 ♚c5 would have led to a drawn pawn ending, e.g. 38 ♖xd5+ ♖xd5 39 cxd5 ♚xd5 40 g3 hxg3 41 ♚g2 ♚e4 42 ♚xg3 ♚e3! Now White once again has the advantage.

**36 c4 ♚c8 37 ♕f2 ♖e8?**

Yet another error, which this time ought to have been the last. 37...♖d7 was correct.

**38 cxd5?**

After 38 ♕f5+! Black would not have been able to hold out for long.

**38...♕c1+ 39 ♚h2 ♖e1 40 ♖xh4?**

And here 40 ♕f5+! was again the move.

**40...♖h1+ 41 ♚g3 ♖f1**

A madcap setting, with each king lacking adequate shelter. The situation is now so complex that Karpov remarked that he felt that he would have lost this position with either colour against a computer where he had an hour and the machine five minutes. As things went the game burnt itself out, after the white king took a stroll.

**42 ♖h8+ ♚b7 43 ♕d4 ♕e1+ 44 ♚g4 ♕e2+ 45 ♚g5 ♕e7+ 46 ♚h6**

♕d6+ 47 ♚g7 ♕g6+ 48 ♚f8 ♕d6+ 49 ♚g8 ♖f4 50 ♕b2+ ♚a7 51 g4 ♕d8+ ½-½

Hair-raising stuff!

---

*Game 61*
### J.Horvath-Jansa
*Czechoslovakian Ch. 1989*

---

**1 e4 c5 2 ♘f3 e6 3 d4 cxd4 4 ♘xd4 ♘c6 5 ♘c3 a6 6 ♘xc6 bxc6 7 ♗d3 d5 8 0-0 ♘f6 9 ♖e1 ♗b7!? 10 b3**

The first occasion on which this move was used.

**10...♗b4**

This move actually forces the win of material, but Horvath had anticipated this. 10...♕c7 was an alternative, and possibly superior, line-up, meeting 11 e5 with 11...♘d7 12 ♕e2 ♘c5.

**11 ♗d2**

Fianchettoing is no longer feasible because of 11...d4.

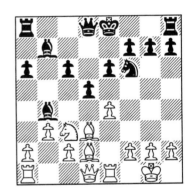

**11...0-0**

11...♕a5 would have won a pawn, but White has fair compensation after 12 a3 ♗xc3 13 b4 ♗xb4 14 ♗xb4 because of his bishop pair, dark-square control and development lead. I suspect that Jansa had intended 11...♕a5 when making his tenth move, but then bottled out.

**12 e5 ♘d7 13 ♕g4**

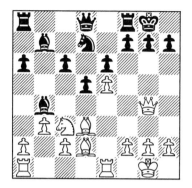

At first sight this is a familiar attacking stance for White, but in fact the weaknesses in his queenside dark squares cause him big problems.

**13...a5**

In conjunction with his next move I find this all wrong. Maybe 13...♗xc3 14 ♗xc3 c5!?

**14 a3**

And here I would have given up the exchange with 14...♗e7!? 15 ♗h6 g6 16 ♗xf8 ♕xf8, when there is no longer an attack and White has queenside troubles.

**14...♗xc3?! 15 ♗xc3**

Now White's edge is indisputable.

**15...♘c5 16 ♖ad1 ♕e7 17 ♕h5 g6 18 ♕h6 ♖fd8 19 ♖e3**

Building up his attack.

**19...♕f8 20 ♕h4 ♖d7 21 ♖h3 ♕g7 22 ♗d4 ♘e4??**

A gross error. Black had to play 22...♘xd3, but White keeps his attack after 23 ♖dxd3 g5 24 ♕g4 ♕g6 25 ♗e3!? ♗a6 26 ♖d2 h6 27 ♖h5, because of the vulnerability of g5.

**23 f3**

Simply trapping the knight.

**23...c5 24 ♗a1 g5 25 ♕g4 ♖ad8 26 fxe4 dxe4 27 ♗e2 ♕g6 28 ♖f1 e3 29 ♖xe3 1-0**

**1 e4 c5 2 ♘f3 e6 3 d4 cxd4 4 ♘xd4 ♘c6 5 ♘c3 a6 6 ♘xc6 bxc6 7 ♗d3 d5 8 0-0 ♘f6 9 ♖e1 ♖b8!?**

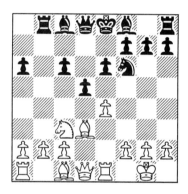

An interesting experiment.

**10 ♕e2 ♗b4!? 11 ♗f4 ♖b6!? 12 ♖ed1**

Presumably to avoid the pin ...d5-d4.

**12...0-0 13 ♘a4 ♖b7 14 c4 ♖d7 15 e5 dxc4!? 16 ♗c2 ♘d5 17 ♗g3 ♗e7 18 ♕xc4 c5 19 ♘c3 ½-½**

A short but fascinating game which raises many questions.

**1 e4 c5 2 ♘f3 ♘c6 3 d4 cxd4 4 ♘xd4 e6 5 ♘c3 a6 6 ♘xc6 bxc6 7**

♗d3 d5 8 0-0 ♗b7!?

An attempt to finesse.

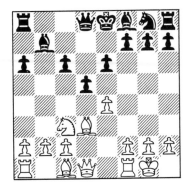

9 b3 ♘f6 10 ♗b2 ♗e7 11 ♕e2 ♕c7 12 ♖ae1 ♘d7 13 ♘a4 ♗f6 14 e5! ♗e7 15 c4! dxc4 16 ♗xc4 ♘b6 17 ♘xb6 ♕xb6 18 ♕g4

White has the better structure and the more active game.

18...g6 19 ♖d1 h5 20 ♕f4 g5

There is nothing for Black to do, and in his frustration he only succeeds in worsening his position.

21 ♕g3 g4 22 ♕f4 ♖d8 23 ♖d6!?

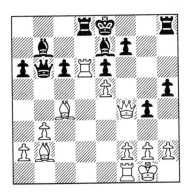

23...♖g8

Capturing would have allowed White to regain the exchange if he wished, e.g. 23...♗xd6 24 exd6 ♖g8 25 ♗h7 ♖f8 26 ♗g7 and, with the black king looking so unhappy, he might have had an even better continuation.

24 ♖xd8+ ♕xd8 25 ♕e4

Winning.

25...♕c7 26 ♕h7 ♖g5 27 ♗c1 ♕xe5 28 ♗xg5 ♕xg5 29 ♕d3 ♕a5 30 ♖d1 ♕b6 31 ♕h7 ♕c5 32 ♗xe6 fxe6 33 ♕g8+ ♗f8 34 ♕xe6+ ♕e7 35 ♕g6+ ♕f7 36 ♖d8+ 1-0

---

Game 64
**Gallagher-Razuvaev**
*Geneva Open 1994*

---

1 e4 c5 2 ♘f3 e6 3 d4 cxd4 4 ♘xd4 ♘c6 5 ♘c3 ♕c7

A useful move-order if one wishes to avoid 5...a6 6 ♘xc6, since now after 6 ♘xc6 bxc6 Black has gained some time since the queen is well placed on c7, while 6 ♘db5 ♕b8 is nothing for White. The drawback of 5...♕c7 is that Black relinquishes the possibility of meeting 5 ♘c3 a6 6 ♗e2 or 6 g3 with the 'pure Taimanov' 6...♘ge7.

6 f4 a6 7 ♘xc6

The same idea under slightly different circumstances.

7...bxc6

It was, of course, quite acceptable to recapture with the queen, as happened in, e.g. Conquest-Pogorelov, Spain 1994: (7...♕xc6) 8 ♗d3 b5 9 ♕e2 ♗b7 10 0-0 (10 ♗d2 can be met by either 10...♗c5 or 10...♘f6) 10...♗c5+ 11 ♗e3 ♘f6 12 ♖ae1 and now 12...0-0 would have left equal chances.

8 ♗d3

8 e5 is considered in the next game.

8...d5 9 0-0 ♘f6 10 ♕e2 ♗b7!? 11 ♗d2 ♗e7 12 ♖ae1 ♘d7 13 ♘d1

---

Joe Gallagher comes up with an attacking scheme that looks less natural and less effective than Spraggett's in Game 63.

**13...0-0 14 ♗c3**

An inferior path to the long diagonal.

**14...♕b6+ 15 ♔h1 d4 16 ♗d2 ♘c5**

About to bump off one of the key attackers.

**17 ♖f3 ♘xd3 18 cxd3 c5 19 b3 f5! 20 ♖h3 e5!**

Stopping the attack, allowing his queen to switch across for defensive purposes and also amplifying the power of his bishops.

**21 ♕h5 ♕g6 22 ♕xg6 hxg6 23 exf5 ♖xf5 24 fxe5 a5! 25 ♔g1 a4 26 ♘f2**

axb3 27 axb3 ♖a2 28 ♘e4 ♖xe5 29 ♗f4 ♖f5 30 ♖f3 ♖b2

Black dominates the board.

**31 ♗g3 ♗d5 32 ♖xf5 gxf5 33 ♘xc5**

A desperate attempt to wangle something.

**33...♗xc5 34 ♖e5**

Regaining the piece, but the game is lost.

**34...♗xg2! 35 ♖xc5 ♗h3 36 ♖c7 ♖g2+ 37 ♔h1 f4! 38 ♖c4**

Or 38 ♗xf4 ♖f2 and White must cede the bishop to avoid mate.

**38...♖d2 39 ♗e1 ♖d1 40 ♔g1 ♖xe1+ 41 ♔f2 0-1**

An excellent strategic victory.

> ## Game 65
> ## Mokry-Benjamin
> *Moscow Olympiad 1994*

**1 e4 c5 2 ♘f3 e6 3 d4 cxd4 4 ♘xd4 ♘c6 5 ♘c3 a6 6 ♘xc6 bxc6 7 e5**

This move gives the game a distinctive character.

**7...♕c7**

The c7-square is more natural for the queen than 7...♕a5.

**8 f4 d6**

You don't have to play this way. In Hellers-Renet, Haifa 1989, the Frenchman preferred 8...f5 9 ♗e3 ♖b8 10 ♖b1 ♘h6 11 ♗e2 ♗e7 12 0-0 0-0 13 ♗f3 d6 14 exd6 ♗xd6 15 ♕d2 ♘f7 with equality, while in Andres-Lebredo, Havana 1987, Black tried 8...c5!? and after 9 ♗d3 c4!? 10 ♗e4 ♖b8 11 0-0 f5 12 exf6 ♘xf6 13 f5!? there were wild complications (drawn in 39 moves).

**9 exd6 ♗xd6 10 ♘e4**

For 10 ♕g4 see the next game.

**10...♗e7**

Taking the f-pawn is not on.

**11 ♗d3 c5**

Black varied in Ulibin-Bashkov, Chelyabinsk 1993, with 11...♘f6 12 0-0 c5 13 ♕e2 ♘xe4 14 ♗xe4 ♖a7 15 ♗e3 0-0, when chances were balanced.

**12 ♕e2 ♗b7 13 0-0 ♘h6 14 b3! ♘f5 15 ♗b2**

White trains a pair of mean bishops on the opposing king's likely residence. The formation of...♘h6-f5 was well known, but Mokry's simple line up calls it into question.

**15...♘d4 16 ♗xd4 cxd4 17 f5 exf5 18 ♖xf5 0-0 19 ♖af1 f6?**

And this is a gross error. 19...g6!?, perhaps.

**20 ♘g5! g6**

Or 20...fxg5 21 ♕e6+ ♔h8 22 ♖f7 and Black cannot defend.

**21 ♘e6 ♕d6 22 ♘xf8 ♖xf8 23 ♖5f2 f5 24 ♕d2 ♔g7 25 ♖e2 ♕d8 26 ♖fe1 ♗h4 27 ♕b4!**

Mokry returns the exchange but keeps a decisive attack.

**27...♖f7 28 ♖e8 ♗xe1 29 ♕xe1 ♕g5 30 ♕f2 ♖d7 31 h4 ♕f6 32 ♕f4 ♖d8 33 ♕c7+ ♔h6 34 ♕xd8 1-0**

---

### Game 66
### Sax-J.Horvath
*Hungarian Championship 1993*

---

**1 e4 c5 2 ♘f3 e6 3 d4 cxd4 4 ♘xd4 ♘c6 5 ♘c3 ♕c7 6 f4 a6 7 ♘xc6 bxc6 8 e5 d5**

This invariably comes to the same thing as 8...d6.

**9 exd6 ♗xd6 10 ♕g4 f5**

The only really sensible way of coping with the threat to the g-pawn.

**11 ♕h5+!?**

A nuance, hoping to weaken the black kingside.

**11...g6 12 ♕f3 ♘f6 13 ♗c4 ♔f7**

The king is not so unhappy here; it is like castling.

**14 0-0**

In Timman-Illescas, Novi Sad Olympiad 1990, White put his king elsewhere with 14 ♗d2 ♗b7 15 0-0-0 c5 16 ♕e2 ♖he8 17 ♖he1 ♗xf4 18 ♗xe6+ ♔g7, and chances were equal.

**14...♗b7 15 ♗d2 c5 16 ♕h3 ♗d5**

Black plans to use the d5-square as a base for either a knight or a bishop and reasons that this important outpost will compensate for his split pawns.

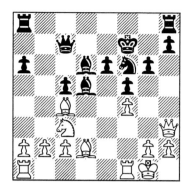

**17 ♛d3 ♛c6 18 ♖ae1 ♖ab8!?**

Allowing Sax an extraordinary tactical chance.

**19 ♘xd5 exd5**

**20 ♗c3! ♖he8!**

The bishop could not be taken because of (20...dxc4) 21 ♛xc4+ ♔g7 (or 21...♛d5 22 ♛xd5+ ♘xd5 23 ♗xh8 ♖xh8 24 ♖d1 ♔e6 25 ♖he1+ and White will be the exchange up) 22 ♖e6 (this pin proves decisive)

22...♖hf8 23 ♖d1 ♖bd8 24 ♖xf6! ♖xf6 25 ♛e6, when Black now has nothing better than 25...♗e5, when after 26 ♛e7+ ♔h6 27 ♖xd8 ♗xc3 28 ♖d7! ♗d4+ 29 ♔h1 the king hunt will hit the target: 29...♔h5 30 ♛xh7+ ♔g4 31 ♛h6.

**21 ♗xf6 dxc4! 22 ♛c3 ♖xe1**

On 22...♗xf4 23 ♗h4 White's superior pawn structure and safer king give him the advantage.

**23 ♖xe1 ♖e8 24 ♖d1 ♖e4**

Another continuation here was 24...♗f8 25 ♗h8 ♗h6 26 ♛xc4+ ♔f8 with obscurity.

**25 ♗h8**

Not a move you see very often.

**25...♔e8 26 ♛d2 ♗e7 27 ♗e5 g5 28 ♛f2 gxf4 29 ♗xf4 ♛e6 30 ♔f1 c3 31 b3 c4 32 ♛f3 cxb3 33 axb3 a5**

Black's weak pawns and insecure king mean that he stands worse, but Horvath continues to struggle resourcefully.

**34 g3 ♗b4 35 ♛d3 ♔f7 36 ♛b5 ♔g6 37 ♔f2 h5 38 h4 ♗e7 39 ♛e8+ ♛f7 40 ♛c6+ ♛e6 41 ♛e8+ ♛f7 42 ♛xf7+**

The position is by now too simplified for White to keep real winning chances.

**42...♔xf7 43 ♖d5 a4 44 bxa4 ♖xa4 45 ♔e3 ♖e4+ 46 ♔d3 ♔e6 47 ♖d4 ♖xd4+ 48 ♔xd4 ½-½**

## Summary

Frankly I am surprised that such a dangerous and high-scoring a system as 6 ♘xc6 is not played more often. (Indeed, a few years ago Kamsky produced the novelty 5 ♘xc6!? against Ribli, without even waiting for Black to 'squander' a tempo with ...a7-a6, and recorded a quick victory.) In the move-order 5 ♘c3 ♛c7 6 f4 a6 7 ♘xc6, firstly Black can satisfactorily recapture with the queen; and secondly after 7...bxc6 8 e5 he is certainly not obliged to vitiate his pawn structure with 8...d5, even though that ought to be okay as well.

**1 e4 c5 2 ♘f3 e6 3 d4 cxd4 4 ♘xd4 ♘c6 5 ♘c3 a6 6 ♘xc6**

> 6 f4 ♛c7 7 ♘xc6 bxc6 *(D)*
>> 8 ♗d3 - *game 64*
>> 8 e5 d6 9 exd6 ♗xd6
>>> 10 ♘e4 - *game 65*
>>> 10 ♛g4 - *game 66*

**6...bxc6 7 ♗d3**

> 7 e5 ♛c7 8 f4 - see 6 f4 ♛c7 7 ♘xc6 bxc6 8 e5

**7...d5 8 0-0 ♘f6**

> 8...♗b7 - *game 63*

**9 ♛e2**

> 9 ♖e1 *(D)*
>> 9...♗e7 - *game 59*
>> 9...♗b7
>>> 10 ♗d2 - *game 60*
>>> 10 b3 - *game 61*
>> 9...♖b8 - *game 62*

**9...♗e7 10 b3 0-0 *(D)***

> 11 ♗b2 - *game 57*
> 11 ♘a4 - *game 58*

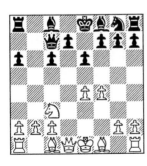

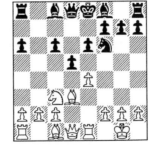

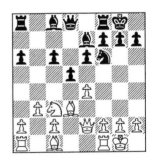

7...bxc6            9 ♖e1            10...0-0

# CHAPTER EIGHT

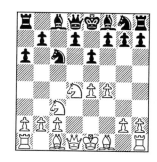

## 5 ♘c3 a6 6 f4 and 7 ♘f3

**1 e4 c5 2 ♘f3 e6 3 d4 cxd4 4 ♘xd4 ♘c6 5 ♘c3 a6 6 f4 and 7 ♘f3**

The set-up with f2-f4 and ♘f3 is not all that common; usually the knight retreats to b3 rather than f3, but on f3 the knight has prospects of joining in a kingside attack. The most striking feature of this move-order is the opportunity it grants Black to seize the a7-g1 diagonal (and thereby stop White from castling kingside) an option he almost invariably takes up, as we see in Games 67-73.

In the selection of games with 7...♗c5 we see two alternative plans for White. First, ♗d3 and ♕e2, to which the response is ...♘d4, before White has chance to play ♗e3. This seems completely playable for Black, as shown in Games 67-70. An alternative idea for White is ♗d3 and e4-e5, making a claim in the centre and on the kingside. However, this also presents no problems for Black. In Games 71 and 72 wild over-exuberance led to White's own swift demise. Indeed, in Game 72 Black was able to stake absolute claim to the important a7-g1 diagonal by reinforcing his control with a subsequent ...♕a7(!).

In this variation the 'pure Taima-nov' ...♘ge7 must be handled with care because the white opposite number, for whom it is so often exchanged, is ready to step back to f3. If you move the knight on e7 to g6, then watch what you are doing: Black was blown off the board in Game 75. However, Black showed a more organised set-up in the final example.

### Game 67
### Tseitlin-Szabolcsi
*Bagneaux 1992*

**1 e4 c5 2 ♘f3 e6 3 d4 cxd4 4 ♘xd4 ♘c6 5 ♘c3 ♕c7 6 f4 a6 7 ♘f3 ♗c5**

Logically occupying the g1-a7 diagonal: we are often told to stop our opponents from castling if we can, and here is a healthy developing move which also serves just that very purpose.

**8 ♗d3 b5**

In Adams-Brenninkmeijer, Groningen 1990, 8...d6 was given its only outing at master level to date, but, as I have stated, the move is not truly integral to Taimanov formations. After 9 ♕e2 ♘d4 10 ♘xd4 ♗xd4 11 ♗d2 ♘e7 12 0-0-0 ♗d7 13 ♕f3 White was slightly better (1-0, 49 moves).

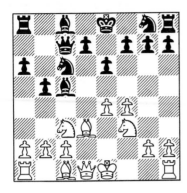

**9 ♕e2**

The direct 9 e5 is considered in Games 71-73.

**9...♘d4 10 ♘xd4 ♗xd4**

One of the features of this position, which will become apparent through study of the next four games, is that White must cede a lot of time to complete his development, and this is the main reason why Black's results have been very good.

**11 ♗d2**

For 11 ♘d1, intending to exchange bishops with ♗e3 or kick the black bishop back with c2-c3, see Games 69 and 70.

**11...b4**

11...♗b7 is considered in the next game.

**12 ♘d1 ♖b8 13 ♖c1 ♕a7 14 ♗xb4 ♖xb4 15 c3 ♖b8 16 cxd4 ♕xd4 17 ♕e3 ♕b4+ 18 ♖c3 ♘e7 19 a3 ♕b6 20 b4 ½-½**

Black was very comfortable here.

---

## Game 68
### Hector-Brodsky
*Copenhagen Open 1994*

**1 e4 c5 2 ♘f3 e6 3 d4 cxd4 4 ♘xd4**

♘c6 5 ♘c3 ♕c7 6 f4 a6 7 ♘f3 ♗c5 8 ♗d3 b5 9 ♕e2 ♘d4 10 ♘xd4 ♗xd4 11 ♗d2 ♗b7

Another, entirely satisfactory way of handling this position.

**12 ♘d1**

The aggressive 12 0-0-0 b4 13 ♘b1 (not 13 ♘a4? ♗c6) 13...a5 is fine for Black, while in Ulibin-Tregubov, St Petersburg 1993, 12 e5 was tried, play continuing 12...f5! 13 ♘d1 (in Tolnai-J.Horvath Hungary 1992, White varied with 13 a4 b4 14 ♘d1 ♕c6 15 ♔f1 ♗c5 16 ♗e3 ♘e7 17 ♕f2 ♖c8, but Black stood better) 13...♕c6!

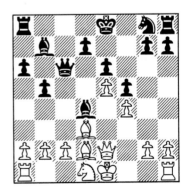

when White's next seven moves were just about forced: 14 ♗e3 ♕xg2 15 ♕xg2 ♗xg2 16 ♖g1 ♗xe3 17 ♘xe3

♗c6 18 ♖xg7 ♘e7 19 ♖g1 ♘g6 20 ♖f1 ♔e7 21 0-0-0 ♖hd8 22 c3 ½-½.

**12...♘f6 13 a4 ♕c6! 14 axb5 axb5 15 ♖xa8+ ♗xa8 16 ♗c3 ♗xc3+ 17 ♘xc3 b4 18 ♘b5 0-0**

Once again Black emerges with a perfectly good middlegame.

**19 e5 ♘e4 20 ♘d4 ♕b6 21 ♕e3 ♘c5 22 ♗f1 ♗d5 23 ♗d3 ♘xd3+ 24 cxd3 ♕b7 25 f5 f6**

**26 fxe6 dxe6 27 exf6 ♖xf6 28 ♖f1 ♕a8 29 ♖xf6 ♕a1+ 30 ♔d2 ♕xb2+ 31 ♔d1 ♗b3+ 32 ♔e1 gxf6 33 ♕g3+ ♔f7 34 ♕c7+ ♔g6 35 ♕g3+ ½-½**

---

*Game 69*
### Rodriguez Lopez-Franco
*Seville Open 1994*

**1 e4 c5 2 ♘f3 ♘c6 3 d4 cxd4 4 ♘xd4 e6 5 ♘c3 ♕c7 6 f4 a6 7 ♘f3 b5 8 ♗d3 ♗c5 9 ♕e2 ♘d4 10 ♘xd4 ♗xd4 11 ♘d1**

Here White pre-empts ...b5-b4 by voluntarily relocating his knight.

**11...♗b7**

11...♘f6 is considered in the next game.

**12 c3 ♗c5 13 ♘f2 ♘e7 14 0-0 ♘g6**

**15 ♕g4 h5!? 16 ♕f3 h4 17 a4 f5**

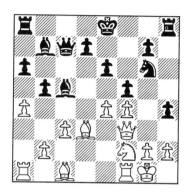

Franco is really going for it. Perhaps his mortgage was due?

**18 axb5 axb5 19 ♖xa8+ ♗xa8 20 ♔h1 0-0 21 ♘h3 ♗e7 22 ♕e2 fxe4 23 ♗xe4 ♗xe4 24 ♕xe4 ♕c4**

Black has the more comfortable game.

**25 ♕e1 ♗d6 26 ♖f3 ♖f5 27 ♗e3 ♕b3 28 ♕d2?!**

With a few incautious moves White first leaves himself prone to back-rank problems, and then ties himself in knots.

**28...♖d5! 29 ♗d4 ♘e7 30 ♖d3 ♕c4 31 ♕d1 ♘f5 32 b3 ♕c6 33 ♔g1 b4**

Knocking the props out.

**34 cxb4 ♖xd4 35 ♖xd4 ♕b6 0-1**

---

*Game 70*
### Shevelevich-Tregubov
*Rostov Open 1993*

**1 e4 c5 2 ♘f3 e6 3 d4 cxd4 4 ♘xd4 ♘c6 5 ♘c3 ♕c7 6 f4 a6 7 ♘f3 ♗c5 8 ♗d3 b5 9 ♕e2 ♘d4 10 ♘xd4 ♗xd4 11 ♘d1 ♘f6 12 ♗e3**

A more direct plan for White is 12 c3 ♗c5 13 e5 ♘d5 14 ♘f2 ♗b7 15 ♘e4, as in Dvoirys-Tregubov from the same tournament, when Black can consider 15...♗e7, planning ...f7-f5.

**12...♗xe3 13 ♕xe3 ♗b7 14 0-0 0-0 15 ♘c3 e5!? 16 fxe5 ♕xe5**

Threatening 17...♕xh2+.

**17 ♖ae1 ♘g4 18 ♕f4 ♕xf4 19 ♖xf4 ♘e5**

A very happy horse now.

**20 a3 ♖fe8 21 ♖d1 ♖ac8 22 ♗e2 ♖c5 23 ♖d4 ♗c6 24 ♖h4 f6 25 ♖h3 ♘f7 26 ♗g4 ♖e7**

As mentioned in the introduction to this book, Sicilian endings very often favour Black. Here the e4-pawn is under pressure.

**27 ♖hd3 ♘e5 28 ♖g3 ♖c4 29 ♖d2 ♘xg4 30 ♖xg4 f5**

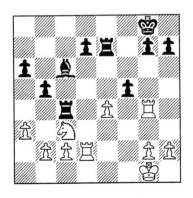

Winning a pawn, but White's blockade makes it difficult to convert this into a win.

**31 ♖g3 fxe4 32 ♔f2 b4 33 axb4 ♖xb4 34 b3 a5 35 ♔e3 ♖e5 36 ♘a2 ♖b8 37 ♘c3 ♖c5 38 ♘e2 a4 39 bxa4 ♗xa4 40 c3 d5 41 ♔d4 ♖bb5 42 ♖a2 ♖c4+ 43 ♔e3 h6 44 h4 ♖b1 45 ♖d2 ♖c5 46 ♔d4 ♖bb5 47 ♖a2 ♖c4+ 48 ♔e3**

How can Black make progress?

**48...♖b3 49 ♖d2 ♗c6 50 ♔f4 ♗b7 51 ♖a2 e3+**

Hoping to get somewhere with tricks.

**52 ♔xe3 d4+ 53 ♔f2 dxc3 54 ♖c2 ♖xh4 55 ♖cxc3 ♖b2 56 ♖b3 ♖f4+ 57 ♔g1 ♖b4 58 ♖xb4 ♖xb4 59 ♖e3**

The position is now far too simplified for Black to win.

**59...♖b2 60 ♔h2 ♔f7 61 ♘f4 g5 62 ♖e2 ♖b3 63 ♘h3 ♔f6 64 ♘f2 ♔f5 65 ♘d1 ♖d3 66 ♘f2 ♖d4 67 ♖e7 ♗d5 68 ♖e1 ♖h4+ 69 ♔g3 ♖a4 70 ♖e2 h5 71 ♘d3 ♖d4 72 ♘e1 h4+ 73 ♔h2 ♗e4 74 g3 ♔g4 75 gxh4 ♔xh4 76 ♘c2 ♖a4 77 ♘e3 ♗f3 78 ♖c2 g4 79 ♘g2+ ♔g5 80 ♖b2 ♖a3 81 ♖b5+ ♔f6 82 ♖b2 ♗d5 83 ♖e2 ♖h3+ 84 ♔g1 ♖b3 85 ♔h2 ♖a3 86 ♖d2 ♗e4 87 ♖e2 ♔f5 88 ♖b2??**

88 ♘e3+ and 89 ♘xg4 draws instantly.

**88...g3+ 89 ♔h3**

Or 89 ♔g1 ♖a1.

**89...♔g5**

*see following diagram*

Suddenly the threat of 90...♗f5+ means that it is all over.

**90 ♖b5+**

Or 90 ♘e1 g2+ 91 ♔h2 ♖h3+! and wins.

**90...♗f5+ 91 ♖xf5+ ♔xf5 92 ♔h4 ♖b3 93 ♔h3 ♔g5 94 ♘e1 ♔f4 95 ♔g2 ♖b2+ 96 ♔g1 ♔g4 0-1**

---

### Game 71
### Dvoirys-Rublevsky
*Russian Championship 1994*

---

**1 e4 c5 2 ♘f3 e6 3 d4 cxd4 4 ♘xd4 ♘c6 5 ♘c3 ♕c7 6 f4 a6 7 ♘f3 ♗c5 8 ♗d3 b5 9 e5!? f5!?**

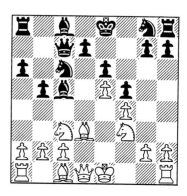

This may be the most logical response; Black stakes out some space for himself on the kingside and fights for control of e4.

**10 g4!?**

Wow! Rather than bother himself with 10...fxg4 11 ♘g5 Rublevsky, one of the rising stars of Russian chess, ignores White's outlandish tenth and calmly completes development.

**10...♘ge7 11 gxf5 exf5 12 a4 b4 13 ♘e2 d6!**

Clearly Black has now solved his opening problems.

**14 exd6 ♕xd6 15 ♘g3 ♗b7 16 ♕e2 0-0 17 ♗d2**

White is the one with troubles. He lags in development and must hurry to secure his king's safety. With the text he offers the exchange, hoping that his initiative will provide compensation.

**17...♘d4 18 ♘xd4 ♗xd4 19 0-0-0 ♗xh1 20 ♖xh1 ♖fe8 21 ♗c4+ ♔h8 22 ♖e1 ♕f6 23 b3 ♗b2+ 24 ♔b1 ♗a1!?**

Not a move you see often.

**25 ♗c1 ♗c3**

Now it will become possible for Black to move his pinned knight and hence remove much of the pressure on his position.

**26 ♖d1 ♘c6 27 ♕g2 ♘d4 28 ♖g1 g6 29 ♘f1 ♖ad8 30 ♘e3 a5 31 ♘d5 ♕c6 32 ♖d1 ♖d6 33 ♗e3 ♖e4 34 ♘xc3 ♖xe3 35 ♕xc6 ♖xc6 36 ♘b5 ♘e2! 37 ♖d8+ ♔g7 38 ♖d7+ ♔h6 39 ♗g8 ♘xf4**

Enabling the king to dig its way out to victory.

**40 h4 ♔h5 41 ♖xh7+ ♔g4 42 ♗c4 ♖c8 0-1**

---

### Game 72
### Hector-Zviaginsev
*Berlin 1993*

---

**1 e4 c5 2 ♘f3 e6 3 d4 cxd4 4 ♘xd4 ♘c6 5 ♘c3 a6 6 f4 ♕c7 7 ♘f3 ♗c5**

**8 e5 f5 9 ♗d3 b5 10 ♕e2 ♕a7!**

Hyper diagonal control.

**11 g4?!**

Another one has a go! This time the move is even looser.

**11...fxg4 12 ♘g5 ♘h6 13 ♘ce4 ♘d4 14 ♕d1 ♗b7**

The gambit is already refuted.

**15 h3 g3! 16 ♕h5+ ♔d8 17 ♗d2 Ndf5 18 0-0-0 g2 19 ♘xe6+**

This won't do either.

**19...dxe6 20 ♕g5+ ♔e8 21 ♕xg2 ♖d8 22 ♔b1 ♗a8 23 ♖he1 ♖f8 24 ♕g5 ♗xe4 25 ♗xe4 ♔f7 26 ♗a5 ♖xd1+ 27 ♖xd1 ♖c8 28 ♕h5+ g6 29 ♕g5 ♗e7 30 ♕g2 ♖c4 0-1**

---

### Game 73
### Hector-Mortensen
*Aarhus 1993*

**1 e4 c5 2 ♘c3 ♘c6 3 ♘f3 e6 4 d4 cxd4 5 ♘xd4 ♕c7 6 f4 a6 7 ♘f3 ♗c5 8 e5 f5 9 ♗d3 b5 10 ♕e2 ♘d4**

This is less ambitious than 10...♕a7, but in principle it is sound.

**11 ♘xd4 ♗xd4 12 ♘d1 ♗b7 13 ♗e3 ♕c5 14 a4 b4 15 ♗xd4 ♕xd4 16 ♕e3**

Hector hopes to stand a little better

in this queenless middlegame.

**16...♕xe3+ 17 ♘xe3 ♘h6 18 ♖g1 ♔e7 19 g4 fxg4 20 ♘xg4**

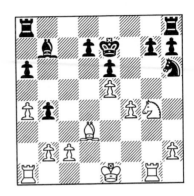

Although White has a slight structural advantage, this position should definitely be tenable for Black.

**20...♘f7 21 h4 ♖ad8**

21...a5! would have prevented White's next.

**22 a5! ♖b8 23 h5 g5**

This backfires, as Black overlooks the strength of White's 29th and 30th moves.

**24 hxg6 hxg6 25 ♗xg6 ♖bg8 26 ♗xf7 ♖xg4 27 ♖xg4 ♖h1+ 28 ♔e2 ♖xa1 29 ♗h5! ♖xa5 30 ♖g8!**

**30...d6**

Black has to cope with the mate

---

threat, but doing so costs him the bishop.

**31 ♖g7+ ♔d8 32 ♖xb7 dxe5 33 ♖xb4 exf4 34 ♗f3 e5 35 ♔d3 ♔d7 36 ♔e4 ♔d6 37 ♖b6+ ♔c5 38 ♖b8 ♔d6 39 ♖d8+ ♔c7 40 ♖d5 ♖a2 41 ♖xe5 ♖xb2 42 c4 ♖c2 43 ♔d4 ♖d2+ 44 ♔c5 a5 45 ♖e7+ ♔d8 46 ♖a7 ♖d3 47 ♗d5 f3 48 ♔d6 1-0**

---

### Game 74
### Rodriguez Lopez-Pogorelov
### *Seville Open 1994*

---

**1 e4 c5 2 ♘f3 ♘c6 3 d4 cxd4 4 ♘xd4 ♕c7 5 ♘c3 e6 6 f4 a6 7 ♘f3 b5 8 ♗d3 b4**

Rather a Mount Everest move; Black kicks the knight because it is there. In Adams-Ninov, Ostend 1989, Black was unsuccessful with 8...♗b7 (8...♗c5! transposes to the earlier games in this chapter) 9 0-0 (Black's inaccurate move-order has allowed White to castle) 9...♗c5+ 10 ♔h1 d6?! 11 a3 ♘ge7 12 b4 ♗b6 13 ♗b2 f6? (quite underestimating White's reply) 14 ♗xb5! axb5 15 ♘xb5 ♕d7 16 ♘xd6+ ♔f8 17 c4 with a raging initiative.

**9 ♘a4 ♘f6 10 ♕e2 d6 11 ♗e3 ♖b8 12 0-0 ♗e7 13 ♔h1 0-0**

A normal kind of Scheveningen set-up.

**14 ♖ac1 ♕a5 15 b3 e5**

As so often in such middlegames there comes a moment when Black has to decide how to arrange his central pawns. This time he advances the king's pawn, but waiting methods, i.e. 15...♖fe8, 15...♗d7 and 15...♘d7, were also feasible.

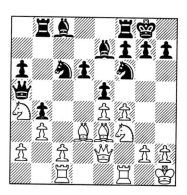

**16 c4 bxc3 17 ♘xc3 exf4 18 ♗xf4 ♘e5 19 ♗b1 ♗g4**

White is more comfortable.

**20 ♕d2 ♔h8**

To avoid ♘d5 tricks, but it is clear that Black can undertake nothing active.

**21 ♘d4 ♖bc8 22 ♕e3 ♘g6 23 ♗g3 ♖fd8 24 h3 ♗d7 25 ♘f5 ♗xf5**

It was difficult to tolerate the knight, but now White has the bishop pair.

**26 exf5 ♘e5 27 ♘e4 ♘xe4 28 ♕xe4 ♗f6 29 ♕b7!? ♖xc1 30 ♖xc1 h6 31 ♗e1!**

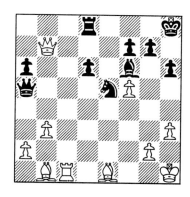

Forcing the queen exchange, after which the bishops' power is amplified.

**31...♕b5 32 ♕xb5 axb5 33 ♗b4 d5 34 ♗c5 ♘c6?!**

34...♖c8 would have been better.

**35 ♗d3 b4 36 ♗b5**

This is decisive.

**36...♖c8 37 ♗xb4 ♘a7 38 ♖xc8+ ♘xc8 39 ♔g1 ♗d4+ 40 ♔f1 ♘a7 41 ♗d7 ♔g8 42 ♔e2 g6 43 ♔d3 ♗b6 44 fxg6 fxg6 45 ♗e6+ ♔g7 46 ♗xd5 ♔f6 47 ♗c3+ ♔f5 48 ♗d4 ♗xd4 49 ♔xd4 1-0**

---

## Game 75
## Hector-Vandrey
### *Hamburg Open 1993*

---

**1 e4 c5 2 ♘f3 e6 3 d4 cxd4 4 ♘xd4 ♘c6 5 ♘c3 a6 6 f4 ♘ge7**

The usual Taimanov alternative to 6...♕c7, but here White can comfortably retreat his knight to f3.

**7 ♘f3 d6**

Black had an unhappy time of it in Svidler-Zapata, New York Open 1995: 7...♘g6 8 ♗e3 ♕c7 9 ♕d2 b5 10 h4! h5 (this is almost certainly a sign that something is seriously amiss) 11 0-0-0 ♗e7 12 e5 ♗b7 13 ♘g5 f5 14 exf6 gxf6 15 f5! and the attack crashed through: 15...♘f8 16 ♘f3 ♖c8 17 ♔b1 ♘a5 18 ♕f2 ♘c4 19 ♗xc4 ♕xc4 20 ♖d4 ♕c6 21 fxe6 dxe6 22 ♖hd1 ♖d8? 23 ♖xd8+ ♗xd8 24 ♖xd8+! ♔xd8 25 ♘d4 and Black resigned. Instead of 8...♕c7, Brendel-Kochiev, Dortmund 1993, went 8...b5 9 f5?! (this does not fit at all) 9...♘ge5 10 ♘xe5 ♘xe5 11 fxe6 dxe6! 12 ♕xd8+ ♔xd8 13 0-0-0+ ♔e8, and with the aid of his splendid knight Black went on to win in 35 moves. The more active 7...b5 is discussed in the next two games.

**8 ♗e3 ♘g6 9 h4!**

Black needs to be very wary of this move after ...♘e7-g6.

**9...♗e7 10 h5 ♘f8 11 ♕d2 b5 12 g4 ♗b7 13 g5 ♘d7**

The knight has taken four moves to reach a square that normally requires just two, yet White seems curiously unable to directly exploit this loss of time.

**14 a4!? b4 15 ♘e2 ♘c5 16 ♘g3 ♕c7 17 ♗h3 0-0-0 18 0-0!?**

Hector has handled the early middlegame very creatively. He correctly perceives that his king is safest here behind the advanced pawns, and not, as one might have assumed, on the queenside.

**18...g6 19 h6 ♖he8 20 b3 ♔b8 21 ♕f2 ♖c8 22 ♖ad1 ♔a8 23 ♗g2 ♘b8 24 ♖d4 a5 25 ♖fd1**

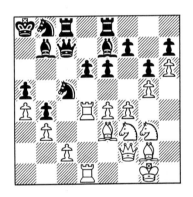

Whilst Black has been trying to make his king as secure as possible (in fact the way he has hidden it in the corner surrounded with a throng of minor pieces reminds me more of the 'bear in the hole' formation from Shogi, Japanese chess, than our own familiar western form of the game), Hector posts his men as dominantly as possible. This is also one of Karpov's favourite methods.

**25...e5**

An attempt at activity which does not succeed.

**26 ♖c4 ♗a6 27 ♗xc5 dxc5 28 ♘xe5 ♗xc4 29 ♘xc4 ♖cd8 30 e5+**

Opening up a monster diagonal into the regal chamber.

**30...♚a7 31 ♖xd8 ♖xd8 32 ♕f3**

Clearly Black cannot survive such an attack

**32...♘a6 33 ♘xa5 ♚b6 34 ♘c6 c4 35 a5+ ♚b5 36 bxc4+ 1-0**

---

*Game 76*
## Gorbatov-Kharitonov
*Moscow Open 1995*

---

**1 e4 c5 2 ♘c3 e6 3 f4 ♘c6 4 ♘f3 a6 5 d4 cxd4 6 ♘xd4 ♘ge7 7 ♘f3 b5 8 ♗d3 ♗b7 9 0-0 ♘c8**

We have already seen the problems that Black can run into if he plays ...♘g6.

**10 a3 ♗e7 11 ♕e2 d6 12 ♗e3 0-0 13 ♖ad1 ♕c7**

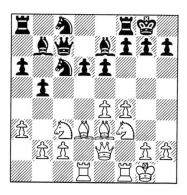

A Sicilian formation which only differs from normalcy in the placings of the king's knights.

**14 ♕f2 b4 15 axb4 ♘xb4**

From here the knight is poised to knock out the bishop at d3, thereby reducing the threat of a white attack.

**16 ♕g3 ♘b6 17 ♗d4 f6 18 ♕h3 ♗c8! 19 e5**

Determining the pawn structure.

**19...♘xd3 20 ♖xd3 dxe5 21 fxe5 f5! 22 ♕g3 ♗b7 23 b3 ♖ad8 24 ♚h1 ♘d7 25 ♘g5 ♗xg5 26 ♕xg5 ♘c5 27 ♖d2 ♘e4 28 ♘xe4 ♗xe4 29 c3?! a5!**

Fixing a soft spot on b3.

**30 h4 ♖b8 31 ♖fd1 h6 32 ♕g6 ♕c6 33 ♖a1 f4**

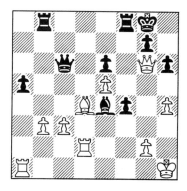

In a middlegame with opposite-coloured bishops, the player who gets his threats in first will usually emerge the winner. This time it is Black.

**34 ♕g4 f3 35 ♖xa5 fxg2+ 36 ♚h2 ♖f1 37 ♖xg2 ♗xg2 38 ♕xg2 ♖f3 39 ♖a7 ♖b7 40 ♖a8+ ♚h7 41 h5 ♕e4 42 ♕g6+ ♕xg6 43 hxg6+ ♚xg6 44 b4 ♖d3 45 ♖d8 ♚f5 46 ♚g2 ♚e4 47 ♖d6 ♖d2+ 48 ♚g3 ♖f7!**

Weaving a mating net.

**49 ♖xe6 ♖f3+ 50 ♚h4 ♖h2+ 51 ♚g4 ♖g2+ 52 ♚h4 ♚f5 0-1**

## Summary

Frankly I would expect this system to be played less and less at master level since there is so much evidence that 6...♛c7 7 ♘f3 ♝c5 provides full equality. White has to lose time in struggling to find an aggressive formation and this allows Black to fully mobilise his forces. After 6...♘ge7 7 ♘f3 Black needs to exercise great care to avoid being swamped by an onrush of white pawns.

**1 e4 c5 2 ♘f3 e6 3 d4 cxd4 4 ♘xd4 ♘c6 5 ♘c3 a6 6 f4**

**6...♛c7**
>    6...♘ge7 7 ♘f3 *(D)*
>>        7...d6 - *game 75*
>>        7...b5 8 ♝d3 ♝b7 - *game 76*

**7 ♘f3 ♝c5**
>    7...b5 - *game 74*

**8 ♝d3**
>    8 e5 f5 9 ♝d3 b5 - see 8 ♝d3 b5 9 e5 f5 below

**8...b5 9 ♛e2**
>    9 e5 f5 *(D)*
>>        10 g4 - *game 71*
>>        10 ♛e2
>>>            10...♛a7 - *game 72*
>>>            10...♘d4 - *game 73*

**9...♘d4 10 ♘xd4 ♝xd4 *(D)***
>    11 ♘d1
>>        11...♝b7 - *game 69*
>>        11...♘f6 - *game 70*
>    11 ♝d2
>>        11...b4 - *game 67*
>>        11...♝b7 - *game 68*

*7 ♘f3*

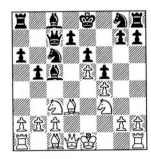

*9...f5*

*10...♝xd4*

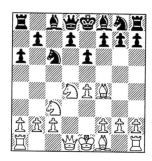

# CHAPTER NINE

## 5 ♘c3 a6 6 ♗f4

---

**1 e4 c5 2 ♘f3 e6 3 d4 cxd4 4 ♘xd4 ♘c6 5 ♘c3 a6 6 ♗f4**

The 6 ♗f4 variation has never really been regarded as anything more than a sideline, although it has been frequently adopted by former World Championship Candidate Gyula Sax. There is still very little theory though.

Games 78 and 79 demonstrate the dangers of 6...d6 7 ♗g3 ♘f6 8 ♗e2 ♗e7 9 ♘xc6 bxc6 10 e5!, but in Game 77 Portisch produces what I am confident must be one of more rational responses, 6...d6 7 ♗g3 ♗e7!? 8 ♗e2 e5, which elegantly solved all of Black's problems. Indeed at move eight of that game he had a few other alternatives, apart from the fixing of the pawn structure (which I personally find preferable), e.g. 8...♗d7, 8...♕c7 and 8...♕b6.

The final three games of this chapter show two unusual ideas. In Game 80 White retreated his knight to f3 without the standard preface of f2-f4, which hardly troubled Black, while in Game 81 Black went for a 'pure Taimanov' approach, exchanging on d4 and the playing ...♘e7. Finally, in the final game we see the very odd 5 ♗f4, followed by the unheralded advance

of Black's h-pawn, which created a very bizarre game.

Please do not try 6...♕f6 7 ♗e3 ♗c5, as after 8 ♘xe6! ♗xe3 9 ♘c7+ ♔d8 10 fxe3 Black is done over.

---

### Game 77
### **W.Watson-Portisch**
### *New York Open 1987*

---

**1 e4 c5 2 ♘c3 ♘c6 3 ♘ge2 e6 4 d4 cxd4 5 ♘xd4 a6 6 ♗f4 d6 7 ♗g3 ♗e7!? 8 ♗e2 e5**

Portisch's move-order is very precise: by deferring ...♘f6 he avoids any problems associated with White capturing on c6 and then disturbing the black structure with e4-e5, which we shall see in the next two games. The text takes play into something akin to a Najdorf variation with 6 ♗e2. The alternatives are 8...♗d7, 8...♕c7 or 8...♕b6, but I know of no theoretical examples.

**9 ♘b3 ♘f6 10 0-0 0-0 11 ♕d3**

Perhaps 11 f4 was best.

**11...♗e6 12 a3 d5**

Black has completely equalised.

**13 exd5 ♘xd5 14 ♖ad1 ♘xc3 15 ♕xc3 ♕b6!?**

An interesting sacrifice.

**16 ♗xe5 ♘xe5 17 ♕xe5 ♖ac8**

With his bishop pair and piece activity Black has full compensation and Watson soon feels obliged to return the pawn.

**18 ♗d3 ♗f6 19 ♕e4 g6 20 ♕b4 ♕xb4 21 axb4 ♗xb3 22 cxb3 ♗xb2**

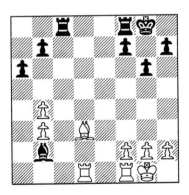

This endgame should be drawn, but William must have fallen asleep.

**23 b5 a5 24 ♗e4 ♖c3 25 ♗d5 b6 26 ♖fe1 ♗a3 27 ♖e3 ♖c2 28 g3 ♗c5 29 ♖f3 ♔g7 30 ♗c6 f5 31 h4 ♖f7 32 ♔g2 ♖e7 33 ♖d7 ♖xd7 34 ♗xd7 ♔f6 35 h5 ♖d2 36 ♗c8 ♔e5 37 hxg6 hxg6 38 ♗b7 ♔d4 39 ♗c6 ♖e2 40 ♔f1 ♖e7 41 ♔g2 ♗a3 42 g4 fxg4 43 ♖g3 ♗c5 44 ♖xg4+ ♔c3 45 ♗d5 ♖e5 46 ♗g8 g5 47 ♔g3 ♗d4**

**48 f4 gxf4+ 49 ♔xf4 ♖xb5 50 ♖g3+ ♔b2 51 ♔e4 ♖b4 52 ♗c4 ♗c3 53 ♔d3 ♗e5 54 ♖e3 ♗d6 55 ♖e6 ♗c5 56 ♖e5 b5 57 ♖xc5 bxc4+ 58 bxc4 a4 0-1**

> *Game 78*
> **Moldovan-Popa**
> *Romanian Team Ch. 1994*

**1 e4 c5 2 ♘c3 ♘c6 3 ♘ge2 e6 4 d4 cxd4 5 ♘xd4 a6 6 ♗f4 d6 7 ♗g3 ♘f6 8 ♗e2 ♗e7?!**

After these natural moves Black quickly runs into trouble. He might instead consider 8...♗d7!?, 8...♕c7!? or 8...♕b6.

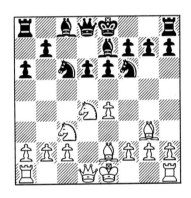

**9 ♘xc6 bxc6 10 e5**

After this rupturing Black already faces an uphill struggle.

**10...dxe5**

10...♘d5 is considered in the next game.

**11 ♕xd8+ ♗xd8 12 ♗xe5 0-0 13 0-0-0 ♗b6 14 ♖hf1 ♗b7 15 ♘a4 ♗a7 16 ♗d6 ♖fd8 17 ♗c5**

White has a superior pawn structure and his pieces suppress all black activity: the sort of scenario with which Karpov pays the rent.

17...♖e8 18 ♗xa7 ♖xa7 19 ♘c5 a5 20 c4 ♔f8 21 ♗f3 ♗a8 22 ♖fe1 ♔e7 23 ♖e3 g5 24 g3 ♖c8 25 ♖a3 ♖cc7 26 ♖b3

Popa has struggled well, and might just have been able to hold out, but now he seems to experience a rush of blood to the head.

26...a4?! 27 ♖a3 ♘d5? 28 ♖xa4?

Spoilt for choice, White passes over the simpler 28 cxd5 cxd5 29 ♖c3 and wins.

28...♘b6 29 ♖b4 ♘d7 30 ♖xd7+ ♖xd7 31 ♘xd7 ♔xd7 32 ♖b8 ♖xa2 33 ♖h8 ♖a4 34 ♔b1 ♔d6 35 ♖xh7 f5 36 b3 ♖b4 37 ♔c2 ♖b8 38 ♖a7?

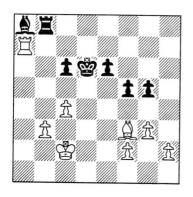

Too casual. 38 h3 kept the win easy.

38...g4! 39 ♗h1 ♖h8!

Black has cleverly found the counterplay that he needs to draw.

40 b4 ♖xh2 41 c5+ ♔e5 42 ♖xa8 ♖xh1 43 ♖d8 ♖h2 44 ♖d2 ♖h7 ½-½

*Game 79*
**Sax-Etchegaray**
*Benasque Open 1993*

1 e4 c5 2 ♘c3 ♘c6 3 ♘ge2 e6 4 d4 cxd4 5 ♘xd4 ♘f6 6 ♗f4

This is not the direct Taimanov move-order, but we shall soon transpose back to it.

6...d6 7 ♗g3 a6 8 ♗e2 ♗e7 9 ♘xc6 bxc6 10 e5 ♘d5

This does not really equalise either.

11 exd6 ♗xd6 12 ♘e4!

Grabbing the dark squares.

12...♗xg3 13 hxg3 0-0 14 c4 ♘f6 15 ♕xd8 ♖xd8 16 ♗f3 ♖b8 17 b3 ♘xe4 18 ♗xe4

18...c5

Black's structural defects give him a sad life. With 18...c5 he secures some freedom and dark-square control, but at the cost of an important pawn.

19 ♗xh7+ ♔f8 20 ♗e4 ♔e7 21 ♖h7 ♖d4 22 ♗f3 g6 23 ♖d1 ♖xd1+ 24

♔xd1 a5 25 ♖h8 ♔d7 26 ♔c2 a4 27 ♖f8 ♔e7 28 ♖g8 ♔d7 29 g4 axb3+ 30 axb3 ♖b6 31 ♖f8

Black is still so tied up by White's domination that he cannot hope to save himself.

**31...f5 32 ♖f6 ♖a6 33 ♖xg6 ♖a2+ 34 ♔c3 ♖xf2 35 g5 e5 36 ♖f6 ♔e7 37 ♗d5 e4 38 ♗xe4 ♗e6 39 ♗f3 ♖a2 40 ♖h6 1-0**

In the last two games Black went from the opening moves straight into a prospectless ending, so I trust that you will take care to avoid the chance of it befalling you.

---

## Game 80
### De la Villa-Sion Castro
*Leon 1994*

---

**1 e4 c5 2 ♘f3 e6 3 d4 cxd4 4 ♘xd4 ♘c6 5 ♘c3 a6 6 ♗f4 d6 7 ♘f3**

To avoid the fork at e5, but 7 ♗g3 seems better to me.

**7...b5 8 ♕d2 ♘f6 9 a3 ♖a7!? 10 ♗e2 ♖d7**

A grandiose but acceptable scheme. In principle Black has a fine Sicilian middlegame and White lacks any purposeful plan.

**11 0-0 ♗e7 12 ♖ad1 ♗b7 13 h3 0-0 14 ♕e3 ♕a8!? 15 ♖fe1 ♖c8 16 ♗f1 ♘a5 17 ♘d2 h6?!**

Dithering. 17...d5! was more consistent.

**18 ♗e2 ♔f8?!**

And neither is it clear to me what this was supposed to be about. 18...♗f8, which is a standard regrouping and here has the additional point of shoring up the king's defences, would have made much more sense, as would 18...♔h8 or 18...e5 19 ♗h2 ♖dc7.

**19 ♗xh6**

Yes, please!

**19...gxh6 20 ♕xh6+ ♔g8 21 ♗d3**

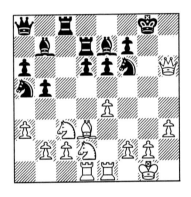

Black's lackadaisical play has given White a dangerous attack. The problem with placing your major pieces offside is that if activity does break out on the other wing (it should not have been allowed to) then you may encounter big logistical problems in transferring the heavy artillery back over for defence. To expedite the queen's swing to f8, Black now makes the standard Sicilian exchange sacrifice.

**21...♖xc3 22 ♖e3!**

Not 22 bxc3 ♕f8 with the end of the attack.
**22...♖xd3**
Causing maximum damage as he dies.
**23 cxd3 ♘h7**
Forced.
**24 ♖g3+ ♘g5 25 ♖xg5+**
Perhaps underplaying it. He could have kept it going with 25 ♘f3!?
**25...♗xg5 26 ♕xg5+ ♔f8 27 ♕h6+ ♔e8 28 ♕h8+ ♔e7 29 ♕h4+ ♔f8 30 ♕h6+ ½-½**
A sloppy game but one that is noteworthy for the novel development scheme that Black chose.

---

### Game 81
### Damaso-Costa
*Lisbon 1995*

**1 e4 c5 2 ♘f3 ♘c6 3 d4 cxd4 4 ♘xd4 e6 5 ♘c3 a6 6 ♗f4 ♘xd4!? 7 ♕xd4 ♘e7**

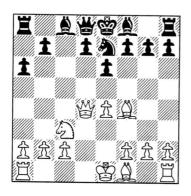

By far the simplest treatment. Black ignores White's unusual sixth move and treats it like any other ...♘ge7 game.
**8 h4!?**
Signalling the side on which he will

be castling. 8 ♗e2 would have transposed to Chapter 4.
**8...♘c6 9 ♕d2 ♗e7 10 0-0-0 ♕a5**
On the exceptional occasions when White castles long, this is often the right square for the black queen.

**11 ♔b1**
To meet the threat of ...b7-b5-b4, but White almost certainly wants to play this move in any case.
**11...b5 12 h5**
Both sides are going for it.
**12...h6 13 ♖h3!?**
A known way of probing the kingside, and one popularised by the younger Jonathan Speelman.
**13...b4 14 ♘e2 e5 15 ♗e3 d6 16 ♖g3 ♗e6 17 ♘c1 ♔f8**
A rich and complex middlegame has arisen.
**18 ♗e2 ♕c7 19 ♗g4**
I would have played 19 f4. Perhaps White overlooked his opponent's reply.
**19...♗h4! 20 ♗xe6 ♗xg3 21 ♗d5**
Even though he has dropped the exchange, White's bishop pair and the general disorder in the black camp mean that he has mighty compensation.

**21...♗h4 22 ♘d3 a5 23 g3 ♗f6 24 c3 ♖b8 25 ♖c1 ♕d7 26 cxb4 ♘xb4 27 ♘xb4 axb4 28 ♖c6 ♔e7 29 ♖c4 b3 30 axb3 ♖hc8 31 ♕c2 ♔f8 32 b4 ♗d8! 33 b5 ♖xc4 34 ♗xc4 ♗b6**

Completing an effective repositioning. The chances are now about equal.

**35 ♗xb6 ♖xb6 36 ♕d3 ♔e7 37 ♕f3 ♔f8 38 ♕d3 ½-½**

---

## Game 82
### Vydeslaver-Gershon
*Rishon le Zion 1995*

---

**1 e4 c5 2 ♘f3 e6 3 d4 cxd4 4 ♘xd4 ♘c6 5 ♗f4!?**

A total novelty.

**5...d6 6 ♗g3 e5 7 ♘b3 ♗e6 8 ♘c3 h5!?**

*see following diagram*

---

Remarkable, but I cannot really advise it. 8...♘f6 was better.

**9 f3 g6 10 ♕d3**

Eschewing the more natural d2-square, presumably through concern of a later ...♗h6.

**10...♕d7 11 0-0-0 0-0-0**

Very unusual stuff indeed.

**12 ♗f2 ♔b8 13 ♕b5 ♕c7 14 ♘d5**

**♗xd5 15 exd5 ♘ce7 16 ♖d3 ♘f6 17 ♖c3 a6**

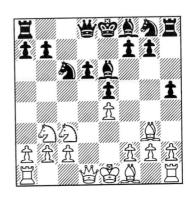

Cool as you like!

**18 ♕a5 ♗h6+ 19 ♔d1 ♕xa5 20 ♘xa5 ♖d7 21 ♖b3 ♖hd8?**

In a most obscure game, this is the most obscure of the moves!

**22 c4?**

I can't tell you why White did not take the a-pawn either.

**22...♖c8 23 ♖c3 ♘f5 24 ♗d3 ♘e3+ 25 ♗xe3 ♗xe3 26 ♔e2 ♗b6 27 ♘b3 ♘h7 28 ♘d2**

Both sides prepare to mobilise their pawn rollers.

**28...f5 29 b4 ♘f6 30 ♖hc1 ♗d4 31 ♖3c2 ♖e8 32 ♘b3 ♗a7 33 ♔f1 e4**

I believe 33...h4 is superior, because it denies the knight access to e6 via d4.

**34 ♗e2 h4 35 ♖d1 g5 36 ♘d4**

Naturally.

**36...exf3 37 gxf3 ♖e5 38 ♘e6 g4**

I suspect that this was a time scramble. Black loses his way and emerges in an endgame where he is struggling.

**39 f4 ♖e3 40 ♖d3 ♖e4 41 ♖b3**

With a sneaky intent.

**41...♘h5 42 ♗d3! ♖e3 43 ♗xf5 ♖xb3 44 axb3 ♘xf4 45 ♘xf4 ♖f7**

Regaining the piece.

**46 ♖e2 ♗b6!? 47 ♖e4 ♖xf5 48 ♔g2 ♔a7 49 h3 gxh3+ 50 ♔xh3 ♗f2 51 ♔g4 ♖f8 52 ♘g6 ♖g8 53 ♖e6 ♗g3 54 ♔h3**

Sealing the fate of the fragile h-pawn.

**54...♔b8 55 ♘xh4 ♗xh4 56 ♔xh4 ♔c7 57 ♖e7+ ♔c8 58 ♖e3 ♔d7 59 ♖g3 ♖h8+ 60 ♔g5**

Often a rook ending of four against three on the same wing is drawn, but this is an unusual structure.

**60...b5?**

Black may have been worried about White bringing his king to d4 and then advancing c4-c5, but allowing that was surely better than this.

**61 ♔f5 ♖f8+ 62 ♔e4 ♖f7 63 ♖g6 ♖h7 64 c5 ♖h4+ 65 ♔d3 ♖h3+ 66 ♔c2 ♖h2+ 67 ♔c3 ♖h3+ 68 ♔b2 ♖h2+ 69 ♔a3**

The only haven.

**69...dxc5 70 bxc5 a5 71 ♖a6 ♖c2 72 ♖a7+ ♔c8 73 c6 ♖c5 74 ♖d7 ♖c2**

Black puts up a spirited resistance, but ultimately in a lost cause.

**75 ♖h7 ♖c5 76 ♖h5 ♖c2 77 ♖h3 ♖d2 78 ♖h5 ♔c7 79 b4 ♖d3+ 80 ♔b2 axb4 81 ♖h7+ ♔c8 82 ♖d7 ♖c3 83 ♔a2 ♖c2+ 84 ♔b3 ♖c4 85 ♖h7 ♖d4 86 ♖h8+ ♔c7 87 ♖h7+ ♔c8 88 ♖d7 ♖c4 89 ♖b7 ♖c5 90 ♖d7 ♖c4 91 ♖a7 ♖c5 92 ♔xb4!**

Finally hitting upon the right plan.

**92...♖xd5 93 ♔a5 1-0**

The b-pawn provides a shelter from checks for the white king when he gets to b6, and so the win is trivial. e.g. 92...♔b8 93 ♔b6 ♖d6 94 ♖h7 ♖d8 95 c7+.

## Summary

Providing Black avoids the positional puncturing that befell the players in Games 78 and 79, then I think you will agree that the theory indicates that he has excellent equalising responses against Sax's 6 ♗f4. I personally would advocate the move-order of Watson-Portisch, but others may opt for 6...♘xd4 7 ♕xd4 ♘e7.

**1 e4 c5 2 ♘f3 e6 3 d4 cxd4 4 ♘xd4 ♘c6**

**5 ♘c3**
    5 ♗f4 - *game 82*
**5...a6 6 ♗f4 d6**
    6...♘xd4 7 ♕xd4 - *game 81*
**7 ♗g3** *(D)*
    7 ♘f3 - *game 80*
**7...♘f6**
    7...♗e7 *(D)* - *game 77*
**8 ♗e2 ♗e7 9 ♘xc6 bxc6 10 e5** *(D)*
       10...dxe5 - *game 78*
       10...♘d5 - *game 79*

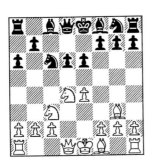
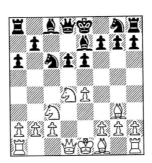
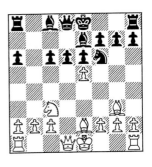

    *7 ♗g3*           *7...♗e7*           *10 e5*

# CHAPTER TEN

## 5 ♘b5

**1 e4 c5 2 ♘f3 e6 3 d4 cxd4 4 ♘xd4 ♘c6 5 ♘b5**

Everybody knows that you should not move a piece twice in the opening, but many of the world's best players do just that with 5 ♘b5. The thinking is that unless Black takes play into a Four Knights or Sveshnikov Sicilian with 5...♘f6 6 ♘1c3 ♗b4 or 6...d6, then he will be forced to either permit a disruptive ♘d6+ or, following 5...d6, allow the establishment of a Maroczy Bind with 6 c4. Twenty-five years ago Maroczy Binds were far more feared things than they are today, and within the confines of his back three ranks Black can shuffle and reorganise himself to the satisfaction of top grandmasters, as we shall see in Games 83-87. Game 88 features a novel fianchetto development from Fischer which is really quite logical since many of the Maroczy Bind middlegames from 6 c4 see White re-deploying his king bishop to suppress Black's projected pawn breakouts ...d7-d5 or ...b7-b5.

Alternatively White may play 6 ♗f4, forcing 6...e5 7 ♗e3, as in Games 88-91. Here the option of the bind has gone, but Black has had to accept a weak d5-square. Of course many modern Sicilian formations, from the aforementioned Sveshnikov to the Boleslavsky (1 e4 c5 2 ♘f3 ♘c6 3 d4 cxd4 4 ♘xd4 ♘f6 5 ♘c3 d6 6 ♗e2 e5) or the Najdorf (1 e4 c5 2 ♘f3 d6 3 d4 cxd4 4 ♘xd4 ♘f6 5 ♘c3 a6 6 ♗e2 e5) see Black voluntarily inflicting that problem upon himself in the anticipation it will be offset by active piece play. Here too results suggest that Black's chances are none the worse.

Game 92 is a joke; the zany 5...♗c5, which Michael Basman and I once looked at and dubbed 'The Black and Horrible', just cannot survive against common sense, but before becoming extinct it left some remarkable fossil traces.

The themes of this variation will become clearer as you play through the material in this chapter. Let us start with the main line, 5...d6 6 c4.

---

*Game 83*
### Jadoul-Karpov
*Brussels 1986*

---

**1 e4 c5 2 ♘f3 e6 3 d4 cxd4 4 ♘xd4 ♘c6 5 ♘b5**

If White wants to establish a

Maroczy Bind, he must play this move first, as the immediate 5 c4 is well met by 5...♘f6 6 ♘c3 ♗b4, e.g. 7 f3 d5! with immediate equality.

**5...d6 6 c4**

This is the most popular move, leading to a very distinctive type of middlegame.

**6...♘f6**

6...a6 makes no sense yet because after 7 ♘5c3 White has the option of developing his knight to d2 instead of a3.

**7 ♘1c3**

Naturally after 7 ♘5c3 Black plays 7...♗e7, refraining from ...a7-a6 for the time being (see Game 88).

**7...a6**

The right timing for this move.

**8 ♘a3**

The knight is obviously not well placed here, but White can always regroup later. Note that after 8 ♘d4 ♗e7 9 ♗e2 0-0 10 0-0 ♗d7 Black is ready to relieve his position with ...♘xd4 and ...♗c6.

**8...♗e7**

In the 16th game of the 1985 World Championship match Kasparov played 8...d5 against Karpov, scoring a

famous victory after 9 exd5 exd5 10 cxd5 ♘b4 11 ♗e2 ♗c5 12 0-0 0-0 13 ♗f3 ♗f5. However, subsequently 12 ♗e3! was discovered, when Black is on the ropes, e.g. 12...♗xe3 13 ♕a4+! ♘d7 13 ♕xb4, and Kasparov's gambit rapidly disappeared.

**9 ♗e2 0-0 10 0-0 b6**

Taimanov's 10...♗d7 is dealt with in Game 86.

**11 ♗e3 ♗b7**

This is the older regrouping. The provocative 11...♘e5 is seen in Game 85.

**12 ♕b3**

12 f4 is premature due to 12...d5! 13 exd5 exd5 14 cxd5 ♘b4 with equal chances, but 12 ♖c1 is a solid alternative.

**12...♘d7 13 ♖fd1 ♘c5!**

13...♖a7 is considered in the next game.

**14 ♕c2**

There is a well-known trap here: 14 ♗xc5? bxc5 15 ♕xb7? ♘a5 and the queen is entombed.

**14...♕c7 15 ♖ac1 ♖ac8 16 ♘ab1**

White has a clear plan of ♘d2, followed by gaining space on the queenside with a2-a3 and b2-b4. There is little that Black can do to prevent this, so he adopts waiting tactics.

**16...♘e5 17 ♘d2 ♘cd7 18 a3 ♖fe8 19 b4 ♘f6 20 h3 ♘g6 21 ♕b1**

Karpov suggested the more straightforward 21 ♘b3, in order to continue with a3-a4-a5.

*see following diagram*

**21...♗a8**

Karpov waits, anticipating that Jadoul will present him with a target.

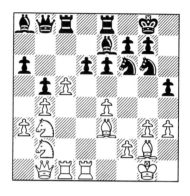

**22 ♘a4 ♖b8**

Not 22...♘d7 because White then has the chance of 23 c5 bxc5 24 ♗xa6.

**23 ♗f1 h6 24 g3?!**

This is the sort of thing that Black was waiting for! The slight weakening of the kingside gives Black more counter-chances.

**24...♘d7**

But first the queenside has to be protected, since c4-c5 was in the air.

**25 ♗g2 ♖bc8**

Now the rook can safely return, because the white bishop no longer controls a6.

**26 ♘b3 ♕b7**

Karpov does not underestimate his opponent. In his notes he draws attention to the possibility that the more natural 26...♕b8 would have given: 27 c5 bxc5 28 bxc5 ♘xc5 29 ♘bxc5 ♕xb1 30 ♖xb1 dxc5 31 ♘b6.

**27 ♕a2**

The knight on d7 is now protected, so Black can answer 27 c5 bxc5 28 bxc5 with 28...dxc5.

**27...♕b8 28 c5**

Jadoul loses his patience. Black is well prepared for this initiative.

**28...b5 29 ♘b2 ♘f6 30 ♕b1 h5!**

The British Grandmaster Tony Miles once observed that Karpov is unsurpassed at probing weaknesses. Here comes a classic case as he takes the white king's position apart. Karpov added these variations to illustrate the vulnerability of that region: 31 cxd6 ♗xd6 32 h4 ♘g4 and the threat of 33...♗xg3 is decisive, or 31 cxd6 ♗xd6 32 ♘c5 ♗xc5 33 ♖xc5 h4 34 g4 ♘f4 with a great positional advantage.

**31 ♘a5 dxc5 32 bxc5 h4 33 g4 ♘f4 34 ♗xf4 ♕xf4 35 ♘d3 ♕c7**

Winning a pawn.

**36 ♕b4 ♘xe4 37 ♗xe4 ♗xe4 38 ♕xe4 ♕xa5 39 c6 ♗xa3 40 ♖a1 ♕c3 41 ♘e5 ♗b2 0-1**

---

*Game 84*
**Nunn-Cebalo**
*Biel 1986*

---

**1 e4 c5 2 ♘f3 e6 3 d4 cxd4 4 ♘xd4 ♘c6 5 ♘b5 d6 6 c4 ♘f6 7 ♘1c3 a6 8 ♘a3 ♗e7 9 ♗e2 b6 10 ♗e3 0-0 11 0-0 ♗b7 12 ♕b3 ♘d7 13 ♖fd1 ♖a7!?**

This was a new move at the time, but the general formation is very similar to the previous game.

**14 ☖d2 ♗a8 15 ♕d1 ♕b8 16 ♕f1 ♘f6 17 ☖ad1**

In his notes Nunn suggests 17 f4, followed by ♕f2 with pressure on b6.

**17...♘e5 18 f3 ♘ed7 19 ♗f4 ♘e5 20 ♕f2**

For the last six moves Nunn has been tacking around. His moves were aimed more than anything at containment. Above all White must always monitor Black's pawn breaks of ...b7-b5, or ...d7-d5.

**20...☖e8 21 ♗e3 ♘ed7 22 g4**

Finally Nunn selects a plan. Typically, it is to attack.

**22...h6 23 h4!? ♘h7!? 24 ♕g3 g5!?**

It is worth remembering this way of holding up a kingside attack.

**25 hxg5 hxg5 26 ♗f1 ♘e5**

From this superb outpost the knight radiates influence.

**27 ☖h2 f6 28 ♕f2 ♗d8 29 ☖h3 ♘f8!
30 ♗e2 ♘fg6 31 ♕h2 ☖g7 32 ♔f2
♗c7 33 ♕h1 ♔f7**

When players start moving their kings towards the centre when all the pieces are still on the board, this is a fair sign that there is not much that can be undertaken.

**34 ♘c2 ♘h4!? 35 ♘d4 ☖h8 36 f4
gxf4 37 ☖xh4 fxe3+ 38 ♔xe3 ♘g6
39 ☖h5 ♕g8 40 ☖f1 ♔e7 41 ♕f3
☖f7 ½-½**

---

### Game 85
### Chandler-Quinteros
*Vienna Open 1986*

**1 e4 c5 2 ♘f3 e6 3 d4 cxd4 4 ♘xd4
♘c6 5 ♘b5 d6 6 c4 ♘f6 7 ♘1c3 a6
8 ♘a3 ♗e7 9 ♗e2 0-0 10 0-0 b6 11
♗e3 ♘e5**

This provocative move is designed to regroup the queen's knight to its optimal square on d7.

**12 f4 ♘ed7 13 ♗f3 ♗b7 14 ♕e2
♕c7 15 ☖ac1 ☖ac8 16 g4!?**

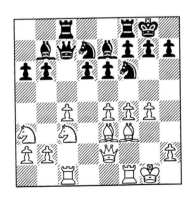

Murray Chandler always likes to

get on with things.

**16...♕b8**

By now you will no doubt recognise this typical crouching spot. 16...h6 would have been met by 17 h4.

**17 g5 ♘e8 18 ♗g2 g6**

To hold up the attack and allow the knight to resurface on g7.

**19 ♗h3 ♘g7 20 f5 exf5 21 exf5 gxf5 22 ♖xf5!?**

22 ♗xf5 would have been met in the same manner, i.e. 22...♘xf5 23 ♖xf5 ♘e5.

**22...♘xf5 23 ♗xf5 ♘e5!**

A necessary defender, and besides, Quinteros is only too happy to return the exchange to reduce White's attack.

**24 ♕h5 ♘g6 25 ♗d4 ♖fe8**

Rapidly organising the defence.

**26 ♖f1 ♗f8**

As you might imagine, precise calculation is demanded in such situations, but the concrete variations affirm that Black's game was sound when the attack began, so he should be able to withstand it.

**27 ♗xc8 ♕xc8**

**28 ♖xf7! ♔xf7?!**

Dubious. There was a remarkable defensive possibility in 28...♗h6!! when many variations reveal the vulnerability of White's own king, e.g. 29 ♖xh7!? (29 gxh6? ♔xf7 or 29 ♕xh6?? ♕g4+) 29...♕f5! and there is no clear win. If 30 ♖h8+!? ♘xh8 31 ♕xe8+ ♗f8 and Black is about to begin checking. Perhaps 32 ♕h5 ♘f7 33 ♘d5 (but not 33 h4?? ♗f3) to block the diagonal, when 33 ...♗xd5 34 cxd5 ♘xg5 with approximate equality is representative.

**29 ♕xh7+ ♔e6 30 ♕xg6+ ♔d7 31 ♕f5+ ♔c7 32 ♕xc8+ ♔xc8**

The two connected white passed pawns mean that Black is the one trying to demonstrate equality in this ending.

**33 ♘c2**

33 h4! was better still.

**33...b5**

Fishing for counterplay.

**34 h4**

Wisely denying the rook access to e2.

**34...♗e4**

Transferring to the action zone.

**35 ♘e3 ♗g6 36 cxb5 axb5 37 a3!**

Not 37 ♘xb5 ♖e4.

**37...♗g7?!**

37...♔d7 was a simpler defence.

**38 ♗xg7 ♖xe3 39 ♔g2 ♔d7 40 ♘xb5 ♖b3 41 a4 ♖b4 42 ♔g3 ♖xa4**

This ending looks drawn to me. The bishop copes with the g- and h-pawns and the king and rook ought to be able to monitor the new passed b-pawn.

**43 ♘c3 ♖a1 44 ♗d4 ♔e6 45 b4 ♔f5 46 b5 ♗e8?!**

Quinteros was running short of

time. 46...♖a3 would have been better.

**47 b6 ♗c6 48 ♘b5 ♖c1?**

And this is a blunder. He should have played 48...♖b1.

**49 ♘xd6+?**

The wrong way round. 49 b7! ♗xb7 50 ♘xd6+ would have won.

**49...♔e6 50 b7 ♖b1 51 ♗c5 ♗xb7 52 ♘xb7 ♖xb7**

This is now simply a 'book' draw.

**53 ♔g4 ♖b5 54 ♗e3 ♖b3 55 ♗f4 ♖b1 56 h5 ♖g1+ 57 ♗g3 ♖g2 58 ♔f4 ♖a2 59 ♔g4 ♖g2 60 h6 ♔f7 61 h7 ♔g7 62 g6 ♖g1 63 ♔f3 ♖h1 ½-½**

**1 e4 c5 2 ♘f3 e6 3 d4 cxd4 4 ♘xd4 ♘c6 5 ♘b5 d6 6 c4 a6 7 ♘5c3 ♘f6 8 ♘a3**

Different knight, same line-up.

**8...♗e7 9 ♗e2 0-0 10 0-0 ♗d7 11 ♗e3 ♕b8!? 12 ♖c1**

12 f3 seems more flexible, to meet 12...♘a7 with 13 ♕d3 ♗c6 14 ♖fd1 ♘d7 15 ♗f1 ♘e5 16 ♕e2, when White is on top according to Agapov.

**12...♘a7!?**

I was one of the first players to be surprised by this squeezing into the top left-hand corner, when Taimanov played it against me in the final round at Plovdiv 1984.

**13 ♕b3**

Stopping 13...b5.

**13...♗c6 14 f3 ♘d7 15 ♔h1 ♗d8!**

A smart idea. Black plans to exchange the dark-squared bishops.

**16 ♖fd1 ♘c8! 17 ♘c2 ♗b6 18 ♘d4 ♕a7**

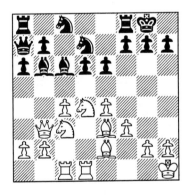

The culmination of this scheme. Black now threatens 19...e5. Frankly I am surprised that Taimanov's idea is not used more frequently.

19 ♗g1 e5 20 ♘c2 ♗xg1 21 ♖xg1 ♘c5 22 ♕a3 ♘e6

In the new pawn structure the knight sits nicely here.

23 g3 f5!? 24 exf5 ♖xf5 25 ♘d5 ♖f7 26 ♔g2 a5!? 27 ♖cd1 b6!?

He is very stuck on the notion of a dark-squared pawn formation.

28 ♖d2 ♖f8 29 ♖f1 ♕b7 30 ♕e3 b5

I am not sure that this was the right way, since the opening of lines will naturally favour the better developed party, and that is not Black. In particular the knight on c8 is not pulling his weight. Perhaps he should just have held back.

31 ♔g1 ♔h8 32 b3 bxc4 33 ♗xc4 ♗b5 34 ♗xb5 ♕xb5 35 ♘a3 ♕b7 36 ♘c4 a4 37 b4 ♘d4 38 ♕e4 ♖a6 39 f4

White is now clearly on top.

39...♕b5 40 ♘a3 ♕e8 41 ♖df2 ♖g8 42 fxe5 ♕xe5 43 ♖e1 ♖c6 44 ♕xe5 dxe5 45 ♖xe5 ♘d6

Finally hopping into the thick of things.

46 ♔g2 ♖c1 47 ♖d2 ♘6f5 48 ♘b5 ♘xb5 49 ♖xf5

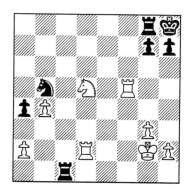

Ultimately this endgame proved too simplified for Ernst to realise his

advantage, and Taimanov held on.

49...♖d8 50 ♖df2 h6 51 h4 ♘d6 52 ♖f8+ ♖xf8 53 ♖xf8+ ♔h7 54 h5 ♘e4 55 ♘f4 ♖c2+ 56 ♔f3 ♘f6 57 g4 ♖xa2 58 ♘g6 ♘g8 59 ♖a8 a3 60 b5 ♖b2 61 ♖xa3 ♖xb5 62 ♖a8 ♖b3+ 63 ♔f4 ♖b4+ 64 ♔f5 ♖b5+ 65 ♔e6 ♖b6+ 66 ♔e5 ♖b5+ 67 ♔f4 ♖b4+ 68 ♔g3 ♖b3+ 69 ♔h4 ♖b4 70 ♘f8+ ♔h8 71 ♔g3 ♖c4 72 ♘g6+ ♔h7 73 ♔f3 ♖b4 74 ♖a7 ♘f6 75 ♖a8 ♘g8

Securing the draw.

76 ♖f8 ♖b3+ 77 ♔f4 ♖b4+ 78 ♔f5 ♖b5+ 79 ♔e6 ♖b6+ 80 ♔d7 ♖b7+ 81 ♔c6 ♖b4 82 ♘f4 ♘f6 83 ♘g6 ♘g8 84 ♘f4 ½-½

---

*Game 87*
### Psakhis-J.Polgar
*Amsterdam (OHRA) 1989*

---

1 e4 c5 2 ♘f3 e6 3 d4 cxd4 4 ♘xd4 ♘c6 5 ♘b5 d6 6 c4 ♘f6 7 ♘1c3 a6 8 ♘a3 b6 9 ♗e2 ♗b7 10 0-0

A natural enough move but John Nunn recommends the aggressive move-order 10 f4 ♘b8 11 ♗f3 ♘bd7 12 0-0 ♗e7 13 ♕e2 0-0, when White can choose between 14 ♗e3, transposing to Game 85, and the dynamic 14 g4!?

10...♘b8!?

This strange-looking move actually comes to pretty much the same thing as going via e5, which we saw in Game 85, except that White cannot play f2-f4 now.

---

*see following diagram*

---

11 f3

Lev Psakhis opts for control now that the bloodlust of the Chandler game is unavailable.

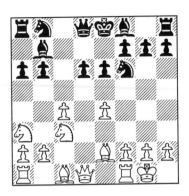

**11...♘bd7 12 ♔h1 ♗e7 13 ♗f4 ♕c7 14 ♖c1 0-0 15 ♕d2 ♖fd8**

Later Black might want to do something on the open e-file after ...d7-d5, so 15...♖fe8 is more accurate.

**16 ♖fd1 ♘e5 17 ♗e3 ♖ab8 18 ♕e1 ♗a8 19 ♕f2**

This is often a good square for the queen in Maroczy formations, especially when combined with a later advance of the a-pawn.

**19...♕a7 20 ♘ab1 ♗c6 21 b4 ♕b7 22 ♘d2**

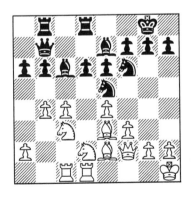

The plan of ♘b3 followed by a4-a5 is a strong one.

**22...d5?**

These positions often hinge upon whether or not Black can time this pawn break accurately. This time Judit got it dead wrong.

**23 cxd5 exd5 24 ♗f4! ♗d6 25 exd5 ♗xd5**

Or 25...♘xd5 26 ♘xd5 ♗xd5 27 ♘e4! and all the tactics work for White, e.g. 27...♗xe4 28 ♖xd6! wins, or 27...♘g4 28 fxg4 ♗xf4 29 ♕xf4 ♗xe4 30 ♖c7! ♖xd1+ 31 ♗xd1 ♗xg2+ 32 ♔g1 and the vulnerability of his back rank causes Black's defeat: 32...♕d5 33 ♖d7!

**26 ♘de4 ♗xe4 27 ♖xd6 ♘d3 28 ♗xd3 ♗xd3 29 ♖d1**

29 ♕d4! would also have worked.

**29...♖xd6 30 ♗xd6 ♖d8 31 ♖xd3 ♕c6 32 ♕d2 ♕c4 33 ♔g1 a5 34 bxa5 bxa5 35 ♖d4 ♕e6 36 ♗g3 ♖e8 37 ♗f2 1-0**

---

### Game 88
### Fischer-Spassky
*Sveti Stefan (21st match game) 1992*

---

**1 e4 c5 2 ♘f3 ♘c6 3 d4 cxd4 4 ♘xd4 e6 5 ♘b5 d6 6 c4 ♘f6 7 ♘5c3 ♗e7 8 g3!?**

Bobby's novelty, which created something of a fashion wave. After the fianchetto the bishop will obviously bear against the liberating ...d7-d5. Fischer's idea was later repeated, with a slightly different move-order, in Anand-Salov, Biel 1993: 7 ♘1c3 a6 8 ♘a3 ♗e7 9 g3 ♗d7 10 ♗g2 ♖c8 11 0-0 ♘e5! (by deferring castling Black sets to work against the soft c-pawn under favourable circumstances) 12 ♗f4, and now Salov should just have taken the pawn, i.e. 12...♘xc4 13 ♘xc4 ♖xc4 14 ♗xd6 ♗c6 and Black is fine.

**8...0-0 9 ♗g2 a6 10 0-0 ♖b8 11 ♘a3 ♕c7 11 ♗e3 ♗d7 13 ♖c1 ♘e5 14 h3 ♖fc8 15 f4**

Now Black cannot take the c-pawn because 15...♘xc4 16 ♘xc4 ♕xc4 17 ♘d5 is massively favourable for White, and retreating to c6 would permit White to change the structure in his favour with 16 ♘d5!, a trick to remember.

**15...♘g6**

So Boris lodges it here.

**16 ♕d2 ♗e8 17 ♖fd1 b6**

The end of the beginning. The same old scene, bar the exceptional squares of the king's bishops.

**18 ♕f2 h6 19 ♔h2?!**

It was better to bring the knight more into things with 19 ♘ab1!, when the consequences of Black grabbing the pawn are dangerous for him, e.g. 19...♕xc4 20 b3 ♕b4 21 ♖d4 ♕c5 22 ♖c4 ♕h5 23 ♗xb6 or 21...♕a5 22 f5! exf5 (22...♘e5 23 b4 traps the queen) 23 exf5 ♘f8 and White can still hunt down the poor lady with 24 b4 ♕e5 25 ♖e1, etc. So Black should do something else, 19...♗c6 maybe, whereupon the reor-

ganisation of the white queenside continues, viz. 20 a4 ♕b7 21 ♘d2 with control of the proceedings and a slight edge. Fischer starts to dither.

**19...♕a7 20 ♕e2 ♕c7 21 ♗f3?!**

Here 21 ♖e1 was more precise.

**21...♗c6! 22 ♘ab1**

In this exceptional instance the drop 22 ♘d5 can be rendered harmless just by sidestepping with 22.. ♕b7.

**22...♕b7**

Boris is all set to make a break, an opportunity which Fischer's inaccurate handling of the early middlegame has presented to him.

**23 ♘d2 b5 24 cxb5 axb5 25 b4 ♕a8!**

Réti's favourite square for the queen, and here it is very effective. Black has rather more than equalised.

**26 ♖c2**

**26...d5**

A good move, but a better one was available, tactically exploiting of White's disharmony with 26...♕a3! when there is no adequate defence of the b-pawn since 27 ♖b1 allows 27...♗xe4!, e.g. 28 ♗xe4 ♖xc3 or 28 ♘dxe4 ♘xe4 29 ♘xe4 ♖xc2 30 ♕xc2

♕xe3. Fischer can now battle on.

**27 e5 ♘e4! 28 ♗xe4 dxe4 29 ♗c5**

Just about forced.

**29...♗xc5 30 bxc5 ♖d8! 31 ♖e1
♘e7! 32 ♘cxe4 ♘f5 33 ♘b3 ♘d4
34 ♘xd4 ♖xd4**

Obviously Black has splendid activity for his pawn.

**35 ♘d6 ♕a4 36 f5**

Just about the only move.

**36...♖a8?!**

Once again not the best way to prosecute his advantage. 36...♖d5 37 ♖b2 ♕d4! was also good.

**37 ♖b2! ♕a3 38 fxe6 fxe6 39 ♘xb5
♗xb5 40 ♕xb5 ♖d3 41 ♖g2**

The upshot is that Fischer has scrambled out to actually have slightly the better chances.

**41...♕c3 42 ♖ee2 ♖a3 43 ♖c2
♕xe5 44 ♖ce2 ♖e3 45 ♖xe3 ♖xe3
46 a4 ♖c3 47 c6!**

This pawn will perish but the a-pawn remains as a big plus.

**47...♕d6 48 c7 ♖xc7 49 ♕b8+ ♔h7
50 a5 h5! 51 h4 ♕c5?**

A serious misjudgement. Instead 51...♖c6! would have drawn, because after the queen exchange the black king would be able to become more active than it did in the game, and thus generate sufficient counterplay.

**52 a6 ♖f7 53 ♕b1+ ♔h6 54 ♕a2
♖e7 55 ♕d2+! ♔g6 56 ♖e2! ♔h7 57
♕c2+**

Last move this would not have sufficed, but with the black king further away it does the trick.

**57...♕xc2 58 ♖xc2**

This position is a simple win. The superb placement of the white rook, behind the outside passed pawn,

means that Black will quickly find himself in zugzwang.

**58...♔g6 59 ♖a2 ♖a7 60 ♖a5 e5
61 ♔g2 ♔f6 62 ♔f2 ♔e6 63 ♔e3
♔f5 64 ♔f3 g6 65 ♖a3 g5 66 hxg5
♔xg5 67 ♔e4 1-0**

*Game 89*
## Westerinen-Taïmanov
*Palma (GMA) Open 1989*

**1 e4 c5 2 ♘f3 e6 3 d4 cxd4 4 ♘xd4
♘c6 5 ♘b5 d6 6 ♗f4**

With this move White does not try to set-up the Maroczy Bind, but prefers to 'dent' Black's structure. All the same the evidence suggests that although it is a different type of Sicilian that Black has forced upon him, it is still a perfectly viable one.

**6...e5 7 ♗e3 a6**

7...♗e6 is considered in Game 91.

**8 ♘5c3 ♘f6 9 ♗c4**

An alternative means of controlling d5 is 9 ♗g5, which is dealt with in the next game.

**9...♗e7**

The usual procedure, but in Brunner-Spraggett, Biel 1990, the interesting novelty 9...♘a5 was tried. Play continued 9 ♗e2 ♗e7 10 a4 ♗d7 11 ♘a3 ♖b8 12 ♘d5 ♘xd5 13 exd5 b5 14 axb5 axb5 15 b4 ♘c4 16 ♘xc4 bxc4 17 c3 ♗b5 18 0-0 0-0 19 ♖a5 ♖b7 20 ♕d2 f5 21 ♖fa1 f4 22 ♗a7 ♕d7

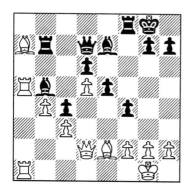

and chances were equal.

**10 ♘d5**

The only real way to play for an advantage, as 10 ♘d2 is met by 10...♗e6! and 10 0-0 0-0 11 ♗b3 by 11...♘a5.

**10...♘xd5 11 ♗xd5 0-0 12 ♘a3 ♘b4**

A radically different treatment is to prepare to advance the f-pawn with 12...♔h8. Trepp-Krnic, Rome 1986, for example, went 13 0-0 f5 14 f3 f4 15 ♗f2 ♖f6 16 ♘c4 ♖g6 17 ♗f7!? ♖h6 18

♘b6 ♖b8 19 c3! ♗h4 20 ♕e1 ♗xf2+ 21 ♕xf2 ♘e7 22 ♖fd1 g5 23 h3 with White standing better. Frankly I am a bit suspicious of this plan of attack, when Black stands so much worse off in the centre and on the queenside.

**13 ♗b3 b5 14 c3 ♘c6 15 ♗d5 ♕c7 16 ♘c2 ♖b8 17 0-0 ♗e6**

Black has equalised.

**18 ♕d3 ♗xd5 19 ♕xd5 a5 20 ♖fc1 ♗f6 21 b4?!**

It is strange that White should choose to become active in this sector of the board. His idea is swiftly shown to be a poor one.

**21...♘e7 22 ♕d3 d5 23 exd5 ♖fd8 24 bxa5 ♘xd5 25 a6 ♘xc3 26 ♕f1 ♕a5 27 a3 e4! 28 ♘b4 ♖bc8 29 ♕e1 ♖c4 30 ♗d2 ♕c7**

Taimanov has managed to establish and coordinate his army on dominating squares, and White is hard pushed to avoid material loss.

**31 h3 h6 32 ♔h1 ♘a4 33 ♖ab1 ♗b2!**

In Game 83 we saw Karpov also winning material by moving his bishop to this square.

**34 ♖xc4 ♕xc4 35 a7 ♗xa3 36 ♗f4 ♖a8 37 ♗b8 ♘c3 38 ♘a6 ♘xb1 39**

♕xb1 b4 40 ♘c7 ♖xa7 0-1

> ## Game 90
> ### Berg-Eingorn
> *London (Lloyds Bank) Open 1989*

**1 d4 e6 2 ♘f3 c5 3 e4 cxd4 4 ♘xd4 ♘c6 5 ♘b5 d6 6 ♗f4 e5 7 ♗e3 a6 8 ♘5c3 ♘f6 9 ♗g5**

Another way of trying to establish hegemony over d5, and to my mind a more consistent one than 9 ♗c4, although it does involve a third(!) move for this bishop.

**9...♗e7 10 ♗xf6**

In Leko-Topalov, Wijk aan Zee 1996, White attempted a refinement in move-order with 10 ♘d2!? 0-0 11 ♘c4 ♗e6 12 ♗xf6 ♗xf6 13 ♕xd6 ♕xd6 14 ♘xd6 b5 15 ♗d3 (here 15 ♘f5 might have been an improvement, since after 15...♗xf5 16 exf5 e4!? 17 ♘xe4 ♖fe8 18 ♗d3 ♗xb2 19 ♖b1 ♗c3+ 20 ♔f1 ♗d4 we reach the same position as in the main game, but with the difference that the black queen's rook is unmoved and not at d8. How much of a deficiency that is for him is debatable) 15...g6 (trying to trap the stray knight) 16 ♘b7 ♗e7 17

♘d5 ♗xd5 18 exd5 ♘b4 19 ♗e4 f5 20 a3 fxe4 21 axb4 ♗xb4+ 22 c3 ♖f7! 23 cxb4 ♖xb7, and the chances are approximately equal. The game was eventually drawn after an eventful 42 moves.

**10...♗xf6 11 ♘d2 0-0 12 ♘c4 b5!**

This was new.

**13 ♘xd6**

Best. On 13 ♕xd6 bxc4 14 ♕xc6 ♗e6 15 ♖d1 ♕b8 Black has a nasty initiative.

**13...♗e6 14 ♘f5 ♗xf5 15 ♕xd8 ♖axd8 16 exf5 e4 17 ♘xe4 ♖fe8 18 ♗d3 ♗xb2 19 ♖b1 ♗c3+ 20 ♔f1 ♗d4**

The extra pawn does not mean so much, especially taking into account the presence of opposite-coloured bishops.

**21 g3 ♘e7 22 g4 ♘d5 23 ♔g2 g6 24 ♔f3 gxf5 25 gxf5 ♘f6 26 ♘xf6+ ♗xf6 ½-½**

In both of these games we saw Black sacrificing his d-pawn and generating enough activity to compensate for it. But in neither instance was he granted any real possibility to complicate and thus play for a win.

1 e4 c5 2 ♘f3 e6 3 d4 cxd4 4 ♘xd4
♘c6 5 ♘b5 d6 6 ♗f4 e5 7 ♗e3
♗e6!?

Another worthwhile variant.

**8 ♘d2!?**

Attempting to pressure either the
d6-pawn, or the anticipated weaknesses in the black queenside.

**8...a6 9 ♘c3 ♘f6 10 ♘c4 b5 11
♘b6 ♖b8 12 ♘bd5 ♗e7**

This simple move was actually
new! Previous games had seen
12...♘g4.

**13 ♘xf6+**

Afterwards Ehlvest thought that 13
♘xe7 might have been better.

**13...♗xf6 14 ♕d2 0-0 15 ♗d3 h6!
16 0-0 ♗g5**

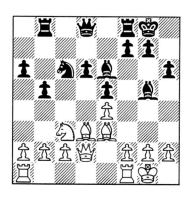

With this exchange it is clear that
Black's experiment has been a total
success.

**17 ♖fd1 ♗xe3 18 ♕xe3 ♕g5!**

Another good swap. Ehlvest will
try to demonstrate that a dark-squared
pawn formation is favourable for

him, because of the colour of the
squares upon which the remaining
bishops move.

**19 ♕xg5 hxg5 20 ♖d2 ♖fd8 21 ♗f1
♔f8 22 ♖ad1 ♔e7 23 ♘d5+ ♗xd5
24 ♖xd5 g6**

Now the advantage is of a similar
type. Black still has a better minor
piece than White's bishop, only this
time it is the knight.

**25 c3 ♖b6 26 b4 ♘b8! 27 a4 bxa4
28 ♖a1 ♖c8 29 ♖a3 ♖bc6 30 ♖d3?!**

This was his last serious error. 30 c4
might well have held out.

**30...a5! 31 b5**

Or 31 bxa5 ♘d7-c5 with advantage.

**31...♖c5 32 ♖e3 ♘d7**

Now it is an indisputable good
knight versus bad bishop situation.

**33 ♖xa4 ♖a8 34 ♖g3 ♘f6 35 ♖xg5**

This guy is now misplaced.

**35...♖xc3 36 ♖g3 ♖xg3 37 hxg3
♘d7 38 f3 f5!**

Mobilising his pawn roller.

**39 exf5 gxf5 40 ♖a3 d5 41 ♔f2
♘c5 42 b6 ♔d6 43 ♗b5 a4 44 b7
♖b8 45 ♗xa4 ♖xb7 46 ♖a2 d4 47
♗e8 e4 48 ♗g6 ♖b1 49 ♔e2 ♔e5
50 fxe4 fxe4 0-1**

The pawns are sweeping all before
them, so White resigned.

To finish with, some light entertain-
ment.

1 e4 c5 2 ♘f3 ♘c6 3 d4 cxd4 4
♘xd4 e6 5 ♘b5 ♗c5

Not a good move, but fun for blitz
games.

**6 &f4!**

6 ♘d6+ ♔e7 7 ♘xc8+ ♖xc8, as arose in a game Chandler-Plaskett from an event in Brighton the year before, is fine for Black.

**6...♕f6**

6...e5 7 &e3 would transpose to a sub-variation of the Lowenthal Sicilian that is known to favour White.

**7 &g3**

Although this is very likely a good move, the simpler 7 ♕c1! guarantees White a clear edge, although I did once scrape a draw with Judit Polgar after 7...♔f8.

**7...h5!?**

More fun. Black will meet 8 ♘c7+ with 7...♔d8 8 ♘xa8 h4 9 e5 ♕h6 or 9 &c7+ ♔e7, when the threats to f2 and b2 leave him with a very good game.

**8 h4 ♘h6!?**

In for a penny...

**9 ♘c7+**

Otherwise Black simply castles.

**9...♔d8 10 ♘xa8 ♘g4 11 f3 ♘e3**

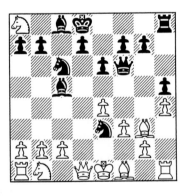

**12 &c7+?**

Bonkers! The critical line is 12 ♕c1, when Black must keep chucking

wood onto the fire with 12...♘d4 13 ♘a3 ♘xf3+ 14 gxf3 ♕xf3. In fact this unlikeliest of scenarios did once grace a chessboard, (upon checking the manuscript I saw that my first draft contained the misprint 'cheesboard', which is perhaps just as credible); Large-Plaskett, London (rapidplay) 1981, continued 15 ♖g1, which seems the most sensible way of coping with the threats to g3 and h1.

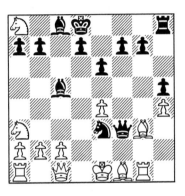

Now, after 15...♘xf1??, White could have finished things with 16 ♕g5+! &e7 17 ♕f4, but he missed this and lost. Instead of 15...♘xf1?? Black could try 15...♕xe4!?, as after 16 &e2 ♘f5!? White would still have to negotiate some tricky territory to bring home the victory: merry mayhem follows 17 &f2 &xf2+ 18 ♔xf2 ♕xh4+!?, 18...♖h6!? or 18...b5!?

**12...♔e8**

Now, however, Black has an unstoppable offensive.

**13 e5 ♕f4 14 ♕d2 ♘d4 15 ♖h3 ♘dxc2+ 16 ♔e2 b6 17 ♕d3 ♘d4+ 18 ♔e1 ♘dc2+ 19 ♔e2 ♘xf1 20 ♘d2 &a6 0-1**

## Summary

5 ♘b5 remains one of the most popular responses to the Taimanov. Statistically White continues to score better with 6 c4 than 6 ♗f4, indicating that despite all of the refinements in strategical thinking of the last twenty-five years, the restrictive effect of the Maroczy Bind is still potent. Most of the crouching postures that Black can adopt against it are well documented, and his pieces ineluctably gravitate towards ...♖fe8, ...♗f8, ...♗b7, ...♖ac8 and ...♕c7-b8. I would also advocate further investigation of Taimanov's idea of ...♘a7 and ...♕b8. After all, he thought up the very opening itself.

**1 e4 c5 2 ♘f3 e6 3 d4 cxd4 4 ♘xd4 ♘c6 5 ♘b5 d6**
  5...♗c5 - *game 92*
**6 c4**
  6 ♗f4 e5 7 ♗e3 *(D)*
    7...a6 8 ♘5c3 ♘f6
      9 ♗c4 - *game 89*
      9 ♗g5 - *game 90*
    7...♗e6 - *game 91*
**6...♘f6 7 ♘1c3**
  7 ♘5c3 - *game 88*
**7...a6 8 ♘a3 ♗e7**
  8...b6 - *game 87*
**9 ♗e2 0-0 10 ♗e3 *(D)* b6**
  10...♗d7 - *game 86*
**11 0-0 ♗b7**
  11...♘e5 - *game 85*
**12 ♕b3 ♘d7 13 ♖fd1 *(D)***
  13...♘c5 - *game 83*
  13...♖a7 - *game 84*

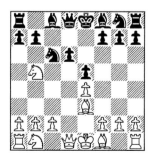

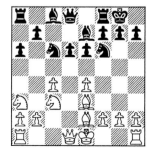

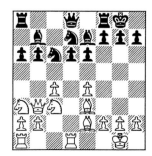

7 ♗e3          10 ♗e3          13 ♖fd1

# INDEX OF COMPLETE GAMES